JUST LIKE FAMILY

Just Like Family

*Inside the Lives of Nannies,
the Parents They Work For,
and the Children They Love*

TASHA BLAINE

Houghton Mifflin Harcourt
BOSTON   NEW YORK
2009

For information about permission to reproduce selections from this book, write to Permissions, Houghton Mifflin Harcourt Publishing Company, 6277 Sea Harbor Drive, Orlando, Florida 32887-6777.

www.hmhbooks.com

Library of Congress Cataloging-in-Publication Data

Blaine, Tasha.
Just like family : inside the lives of nannies, the parents they work for, and the children they love / Tasha Blaine.
p. cm.
ISBN 978-0-15-101051-6
1. Nannies—United States. 2. Child care—United States. I. Title.
HQ778.63.B52 2009
649'.10922—dc22   2008052949

Book design by Robert Overholtzer

Printed in the United States of America

DOC 10 9 8 7 6 5 4 3 2 1

For Michael:

Hello, my life, I said.

—GRACE PALEY, "Wants"

JUST LIKE FAMILY

FATIMA WORKED in a house of light. She showed me around the apartment as if it were her own, pointing out the four bathrooms, the formal dining room, the master bedroom suite. I told her that the family I worked for lived in a dark railroad apartment, that Mia's crib was shoved in a corner of her parents' bedroom, up against the window where the street noise was loudest. In the apartment where Fatima worked, we watched the sun pouring in through the floor-to-ceiling windows. Perched up on the twenty-third floor, we took in sweeping views of the Hudson River and Upper Manhattan.

After the children's music class one day, Fatima had unexpectedly invited me on a play date with Theo, who was the same age as Mia. Since then, she had been after me to "train" Mia better. She disapproved of a fourteen-month-old sucking her thumb, of the way she ran through the classroom and climbed on chairs. "She's hyper," she observed. "But it's not your fault. You don't know what the woman who took care of her before you did. She probably taught her bad things."

We went into the kitchen and Fatima got started on lunch. Her bracelets rang as she cooked. Fatima was a fifty-year-old Pakistani woman with elegant cheekbones, long black hair, and a gold stud in her nose. She had moved to the United States in 1991 with her children and husband, who was a lawyer in Pakistan. Her children did well here; one was in law school, another was on full scholarship at a business school in Boston. One drove a Lexus, the other had just bought an Acura.

Fatima had been a nanny for a decade, and she saw right away that I was new at the job. I admitted that caring for Mia was only my second job as a nanny, after a brief stint caring for twelve-year-old twins, and I'd only been with her for two months. Fatima took me under her wing, gave me advice, asked me how much I made, and told me to ask for more — I was white and American-born, after all.

The children went off into separate corners of the living room, immersed in their own toys and ignoring each other. When lunch was ready, Fatima slipped Theo into his highchair. I let Mia play, but once she saw Theo, she ran over to me and I pulled her up to my lap to feed her from the table. We were all quiet as the eating began and then I heard Fatima cooing.

"Who's your mommy? Who's your mommy?" she asked Theo, pointing to herself as she smiled. I stopped feeding Mia and stared. Fatima laughed at the stunned expression on my face. "His mother doesn't like it when I say that. But I tell her it's okay. I'm Theo's daytime mommy, and she's his nighttime mommy."

In my early thirties, before I had children of my own, I left my full-time office job and dove headfirst into the nanny world. My plan was to find work for one year that would enable me to pay my bills but leave me enough time, as an MFA graduate, to finally do my own writing. All of my office jobs had been time-consuming and distracting. Working with children, I naively thought, was something I could leave behind at the end of the day.

I lasted only six months — in two different positions. Compared with real nannies working across the country, I was a total lightweight. I couldn't take the long hours, the isolation, or the repetitive nature of the work. I struggled with my instinct to protect the children from their parents and my guilt over knowing I wasn't in it for the long haul.

I encountered all kinds of women working as nannies, from women like Fatima who were too attached to their charges to nannies who snapped at children or ignored them. If I learned anything about the nanny world, it was that nothing could be neatly summed up. I saw energetic nannies, bored nannies, loving nannies, stern nannies, distracted nannies, and hovering nannies. The only thing they had in common was that they were all in it together — the messy, relentless work of childcare — while the parents lived in another orbit.

I wrote this book not as a mother with her own feelings to explore but as a reporter fascinated by a world that slowly unfolded before my eyes. The more I dug in, long after I stopped working as a nanny myself, the more riveted I became. Inside homes across the country, domestic dramas are playing out quietly every day. Nannies, often underpaid, overburdened, and isolated, have a tremendous impact on the families that hire them. It is an odd contradiction: a nanny who feels powerless at work is incredibly powerful in her employers' eyes.

Parents often remain in the dark about their nannies' true emotions and point of view because nannies dread confrontation or don't feel that their thoughts are valued. Many nannies I met kept their anger and opinions to themselves because they feared that being open with their employers would lead to an ugly argument or, worse yet, termination. As one nanny with an overweight charge put it, "They don't want to hear, 'Your daughter is medicating herself with food because she wants her mother to be home with her, not working sixty hours a week.'"

Meanwhile, parents were equally hesitant to bring up problems, because they didn't want to offend the person taking care of their child, felt guilty about hiring a nanny to begin with, or worried the caregiver would quit. What, exactly, does our nanny think of us? many parents wonder. And what exactly happens all day while we are at work?

Fatima's coaching that day after music class is only one of many nightmares parents may have when they hire a nanny to care for their child. Parental anxiety about nannies has popped up everywhere: morning talk shows, books, magazine and newspaper articles, and of course the Internet. Parents have learned how to hire nannies, fire nannies, and spy on nannies. They have learned how to acknowledge their guilt over hiring women from poorer countries and then how to get over that guilt.

On local Internet message boards, parents look for nannies recommended by other parents and get advice on all kinds of issues, from whether to dock a nanny's pay when she loses a child's toy on the playground to the protocol for providing lunches. Informal networks of parents — online and on the streets — have sprouted up to get the word out when a nanny is spotted misbehaving. Formal networks have also appeared, including one New York City–based site called Howsmynanny.com, which provides stroller license plates for an annual fee of $50 so people can report on a specific nanny's behavior by posting to her plate number on the site. The idea is to track all behavior — abuse, neglect, and affection — through a stranger's observation on the street. And if parents want to see for themselves how their nannies behave, they can easily order a nanny cam small enough to fit inside a clock or a smoke detector.

By now, as nannies have become increasingly common in both upper-middle-class and middle-class families across the United States, we've heard and read it all, from a nanny who suffocated a toddler when she duct-taped his mouth shut to a nanny who drowned trying to rescue her three-year-old charge from a pool. Parents, taking in all these tales, are left worrying what kind of nanny they have hired, the good or the bad.

"You're definitely handing over too much power," says Samantha, a nanny working on Manhattan's Upper East Side. "I'm not the kind of person who would abuse that power. But people do. I know nannies who take the children to their own homes, and they clean their apartments while the children sit on the floor."

But it is in between these extremes that I saw most nannies living, and while the nanny world can be full of high-stakes drama, there is no denying the everyday monotony of childcare. This book follows three nannies — Claudia Williams, Vivian McCormick, and Kimberley Falls — as they navigate conflicts at work and home, in order to portray, for the first time in this level of detail, what a nanny's life is really like and what nannies really think about their jobs. If parents wonder what happens all day long, nannies wonder why so few of them bother to ask. By presenting an almost exclusive nanny point of view, it was my hope to give caregivers a voice while also providing a keyhole for parents into a world they never really enter but always speculate about. Most families don't hire a nanny like those portrayed in either *Mary Poppins* or *The Hand That Rocks the Cradle*. They hire a woman who appears in the morning to run the household as best she can while they are away. It is the cumulative effect of spending all day, every day with another person's child that is so compelling. It is what happens when parents hire strangers to be second mothers, paid by the hour to love, that is so important.

It was no surprise that Lauren and Nathaniel Martin, multimillionaires who lived on Manhattan's Upper East Side, hired me. The first family I worked for, the Martins were used to hiring white nannies, and my background suited them perfectly. While many of the other families who interviewed me came up with little lies to explain why I wasn't right for them, others were surprisingly candid. I unnerved them. Why would a white, college-educated U.S. citizen want to be a nanny? A few women saw themselves in me and wondered how I could stay home with their kids full-time when they didn't want to do it themselves. As one mother said, "Nobody smart wants to be a nanny."

Some families were simply afraid I wouldn't fit in with the nannies in their neighborhoods, limiting their children's social networks, but others were altogether uncomfortable having someone like me work in their homes. After one hourlong interview, a mother looked at me and said, "You know, I just don't think my husband will feel comfortable asking you to make our bed." Another mother ended our interview with, "Are you sure you won't think this job is beneath you?"

There were also families I didn't want to work for. One mother called me from a taxi, huffing into the phone as though I was already wasting her time. She listed her many requirements for a nanny, including working holidays like Christmas. I explained that I saw this as a one-year job, and she sighed into the phone, "Well, you know, nannies really only have a shelf life of one year anyway."

I realized I was looking for a job in the most intimate arena of people's lives: their homes. There was no office protocol. There were no hard and fast rules. Every family had a different set of priorities. Every family had a different philosophy on child rearing. Each time I talked to a new family, I had to be a quick study, gauging their wants within a matter of seconds. I became a chameleon of sorts, ready to blend in to whatever private family world I happened to encounter.

The job with the Martin family was just what I was looking for. I was paid $500 a week to pick up the twelve-year-old twins from school, take them to their tutor, and then bring them home to give them dinner. I was, by definition, more of a babysitter than a real nanny. When the kids were on vacation from school, I had them all day long, but their mother, Lauren, gave me up to $200 a day, on top of my regular salary, to keep them entertained.

We had a ball during that vacation. We ate all our meals out, rode only in cabs, saw countless movies, went ice-skating, and played video games all day at ESPN Zone. Even when the twins were frustrating, they made me laugh, and the three of us had a set of long-running jokes. Tyler talked nonstop and wanted constant attention. Sarah was more reserved and introspective, but I enjoyed the challenge of bringing her out of her shell.

My first week working for the Martins, I was admittedly starry-eyed. I was in awe of the five-story townhouse, the perfectly restored moldings, the claw-foot bathtubs, the greenhouse leading off of Sarah's bedroom. When I stepped inside their home, I left New York City behind. I forgot about the bus and subway I had taken to get there. I forgot about the leak under my kitchen sink. I forgot about the piles of bills waiting for me, the credit-card and student-loan payments I was late for again. For a moment, standing in the quiet of the foyer, this was my home too.

It didn't take long for the thrill of someone else's money to wear off. I quickly realized I was just another domestic worker on this family's payroll. Even the children, usually kind and good-natured, made fun of the long line of nannies who had come before me.

"Remember Penelope?" Sarah asked Tyler.

"She was a fat pig."

"Remember Maria?" Tyler asked Sarah.

"She couldn't even speak English. She had to point at everything."

The Martins had houses in Martha's Vineyard and Connecticut; they owned apartments in London and Paris; a maid appeared silently each day to make their beds, sweep their floors, and fold their laundry. But underneath all the luxury, they were still just a family. When I looked close, I saw smudges on their walls. Their old stairs creaked and the windows rattled when the wind blew strongly.

The mood changed when Nathaniel Martin came home. You could almost feel everyone holding their breath. The children sat up straighter on the couch. Sarah whipped a headband out of her pocket and placed it neatly on her head. Lauren poured a drink and lit a cigarette.

Then the criticism and nitpicking began. "I think those pants are too tight on you. Stand up," Nathaniel said to Sarah. Then he whispered to me, just loud enough for Sarah to hear, "She's been gaining a lot of weight lately."

Later it was Tyler's turn. "Did you buy Tyler's pull-ups?" he asked me in front of his son. "You know he still wets the bed."

This was my first taste of the complex role a nanny plays in a family. Within days, I witnessed several family fights and, almost immediately, my instinct to protect the children sprang up. I was employed and paid by the parents, but my true loyalty was to the children.

I quickly saw the effect these comments had on the twins. "People who are ugly when they're young grow up to be pretty,"

Sarah said to me one day after school. "That's like me. I'm ugly now, but I won't be forever." A few days later, Tyler confided, "I'm stupid." When I argued with him, he continued, "Really, I am. But it's okay because I'm popular." Nathaniel was a very generous employer — he paid me well and often let me leave early — but that didn't seem to matter. After I saw how he treated the children, I knew whose side I was on.

I did whatever I could to avoid bringing Nathaniel's wrath down on the kids. I stayed silent when Sarah lied to her father's face about wearing her hair back in her headband all day or about eating a turkey sandwich instead of french fries. I stayed silent when Tyler pretended he'd had a great day at school even though he'd just told me he did poorly on a test. I learned to walk a line between giving in to the children and letting them have fun when we were alone, and asserting my own authority. This wasn't always easy to do. When I gave in too much, they realized they could run all over me. They would lie to me just like they lied to their father. I learned to spot those white lies: We don't need to go to the tutor because we don't have any homework; I have to buy this candy for a friend at school; Mom doesn't care if you buy us lottery tickets.

When I became a nanny, I didn't know that I would be spending my free hours at home running scenes from my time with the twins through my mind. Did I let the children watch too much television? Should I have sent them to bed at nine as I was told or let them stay up later? Why wouldn't Sarah show me the short story she wrote for class? Did the children like me or had they simply been trained to put on a happy face for the help? I was in much deeper than I had planned to be when I took the job. The children were becoming part of the fabric of my life.

And then over the course of a week, odd things began to happen, and I realized that this family probably didn't think about me nearly as much as I thought about them. On a Friday while I was on line at the bank, Tyler looked up and said, "You know, I'm going to inherit twenty-three million dollars." The next Monday, he refused to eat anything but fast food because Nathaniel had told the children they were going broke. On Tuesday, Lauren told me the family was moving out of the country. Nathaniel suggested I look for moving boxes at the local supermarket and ask the doormen in the buildings lining Park Avenue if anyone had thrown any boxes away. By Thursday, the family had packed those boxes with their most important belongings and left the country.

I haven't heard a word from the Martins since they left, but I like to imagine the children's conversations.

"Remember Tasha?" Tyler asks.

"She was our last nanny in New York," Sarah answers and laughs. "She always wore that big red coat."

After only three months of working for the Martin family, I was a different person. Before, I had passed playgrounds and schools and seen only the children, heard only their laughter, the collective chatter of their voices. Now my eyes went straight to the nannies, who, it seemed, were suddenly everywhere. While I obviously wasn't like these women at all — in New York City, the majority of full-time nannies are from other countries, in the job for years, sending money back home to their own families — I did have an understanding of the complicated nature of their work. And, back in the job market again, I was about to get a sense of what their daily life was like.

My second job couldn't have been more different from the first. I was solely responsible for fourteen-month-old Mia for fifty hours a week at a salary of $350. Even on my first day at work, her parents never called to check in. They didn't stop by unannounced, and as soon as I walked in the door, they walked out. I took Mia to music class, spent mornings in the park talking to other nannies, ducked into Barnes & Noble on rainy days, and arranged play dates if I could.

Outside the apartment, I witnessed the nanny culture in the playgrounds, museums, toddler classes, and on play dates. I saw the wide range of care, from nannies who were as conscientious as the best mothers to nannies with vacant looks on their faces or an edge to their voices. I saw the nanny community: tight-knit groups of women who gossiped, laughed, complained, and supported each other as they watched their children and looked out for each other's.

Mia was a slight child with huge brown eyes and rail-thin arms. When I picked her up, I felt her spine through her shirt, her jutting shoulder blades. Lying still, she was a frail baby bird just out of the egg. Wide awake, she was a burst of energy, climbing, pushing, constantly exploring. She ran. She collapsed. She ran. She collapsed. I did what I could to keep up.

I was immediately struck by her detachment. Rather than seeking out affection from others, she comforted herself. When she was tired or upset, she simply sucked her thumb and played with her hair. When she hurt herself or became angry, she thrashed on the ground. After one month together, she finally let me pick her up and, on occasion, she came to me when she needed affection. But I still didn't feel a true connection between us. Mia had very few toys, shared a bedroom with her parents, and half her clothes were too small. She was anemic and still ate mostly bottled baby food. She was often exhausted because one of her parents regularly brought her back to the office for a few hours after I left at 6:00 P.M. I was faced with my inability to feel a strong attachment to a withdrawn child. I wavered dramatically between anger and sympathy toward the parents, Natalie and Jack, who lived modestly and worked long hours.

My first week with Mia, I set out to discover all the nanny hang-outs in the neighborhood. On a freezing day, with sleet falling from the sky, Mia and I bundled up and headed for Barnes & Noble. We rode the elevator up to the second floor with three other nannies. The doors opened and I was immediately hit by the noise of stir-crazy children. They were running through the aisles, pulling books off of shelves, eating in corners, playing around the water fountain, and grabbing toys from each other's hands. Their nannies were everywhere and way outnumbered mothers. I began to count but lost my concentration at twenty-three.

Mia and I settled into a corner, next to a basket full of soft books and stuffed animals. She threw herself into her version of a game, picking up objects, inspecting them, tossing them to the floor. I read her a book, although she paid only sporadic attention. Eventually she found a stuffed dog and crammed its entire face into her mouth.

"You shouldn't let her do that," said the nanny next to me.

"Her mother says she does it all the time. She lets her do it," I answered.

The nanny sighed and shook her head. I told her I was new at watching children, and she showered me with advice: It's best to work with young children. If you start with a child over a year old, it's hopeless. The parents have already spoiled them and they've learned all kinds of bad behavior — like putting things in their mouths. She had made a mistake with her current job. The child was four when she started, and now she was battling every day with the child's behavior: The child had tantrums. She was overweight. She thought she could have whatever she wanted.

"I try to love this child," she told me. "I swear to God I try to love her. But she's the kind of kid who always has her underwear up her ass."

Most of the nannies I met didn't talk about their children like this, but there were days when I understood the impulse. These women were dealing with all the daily challenges of full-time motherhood without many of the rewards, and that could be hard to take.

If my experience was so intense, what must life be like for a career nanny? I kept wondering. In bookstores and libraries, in playgrounds, on the subway, just walking down the streets of the city, I saw women taking care of other women's children. How, when I had such a tough time getting through a single day, did these women do it for decades? How did this job, which required so much sacrifice and so much genuine love to do it right, affect these women's home lives?

After I quit my job taking care of Mia, I began formally researching my book in the best place I knew: the playground. I started on a spectacular summer day at a downtown park known as a major nanny hangout. The sandbox and slides were packed with children, and the park was just as packed with nannies. I approached one nanny, hoping she would be willing to talk. Once I introduced myself and said I was interested in writing a book that showed life from the nannies' point of view, I was stunned by the response. Within minutes I was surrounded. Every woman wanted to tell her story. They all wanted to be heard.

I then began one-on-one interviews with nannies, in person and by phone. Each woman was different from the other, from a well-paid American nanny in California, to a Jamaican woman dreaming of marrying her boyfriend and gaining citizenship in New York, to a mother in suburban Chicago who became a nanny to earn a living after her divorce. Yet their complaints were frighteningly similar. Everyone had at least one horror story to tell. Most stayed in unhealthy situations for what they believed was the sake of the children. Many were unhappy or felt taken advantage of in their current jobs.

Some of the stories I heard were hair-raising. Dawn, a nanny on Long Island, hid in her room every night as her employers fought, and was eventually dragged into divorce court to testify against the husband. Sylvia, a nanny in Brooklyn, spent over an hour every day marching up and down the same set of stairs with a baby strapped to her in a BabyBjörn, because her employers were convinced it was the only way their child would nap.

Pam, a live-in New York City nanny, was chased around the house by her drunk employer, in a rage because she forgot to buy bread, as his wife stood silent. Pam ran into her room and started packing her bags, but the husband followed her, breaking the lock and pushing the door open. She did manage to escape and stayed with friends for a few days. Later, the father apologized. "He asked if I could stay until Sam graduated from preschool, and I said yes. My whole thing was that I wanted to do right by Sam and I wanted to be able to see him again. I knew if I left on bad terms, his parents wouldn't let me see him. So as much as I was having to really lower myself to do it, I did it."

Even when the stories weren't so dramatic, they were quietly devastating. All the nannies I interviewed repeated a single line: "We don't get any respect." Kathleen, a New York City nanny, said, "These people pay their dog walkers more than their nannies." Barbara, a Texas nanny, said, "I don't want to be treated as someone who just changes kids' messy diapers." Cynthia, a nanny in Los Angeles, said, "I'm taking care of these people's most prized possession. You would think they would show me more respect."

One theme that ran throughout my discussions was that nannies often, in some way, felt like victims. In their eyes, they were underpaid, underappreciated, overworked, and overlooked. On the other hand, nannies often show intense loyalty to the families they work for, and an overwhelming love for the children under their care. I went forward with my research almost as though I were on a mission for my own benefit. After all, I hoped to have children someday. Was it possible that the majority of in-home childcare situations were flawed? Were millions of children in the United States in the middle of an emotional tug of war between nannies and parents? What kept these women — who gave so much but felt they got so little in return — coming back to work each day?

For many nannies, one of the hardest parts of the job is the sense of intimacy they feel from participating in a family's most personal moments, while remaining aware that they do not truly belong. Emma, a nanny in California, described her heartbreak over one job she had for more than three years. She fell in love with the boys under her care, sharing every meal with them, spending days by the pool, and discussing their innermost thoughts. The boys' mother lavished her with gifts, remembered her birthday every year, and bragged to her friends about her great nanny. "Emma is like our daughter. We love her. The boys love her," she would say, and Emma wanted to believe she was just like family. The reality was far more complicated. Within two years of Emma's leaving the job, the family had essentially forgotten her, not even responding to her wedding invitation. "I think of nannying again," Emma says, "but I don't think I can handle the unnatural role of being inside the family but always outside."

Even beneath the best in-home childcare situations there lies the fundamental fact that one person is being paid to take care of another person's child for the majority of that child's waking hours.

Parents who trust and respect their nannies can still feel jealous, nervous, and guilt-ridden. Nannies who gain their employers' respect can still be resentful or frustrated because they have bigger dreams for themselves or for their own children. It is impossible for a nanny to walk into a family and replicate the parents' values and child-rearing philosophies as if they were her own, raising a child exactly as his parents would if they were home full-time. It is also impossible for parents to leave their children all day, five days a week, without trying to control and influence those hours in some way. The two sides perform a domestic dance as a working relationship evolves. Both sides compromise; both sides win and lose.

It was the nanny side of this dance that I wanted to show. I wanted to give nannies their say, to give them a chance to be perfectly honest about their feelings; as a result, parents could finally learn what happened when they closed their front doors, leaving their children in the care of paid strangers. If I really wanted to know what life was like for a full-time caregiver, I decided, the best way to do that was to earn her trust, let her open up as I followed her over an extended period of time, and then retell her story as it was told to me. I have attempted to take my readers on the same journey I took and let them come to their own conclusions. While protecting privacy by changing names, locations, and some other specifics, I have preserved the rest of the stories as I heard and saw them in order to give the most authentic account of the nanny experience that I can.

The three nannies I chose to focus on — Claudia, Vivian, and Kimberley — also chose me. Taken as a whole, they represent a broad swath of the very complicated and diverse world of full-time caregivers. They are, together, immigrants and American-born, live-in and live-out, dedicated and frustrated, part of the family and hired help, full of love and full of resentment. All three have a desire to be seen by the world as proud and smart and for their work to be respected and acknowledged.

My second visit to Barnes & Noble was much calmer. The sun was shining, and it was unseasonably warm. Most of the nannies were outside enjoying the weather, but Mia and I had already been to the park. I let her run through the long aisles in the fiction section until she started climbing on tables; then I took her to the children's books. We settled back into our corner and I noticed the nanny sitting next to me, who was totally engaged with her child. As she read him a book, she pointed out all the other objects on the page and their colors. When she pointed out an animal, she made the sound that the animal made and the child laughed.

"He needs a lot of attention right now because he will be getting a new little brother any day," she told me. "He already knows things are going to change, so his mother and I want to make it as smooth as possible."

She continued reading, rocking the little boy in her lap. Mia inched over to her, drawn in by the sound of her voice and the farm-animal noises she was making. I watched her face as the nanny read, and she began to giggle. She didn't usually laugh easily, and I felt inspired as I took her home for her nap. I vowed to be more attentive. On the way out, I stopped to buy a book on child development.

Back home in the apartment, Mia threw a tantrum when I tried to take off her coat. I stood above her tiny body and watched. She was squirming, her mouth curled up in anger, thrashing her hands on the floor. For the past month, I had done all the basics: feeding, clothing, and playing with Mia. Thinking about the nanny I had just met, I realized I was still holding back. I was just as detached with Mia as she was with me.

She continued crying and banged her head on the floor repeatedly. I reached down and picked her up. We began to rock, and slowly she calmed down. The room went quiet except for the humming of the refrigerator and my soft singing. She fell deeper in my arms, resting her head on my shoulder. Taking a breath, I finally gave in. I smelled her head. I kissed her cheek. I held her tighter. She was not mine, but I willed myself to love her anyway. It was the only way to get through the day, the only way to do this job right.

After I left Mia, I often wondered about her next caregiver. That unknown frightened me. What if she had fallen into the wrong hands? What if her new caregiver didn't know how to calm her down during a tantrum or how to get her to eat when she refused? And, even worse, what if the next nanny was bored, uninterested, and neglectful?

The first time I took Mia to the playground, I learned about the disappearance of her former nanny, Nancy. It was January, but the weather was a gift. I was relieved to be out of Mia's tiny apartment, breathing the air, watching the bright colors of children's clothes flash against the bare trees, the brown grass, the cloud-heavy sky.

Mia ran over to a bench where three Caribbean nannies were sitting together, one of them holding a baby in her arms. I was surprised as I watched Mia approach them without an ounce of trepidation and put her head in one woman's lap. It was almost painful to see her seek out affection from a stranger.

"It's Mia!" the woman called out, covering her face in kisses. The other two women knew her, too, and they all began hugging her. After I introduced myself and let them know up front that I wasn't Mia's mother, they took on a different tone. They told me that Nancy was a friend of theirs. One day she was there — in the parks, in Barnes & Noble, in the store where they all bought formula and baby food — the next day she was gone.

"I guess they just fired her and she disappeared. You better watch out, you could disappear too," warned one of the women.

"Don't listen to her," said the woman next to her. "She's angry. She lost her job yesterday after seven years."

"The mother said I was too attached to the children and then she told me to leave," the first woman said, staring at the ground. "I haven't seen my own children for five years and now I can't even say goodbye to these children? I keep hoping I'll see them on the street so I can explain why I'm gone."

It was only as I was leaving a few minutes later that I realized this woman had come to the park even though she no longer had a reason to be there. Perhaps to catch one last glimpse of the children she had helped to raise while she could not raise her own. For the rest of the day, I couldn't shake the feeling that Mia and I were being watched. I kept looking over my shoulder, expecting to see Nancy. Maybe she, too, had traveled back to the neighborhood, childless, hoping to run into Mia to say a final goodbye.

Like Claudia, Vivian, and Kim, this nanny in the park gave a part of herself that she would never get back. For most nannies, the ability to love is part of the job. And when her time is up with one family, a great nanny takes that love with her. She keeps pictures of her old charges on her refrigerator or continues to tell stories about them to friends or just pauses once in a while and sighs, remembering a moment they shared or a funny thing a child might have said. She puts her love in a box, stores it away, and labels it for that one specific child. Then she opens herself up again for the next child, for the next family. She starts the process of love and loss all over again.

ONE

CLAUDIA WILLIAMS had a superpower she only used under special circumstances. She could make herself invisible. When her employers bickered or there was tension in the apartment, Claudia retreated to the corners of the living room and silently flipped through a magazine. Bowing her head in the kitchen, she swept the floor, the bristles of the broom touching the tile in a soft, hypnotic swoosh. She pulled glasses and plates out of the dishwasher and placed them in the cabinets above her head so smoothly they didn't even clink. When James and Betsy Hall argued, forgetting Claudia was even in the room, she waited out the storm until it was safe to be seen again.

This was one of the qualities that made Claudia a good nanny. She did not get in the way. Claudia shepherded Jackson, the Halls' eight-year-old son, around the neighborhood, along with Lucy, their three-year-old daughter, but she did not try to lead the family pack. Her job included a number of important and essential tasks — picking the children up from classes, arranging play dates, folding laundry — but there were few complicated decisions to make, and she did not weigh in on issues like schools or extracurricular activities or potential problems with the kids. If asked, Claudia would have offered her opinion. But she was never asked.

Every morning, Claudia entered the building on West Thirteenth Street, rode the elevator up, and opened the front door of apartment 6F. She could immediately sense whether Betsy wanted to chat or be left alone; whether James was looking to play with the children or wanted them out of his hair. Rarely did Claudia have a discussion about the children's development or behavior, even if she was worried about something. She simply felt her way through the changes, taking stock of the vibe in the apartment and acting accordingly.

This kind of familiarity took time to develop. Every family was different, and each time Claudia or her friends started a new job, there was another set of family rules to adapt to. There were mothers who expected a perfectly neat house when they walked in the door — toys put away, dishes washed and in the cabinets — and then there were mothers who eyed their living rooms suspiciously if books and blocks and trains weren't scattered around, tensing up at the thought that their nanny might not have been playing with their child that day. Some mothers wanted their children bathed while others were territorial about the task. Some mothers gave instructions about food and naps and outfits to be worn while others expected their nannies to take the initiative. Claudia was way past the breaking-in stage with the Halls, and if she was ever frustrated at work, she talked herself out of it. She could not leave this family and start all over again with another. It was just too hard.

A forty-year-old native of the eastern Caribbean island of Dominica, Claudia had spent most of the past nineteen years working as a nanny in the New York City area. After she got pregnant for the second time, Claudia married the love of her life, Cap

Williams, a man she first met as a teenager and with whom she reunited years later in Brooklyn. Together they raised their now twelve-year-old daughter, Tanisha, Cap working in construction until he got injured and went on disability, Claudia caring for other people's children in their homes. Of all the families she'd worked for, Claudia had been with the Halls the longest: eight straight years, with no big blowups and relatively little drama.

Originally, Claudia's closest friend and Cap's cousin, Royette, had worked for the Halls. Six months into the job, Royette, who was undocumented, risked taking a trip home to Curaçao. Once out of the country, Royette wasn't allowed back in. In an effort to keep her job, Royette asked Claudia to fill in for her until she figured out a way to return to New York. When Royette finally did come back, Betsy and James decided they were more comfortable with Claudia and asked her to stay on instead.

Claudia had been put in a difficult position, and there was tension between her and Royette for a time, but that was all in the past now. The women were as close as ever, and so were their daughters. Claudia had never had a formal interview with the Halls. Instead, nanny and family fell in with each other, got into a rhythm, and dealt with issues as they came up, often communicating without using words. Things were understood if not spelled out.

By now Claudia knew every inch of the Halls' apartment, from the insides of the closets to the scratches on the walls. She knew where the sunlight would hit at a particular time of day. She had spent endless hours picking up toys, entertaining play dates, negotiating TV time, and answering phone calls from Betsy, who checked in from the office, and Tanisha, who checked in when she got home from school. She had cooked meals and made beds. The seasons passed, and Claudia watched new things appear around the apartment: a retro dining room table and chairs James bought

on eBay; new light fixtures. One year, the Halls' kitchen renova-
tions forced Claudia to commute to Connecticut for six weeks
while the family camped out with Betsy's parents.

The apartment was large, especially by Manhattan standards,
and carefully decorated. Framed family photos lined the walls,
along with a few oversized pieces of art, colorful abstracts that
Claudia dismissed as something Lucy could have thrown on canvas
herself. An open kitchen with soapstone countertops, sleek wood
cabinets, and a Sub-Zero refrigerator led into a living room full of
modern furniture, all covered with the debris of a busy family. The
New York Times and random drawings from the children covered
the shiny rosewood table. Toys were spread out on the rug. Piles
of books, collected by Claudia throughout the apartment, were
stacked around the room. The state of the house reflected a tension
Claudia witnessed every day. James was a neat freak who took
pride in his furniture purchases, while Betsy gave the place over to
the children, too busy to fight a losing battle.

Claudia knew the Hall family as well as she knew her own. She
knew Betsy hated making beds, organizing closets, or pretty much
any domestic chore, while James craved order. Their fights were
often about minor things like cluttered drawers and socks found
on countertops. Lucy was an extrovert, the family drama queen,
butting heads with her father more and more as she got older.
Claudia beamed with pride when she described Lucy's independent spirit. "She can take care of her own self," Claudia said. "I
don't have to worry about her."

Jackson had a special place in her heart because he was the first.
She knew he was more introverted than his sister and sometimes
preferred reading a good book to socializing, just like Claudia herself. "Jackson reads like a plane," Claudia described, buzzing her
hand through the air to show how fast the boy tore through books.

She did not speak with the same certainty when she described her own child. She worried about her daughter constantly, from her health to her academic performance to her developing body and her tendency to be rude. Tanisha was a sarcastic and quick twelve-year-old girl. Claudia worked hard to give her daughter all the things she didn't have growing up in a family of ten children. When her daughter begged for new clothes and shoes, Claudia worried Tanisha's sense of entitlement was too strong. And when she grew sullen or angry, Claudia was consumed with guilt, positive her daughter was reacting to the now rocky state of Claudia's marriage to Cap, who had moved back to Dominica six months earlier.

With Cap gone, Claudia tried to be even more vigilant. Tanisha had watched her parents' marriage crumble but she still retained an air of innocence, a fearlessness, a bold belief that the world would mold for her, giving her whatever she wanted. She called Claudia at work several times a day to complain that her chest hurt from her asthma or to tease her mother or just tell her a story about her day at school. Claudia picked up the phone every time her daughter's low, insistent voice came through the Halls' answering machine: "Mommy. Mommy. Pick up the phone. Pick up the phone." There was a click and the two connected.

Teachers warned Claudia at parent-teacher conferences that Tanisha was smart but did not apply herself if she wasn't interested. She used her intelligence to skate through school, studying at the last minute, passing tests other children would have failed. She was charmed. Claudia knew her daughter's lucky streak wouldn't last, and the thought that life would eventually hurt Tanisha worried Claudia to the point of distraction. She wished for a daughter who focused on school, a daughter who planned for a stable career. But Tanisha didn't like sitting still. She wanted to dance.

"Tanisha, you have to think about schoolwork," Claudia had told her daughter. "Dancing isn't going to get you anywhere."

"Mommy, why are you trying to break my self-esteem? You know I love to dance," Tanisha had answered with a twinkle in her eye.

"You have got to go to college, Tanisha," Claudia said sternly. "Even if I die, I will come back and haunt you until you go to college."

Monday was Claudia's toughest day of the week. After two days of cleaning her own apartment and taking care of Tanisha, she arrived at work to begin the cycle of domestic duties all over again. This new week had barely begun and she already wished it was over. Claudia had woken earlier than usual to go to Tanisha's school in Flatbush, Brooklyn. Tanisha had suffered from asthma since she was a young child, and on September 4, just before the new school year began, she had one of her more serious attacks. She was hospitalized for several days. When she failed to show up at Thomas Jefferson Middle School at the start of the new term, the administration assumed Tanisha was no longer a student. Claudia spent the whole morning at the school trying to get Tanisha enrolled again.

A forty-five-minute subway ride later, Claudia hurried along the Q train platform at Union Square and climbed the subway steps into the bright September sun. Claudia held her head high as she made her way to Lucy's preschool, lost in her own thoughts. Tanisha was taking up her usual space on her mother's list of worries.

For months now, Claudia had been considering a divorce from her husband, but she didn't have the courage. She had known Cap since she was sixteen, and even after many ups and downs, even after she had agreed six months ago that he should move back to

Dominica and use their savings to build the family a house on his father's land, even after hearing rumors of his running around on her, she could not leave him for good. Sometimes anger ripped through her so strongly that she vowed to turn him away the next time he flew to Brooklyn to visit them, pretending he was faithful. But then she looked at her daughter: Tanisha needed her father, especially now.

"They are two peas in a pod," she explained, weaving her fingers together to show how tight they were. "How can I split them up?" Tanisha worshiped her father, laughed at his jokes, danced with him when he came home, looked to him for guidance. Claudia watched them together and could not bear the thought of breaking their bond.

Tanisha was far more physically developed than the other girls at Thomas Jefferson, and Claudia had relied on Cap to keep their daughter away from boys. As Tanisha stood before her at the end of the last school year, her hair still in pigtails secured with gumball rubber bands but her body showing the curves of a woman, Claudia was immediately paralyzed with fear. What if someone hurt Tanisha, or even worse, raped her, when Claudia wasn't there to protect her? It was her worst nightmare. Tanisha had the mind of a girl still untouched by tragedy. She had a round face, chubby apple cheeks, and wide, dark eyes she liked to flutter when she gave her mother grief. If she could have, Claudia would have locked her daughter up until she was eighteen.

"Thank God I got Daddy's body and not yours," Tanisha had taunted her mother over the past weekend. "I have a nice butt!"

"Tanisha, you have to think above your navel," Claudia responded, tapping her daughter's temple with one finger. "There's nothing important going on back there."

• • •

Claudia paid no mind to the beautiful fall weather or the men who threw glances at her or the group of teenage boys who should have been in class but instead stood in a pack on the sidewalk, laughing. She was dressed in typical work clothes: a gray turtleneck and a pair of jeans. Her hair had a slight purple tint and was wrapped in small twists close to her head. Simple, wire-rimmed glasses rested on her face, partly covering the same apple cheeks her daughter had.

When people told Claudia she did not look her age, she giggled and exclaimed, "I know!" At forty years old, she had a straight, athletic figure, with long legs and a short waist. Although she gravitated toward muted, solid colors, she dressed with a flair that kept her looking young and stylish: a newsboy cap or a pair of gold hoops, a new hairstyle if she had the money that week, or airbrushed fingernails. Claudia appreciated quality, but she couldn't always afford it. If it were up to her, she would have owned a completely different wardrobe and a whole different set of shoes. She'd buy at Nine West instead of Parade of Shoes, Macy's instead of Lerner.

Claudia made a left turn on Twelfth Street and the sidewalk fell into shadow. Scaffolding stood above Lucy's school, blocking out the sun, giving the air a slightly damp and dirty feel. Inside, Little Acorns was all noise and bright color. Drawings plastered the walls. Parents and nannies sat in random corners or stood chatting with arms folded. Strollers, mostly expensive Bugaboos and Maclarens, blocked the hallway. Claudia nodded to the women she knew but kept to herself today.

Lucy spotted Claudia from across her classroom and lit up with a smile as she skipped over to her nanny. She climbed into Claudia's lap as the other children, along with the rest of the nannies and a small handful of mothers, sang the goodbye song. "Goodbye to Ella, Goodbye to Clementine, Goodbye to Charlie, Goodbye to Owen."

Outside again, Lucy and Claudia made an intimate team of two, strolling down the street hand in hand, matching their strides. They were striking as they made their way home through the quiet, tree-lined West Village streets, a grown woman with dark skin, a pale little girl in tow. Their colors didn't match, but they walked at the same pace, chatting, holding hands, and falling into natural silences. They belonged to each other.

"I have something for you, Lucinda," Claudia said as she headed north on Eighth Avenue. Her Caribbean accent added a sweet melody to her words, her voice rising and falling with affection.

"A snack?" guessed Lucy, holding out her hand for a cracker.

Five minutes later, while Claudia browsed the aisles of the local drugstore with a circular of specials in hand, the friendly spell broke when Lucy decided she could not live without a lollipop. And the whining began. Lucy dragged her feet and let her red coat fall slightly off her shoulders. She pulled along behind Claudia, who ignored the child and scanned the shelves instead.

"Claudia, can I have a lollipop?" Lucy asked. "Claudia, I want a lollipop. Claudia, can I have a lollipop? Claudia, I need a lollipop!"

At only three feet tall, Lucy was already her own person. Blond and blue-eyed, she was as delicate as Tinker Bell and flitted around just as much. Her moods shifted in seconds, and Claudia couldn't help but laugh when Lucy put her hands on her hips like a little woman and made demands. In the space of an hour, Lucy could be loving and sweet, whining and tiresome, sad and crying, and happy and bouncy all over again. Claudia usually responded with a flat, even tone, doing her best to ignore Lucy's moods, but sometimes relenting in exchange for a few minutes of peace.

Silently, Claudia made her way to the front of the store, where Lucy threw herself into full gear, panicked that they were so close to leaving the store without her candy. She begged and whined relentlessly. Finally, Claudia glanced down at the child and sighed. She did not have the energy to fight today.

"You're going to have to eat your lunch first if you want a lollipop," Claudia said halfheartedly.

Lucy already had the candy unwrapped by the time she and Claudia reached the Halls' building. She rolled it happily around in her mouth, her tongue growing red. It would be a challenge to get the child to eat lunch now, Claudia thought as she pressed the elevator button and said a quick hello to the doorman, who was busy reading the *New York Post*. This wasn't the fanciest building Claudia had ever worked in or the fanciest neighborhood. But it was comfortable, and after eight years it felt like a second home. The worst neighborhood to work in, according to Claudia and many of her friends, was the Upper East Side. They all agreed the people up there were so rich, they often hired nannies for every day of the workweek plus Saturdays, and only took their children out on their own on Sunday mornings, cleaned and pressed like little dolls for show-and-tell with their other rich friends.

Claudia knew every babysitter in this building, including the ones who had come and gone. She was friendly with all of them. But Cynthia, who worked for a family with two boys on the second floor, was her go-to person, a true confidante. They talked about all kinds of things, from their jobs to worries about their own children to problems in their marriages. When Lucy was sick or Jackson had trouble at school, Claudia went to Cynthia, who calmed her down immediately with practical advice.

As the elevator climbed up to 6, Lucy recited the names of her friends and their nannies on each passing floor. Kai and Damien belonged to Cynthia on 2. Maya and Ian had Maria on 3. Nate went with Mala on 4. At one time or another, Lucy had play dates with almost every child in her building. It was a neighborhood in itself, with gossip flying about the state of employers' marriages, how nannies were treated, who was fired, who quit, who was wooed away from one family and hired by another. A nanny on the fifth floor, who worked for a notoriously demanding family with three children, had left her job the week before because her pay was cut when she went to the doctor. She never said a word to the parents, but she mailed a goodbye note to the children. Another nanny on the tenth floor suddenly disappeared after one of the children in her care called her "mommy" and her real mother overheard it.

Claudia didn't have these kinds of problems with the Halls. At the end of her long shift, Claudia sometimes retold the day's building gossip to Betsy, who always recoiled in disgust at the way other nannies were treated. Over the years, Betsy and James had helped Claudia in little ways too. When Claudia's grandmother died, Betsy spent over an hour booking Claudia's plane ticket home for the funeral and gave her the paid time off she needed. After Tanisha begged for an iPod for Christmas, James found the best price online and then bought it for her. And the day Claudia realized Tanisha was no longer a little girl, she confessed her worries to Betsy, who came home that night with an article on adolescent girls.

The elevator doors opened to a long hallway with gleaming floors. Every door on the floor was black. Some had welcome mats in front, others the morning's New York Times still waiting to be picked up. In front of the Halls' apartment sat Jackson's bike and the stroller Claudia hated using for Lucy. As far as Claudia was concerned, it was time for Lucy to give it up, but her parents still indulged their little girl.

Claudia unlocked the Halls' door, and when it swung open she was immediately startled. Someone was in the apartment. She heard the rustling of papers and caught the glow of a lamp in the living room. And then she heard a voice, low and steady, all business. James was on the phone. Lucy rushed over to her father, who put his hand on her head affectionately, then shooed her away. Claudia took one look at her boss standing at his desk with his head bowed, shoulders slightly stiff, and calculated his level of stress. She decided to get in and out as quickly as possible, keeping an eye on Lucy the entire time to minimize the child's damage to the now organized living room. She would have to keep Lucy out of his way today.

James was dressed casually in jeans and a button-down shirt with the sleeves folded up. His dark hair had recently thinned so much that he had shaved it all off. With bright green eyes, thick black lashes, and his shaved head, James looked more hip than middle-aged, the kind of father who hid a tattoo underneath his clothes.

James should not have been home, but Claudia took it in stride. Ever since Claudia began with the Halls, James was mostly out of the house at work. She was fuzzy on the details of his job — it had something to do with the Internet — but she knew he was under a lot of pressure and often traveled. The rare times they were in the house together, James was polite and friendly, making sure the kids thanked her at the end of the day. He never once raised his voice to her, although Claudia knew that he had a temper. She had seen it flare up with the kids.

"Come, Lucy, let's make you some lunch," Claudia whispered, pulling Lucy into the kitchen.

While Lucy sat eating leftover pasta, Claudia picked up a note Betsy had left on the counter. *C — Please buy carrots. Make sure Jackson finishes his homework. Can you start this recipe?* Over the years, Betsy had left Claudia hundreds of little notes. *C — Don't forget Lucy's sunscreen. C — Take the kids to the park and I'll meet you there at 5. C — Pls. pick up milk.* The pieces of paper and yellow Post-its often popped up later in random places — in the cushions of Claudia's couch at home, her jacket pocket, the bottom of her purse — and sometimes they made her laugh when she found them. She could make an entire book out of these daily reminders.

Claudia put the note down and opened the page Betsy had marked in the cookbook. Betsy was a great cook but didn't always have the time to make meals. Claudia, on the other hand, hated few things as much as cooking and usually sent Tanisha to the corner for fried chicken from the Chinese place to avoid it.

Lucy shrugged her shoulders in her toddler-size chair, swaying back and forth. She looked at the bowl in front of her, stuck her finger in the food and swished it around.

"I want my lollipop," she announced. Claudia had taken the half-finished candy away from her temporarily.

"After lunch," Claudia responded, loading the breakfast dishes into the dishwasher. The lollipop sat, back in its wrapper, on the counter.

"Lucy! Eat your lunch now," James said sternly, appearing in the doorway, his phone call over. His daughter looked up, irritated, but she sat a little straighter and placed a single piece of penne on her tongue. The phone rang and James walked back into the living room, pacing in front of the windows.

"I didn't watch any TV this weekend," Lucy said, pushing her food away again. "Can I watch some now?"

"No television," answered Claudia. "We're going to the park when you're done with your lunch."

Claudia leaned against the kitchen counter and flipped through Betsy's magazines. Reading on the job was Claudia's secret weapon, her best defense against boredom. Sometimes she felt so stuck in this job she was sure she would lose her mind. The same routine every day was a quiet but steady form of torture, and as much as she loved Lucy and Jackson, none of it was enough for Claudia.

"Claudia, don't leave," Lucy had recently told her. "I want you to take care of my children. I don't want you to ever, ever leave."

"Claudia has better things to do than take care of your children," Betsy told her daughter.

"I want you to take care of my children too," said Jackson. "I'll even give you permission to spank them."

"Oh no, I don't think I'll be there for that!" Claudia had answered on her way out the door.

Since she had started this job, Claudia hadn't gotten a promotion, been given a new office or more intellectually challenging work. She didn't have a 401(k). She had watched James gain more responsibilities and seen Betsy take a huge step, opening her own gallery in Chelsea. All Claudia had gained over the same eight years was more childcare experience and a cost-of-living increase. The Halls were moving ahead in their lives, and she was right where she'd always been, trying to figure out what to do next.

James caught Claudia just as she was on her way out to the playground with Lucy. The child had finally eaten a few bites, and after an intense fifteen minutes of trying, Claudia got Lucy's shoes on and jacket zipped up. While Lucy squirmed and whined near the front door, Claudia tried to keep her out of her father's line of vision, but James walked right up to them before she could escape and extended his index finger straight down at a patch of the hardwood floor.

"Have you seen these scratches?" he asked.

Claudia didn't speak. She walked in circles, inspecting the floor, turning her head to catch it in different light. It took her several tries to make out a few faint, thin lines.

"They're from the laundry basket," James said. "You can't drag it on the floor anymore."

"How am I going to get the laundry to the basement? It's too heavy to carry."

"Use the grocery cart," James suggested.

"I thought you didn't want it banging in the doorway."

"You can roll it into the hallway folded up. Then unfold it outside the apartment and carry smaller baskets out there one at a time and fill the cart up."

Leaving the apartment with Lucy, Claudia wondered if James had lost his mind. She didn't know many men who would even notice scratches that small on the floor. Betsy certainly hadn't. How would she find the time to fill up a grocery cart with tiny baskets of clothes? It was already a struggle to get the house in order at the end of the day. It was times like this that made Claudia scream inside, even though she kept her expression perfectly calm.

This was not the life Claudia was supposed to live. Growing up in Dominica, a tiny island nestled between Martinique and Guadeloupe, Claudia knew she was meant for bigger things. She planned her escape, imagining a place with more opportunity, a place where she could work hard, earn a nursing degree, and send money home to her family. "I used to see streets of gold and bright lights and enough money to go around for everyone," she said with a laugh, recalling her old dreams of New York. "I really thought the streets were paved with gold!"

Instead, New York was all concrete and brick, with freezing, gray winters and hot, humid summers. Apartments were cramped and expensive. The only work available for those without documents was caring for children or cleaning. It was hard to find a job, tougher to find a family that treated her right, and almost impossible to get by on what they paid her. There was no way Claudia could go to school and still earn enough money to send back home to her family. There weren't enough hours in the day.

She had immediately postponed her dream of going to school, telling herself she'd do it eventually. Now, two decades after Claudia first arrived at John F. Kennedy International Airport in Queens, she found it hard to grasp that she was forty years old and still a nanny. Even the word made her voice crack. "I prefer to be called a babysitter," she said seriously. When she discovered there were white, American-born nannies, she wondered aloud, "Why would they do that? It's so degrading."

Claudia knew that being a nanny was a difficult and important job, but she also knew it carried little status. She felt it in the condescending stares she got on the street, the once-over people gave her when they saw her walking with white children. This job paid her bills and there was nothing wrong with that, Claudia told herself, but inside she felt trapped.

As things had begun to sour with her husband, especially after he'd returned to Dominica, Claudia vowed to change. The Halls would be her last nanny job ever. She would plan a new life, one that stimulated her mind and commanded more respect from the world. A life that did not include working in someone else's home, caring for someone else's kids, sweeping someone else's floors, and buying someone else's groceries. She would have a life to call her own.

The best days, according to many nannies in New York City, are the days that are warm enough to spend outdoors. Parks and playgrounds are the ideal place for them to get away from overbearing stay-at-home moms, whining children, and the four walls they've been staring at for hours at a time. All winter long, nannies scatter, spreading out to the children's sections of Barnes & Noble bookstores, to libraries, dance and music classes, indoor play spaces, and museums. They arrange play dates in one another's homes and scramble to clean up apartments before parents walk through the doors.

Outside, children run wild, and there's no cleanup. Nannies who haven't seen each other through the cold months greet each other with smiles and get caught up. From far beyond the playground gates, when the sun is shining and the air is soft, the swarms of kids, the chatting women, and the gleaming jungle gyms look blissful.

But close up, parks are complicated places with unspoken rules. A first-time mother or nanny new to the neighborhood can be easily intimidated. Groups of women form cliques as tight as those in a high school lunchroom. Mothers stick together; nannies stick together; and the occasional father is simply the odd man out. Even among the nannies, subgroups form according to home country and race.

Claudia had nanny friends who weren't born in the Caribbean, other babysitters in the Halls' building, but she did not always sit with them in public. She nodded hello, gave a smile, and then sat with her own kind. Asian nannies stuck together. Caribbean nannies stuck together. White nannies stuck together. And the groups were often critical of each other.

For instance, Heather, an American nanny from Chicago, scorned women from other countries. "Uneducated, foreign nannies don't burn out because they have it so fuckin' good. They've got a good paycheck. They've got a good place to sleep. They're living a lifestyle they never would have been able to live outside of America." Lubna, a Pakistani nanny on Manhattan's Upper West Side, hated the black nannies working in her neighborhood. "The Caribbean nannies are never in the playground," she explained. "They're sitting outside of it with the children strapped in strollers.

They do it so they don't have to run after them. They don't like to move because they're so overweight."

Claudia had heard that Filipino nannies were more subservient and willing to take abuse, especially when they were new to the country. "Some girls say people hire the Filipino because they can give them anything. They can give them two dollars a week and they will take it," Claudia said, outlining the playground stereotypes. "Caribbean nannies just say no. They will argue."

Caitlin, a nanny from Scotland, once witnessed a fistfight between a Caribbean nanny and a Latina nanny in Washington Square Park. The Caribbean nanny's child came down the slide too fast, bumping the Latina nanny's child. The Latina nanny flew into a rage and picked up the other child by his neck, throwing him on the ground. The Caribbean nanny lunged at the Latina nanny and they began hitting each other, screaming, and pulling hair. All the other nannies yelled, "Fight! Fight!" Eventually, the cops arrived and the crowd dispersed.

Some nannies kept their distance from other nannies altogether because they didn't want to get pulled into the fierce gossip. Alicia, a nanny in Brooklyn Heights, was friendly with the other nannies in the neighborhood but made sure she didn't get in too deep. "The first thing I noticed when I started working here was gossip. There was this little group, and they were always having arguments about 'somebody said this' and 'somebody said that,' and I thought, 'I'm keeping out of this,'" she said. "If they don't like you, you're totally on your own."

Claudia did her best to avoid the gossip mill, but she also relied on the women to help keep an eye on the kids and get her through the day. She brushed off the Caribbean-nanny stereotype, explaining what it was like on the inside of the clique. "I'll be sitting in the park. I know you, you know me. You see a whole bunch of nannies sitting together. They know each other. And everybody knows your kids, and sometimes you see us chatting, but the other women are watching my kids, and I'm watching theirs. Other people don't know that. They think we're just yap, yap, yapping. But Lucy could never run out of the playground without someone I know seeing her and grabbing her."

When Claudia arrived at the park, still irritated by James's new laundry rule, she sat with the women from the islands as usual. She mostly kept quiet, but she said her hellos to the other nannies so she wouldn't seem rude. Claudia's motto was "Be nice to everyone but don't get too close." She was very picky about her true friends, choosing one or two to allow into her private life and thoughts. She didn't like this "chatty-chatty thing" with the local nannies who always told each other's secrets.

She talked with the nannies she saw in her path every day, in the park, around the neighborhood, at school, but she often couldn't remember their names, and if one of them disappeared suddenly, fired for some reason, or deported, Claudia remembered her fondly but she didn't exactly miss her.

Sometimes, Claudia admitted, the group dynamics were too intense for her taste. Recently, while Claudia was spending a morning at the playground with Lucy, she tried to reach Tanisha by phone. When Tanisha didn't answer, Claudia panicked. Her daughter's asthma was acting up again and Claudia worried something terrible had happened to her.

Claudia called James and told him she had to go back to Brooklyn. They agreed that another nanny from the neighborhood, who they all knew, would stay with Lucy. Shortly after Claudia left, Betsy appeared at the park, and the nanny who was looking after Lucy lied to Betsy, along with all the other nannies she was sitting with, telling her Claudia had just run to the store. Unsure whether

Claudia had told her employers the truth about going to Brooklyn, the nannies instinctually stuck together to protect their friend. The women were furious with Claudia when Betsy caught them in the lie.

At the same time, Claudia was angry at the women for covering up. Of course she would tell Betsy and James where she was. But Claudia kept her thoughts to herself and continued to navigate playground politics the best way she knew how — by laying low and avoiding conflict. She depended on the other nannies for help here and there, offered help of her own, and made small talk, but she always maintained a distance, putting up a wall that kept her safe.

Life in a small New York City neighborhood could be as claustrophobic as small-town America. A week before, the mother of a girl at Lucy's school had needled Claudia about the state of Betsy and James's marriage after she saw them having an argument on the street. Claudia was amused, as always, that white people gossiped as much as the black people she knew. But she was also shocked by the woman's nerve in trying to ply her for information.

Claudia sat on the park bench with the other Caribbean nannies, going over their kids' new fall schedules. When one of the women talked about wishing she had time to go to school and earn a bachelor's degree, Claudia did not confess that she had the same dream for herself. She did not complain about James's sudden interest in scratches on the floor. She did not let on that sometimes she felt so bored and stuck and terrified, she feared she would go mad.

"So where have you been?" asked one woman as she smiled and sat down next to Claudia. Daisy was one of the nannies Claudia liked best in the neighborhood. She wasn't as close with her as she was with Cynthia, but she enjoyed her company and spent more time with her than most. A cheerful woman, Daisy cared for a girl named Violet, an intense child Lucy's age with thick hair and penetrating black eyes. Daisy had come to New York from St. Lucia five years ago. She was a shade lighter than Claudia and about twenty pounds heavier. Her face was wide and open, with high cheekbones and bright eyes. At least ten years younger than Claudia, she was optimistic about her future and on her way to earning a degree at Brooklyn College.

"Oh, I've been to London," joked Claudia.

"To see the queen?"

"Yep, to see the queen and have some tea."

A woman dressed in black leather pants, high-heeled boots, and a leopard-print jacket walked into Claudia and Daisy's line of sight, shadowing her child through the jungle gym. They looked the woman up and down and made quick eye contact with each other. They didn't have to say a word to know they were having the same exact thought. This mother was a ridiculous sight, standing alone in a sea of casually dressed nannies, with a full face of makeup and highlighted hair. Claudia and Daisy pegged her as the type to spend ten minutes in the park, declaring nannies were lazy or mean because they sat on benches, only to leave her child with her own nanny when she got bored so she could get lunch or go shopping.

Claudia returned to the apartment at 5:00 P.M. with Jackson, whom she'd picked up at a friend's house, and Lucy in tow. They were overtired, bickering and complaining, but Claudia managed to block them out as she opened the front door. It was quiet and dark. Relief came over her. James was gone again and the place was theirs alone. She could throw her coat on the counter and get to work on dinner, sending the kids into the living room to amuse themselves.

"Jackson, your mom wants you to start on your homework right away," Claudia said.

"Can I watch TV now?" asked Lucy.

"One little show and that's it."

With the children out of the way, Claudia opened the cookbook on the counter. She preheated the oven and pulled a chicken out of the refrigerator. In a little over an hour, dinner needed to be ready or at least on its way. She cut up potatoes and carrots and arranged them around the chicken in the pan. Once the prep work was done, Claudia sat on a stool at the counter. Why had James been home? she wondered. And why was he so tense on the phone?

Jackson had his homework out and Lucy was lost in cartoons. They did not notice when Claudia walked gingerly over to their father's desk. Sometimes James and Betsy forgot to tell Claudia things that would have been helpful for her to know. This was one of those times. What if he was back in the apartment the next day? It would be nice to have a warning ahead of time. She moved some papers around on the desk and found a calendar. Scanning the days of the month, she saw some meetings written down but no real clues. She had no idea what James was doing in the apartment earlier, but she hoped things would get back to normal.

By the time Betsy came home, the smell of chicken filled the air. An attractive woman, Betsy was exactly the same age as Claudia. Betsy knew how to dress: she always looked trendy but classic. Her blond hair was cut in a wispy bob that framed her fine-featured face perfectly. When Betsy opened the front door, a cool breeze shot through the kitchen and her footsteps fell heavy on the floor. She heaved her workbag, a chocolate-brown Kate Spade tote, onto the island in the kitchen next to Claudia's jacket. It was full of papers and binders. An overstuffed wallet slid out.

"How was your day?" she asked without looking at Claudia. She flipped through a stack of mail, pushed her hair out of her face, and called out to the kids.

"Fine, fine. The weather was nice. We went to the park," Claudia answered.

Lucy came running, wrapping her arms around her mother's legs. Betsy unzipped a pair of knee-high boots and pulled her daughter onto her lap. "Hi, peanut," she whispered into her ear. Two blond heads leaned together, foreheads touching. Lucy buried her head in her mother. Claudia zipped up her own jacket, pulled her bag over her shoulder, and said goodbye before walking out of the apartment for the night.

As she drew the door closed behind her, Claudia heard the Halls going about their evening, the children adjusting to the shift change. Betsy opened the refrigerator as Lucy chatted away. Claudia couldn't hear Jackson, but he was probably on the couch, sneaking in a few minutes with his Game Boy. She stood in silence at the elevator and closed her eyes for a moment as she breathed in and let the day ease out of her mind.

Forty-five minutes later, Claudia climbed the stairs at the Church Avenue stop in Brooklyn on the Q line. Flatbush was buzzing with people darting in and out of shops, coming home from work, or running errands. Tiny storefronts overflowed along the avenue, jammed together one after the other like a colorful, chaotic jigsaw puzzle. Claudia loved the energy of Brooklyn, where horns honked, music pumped out of windows, and people greeted each other on the street. She loved the fish markets and the takeout Chinese and the discount furniture stores and the hair salons and sneaker shops, even the squeaking brakes of buses as they came to a stop.

Claudia felt most at home in Flatbush, and walking down the street, she often nodded or smiled or stopped to say hello to someone she knew from back home. She referred to some of them as cousins, distantly related to her or Cap through marriage or blood. This neighborhood was as familiar to Claudia as the tiny town she'd grown up in, only more vibrant and alive. Fruit stands opened up their storefronts to pile cardboard boxes high with cilantro and yams and yucca. Tiny travel agencies posted discounted airfares to Trinidad, Tobago, Haiti, St. Martin, and St. Lucia in their windows, along with international phone cards.

But tonight Claudia was overcome with a wave of exhaustion even Flatbush couldn't lift. She pulled her bag higher on her shoulder, practically empty compared with Betsy's, and wondered what she could put together for dinner and whether Tanisha would demand a lot of her attention. It was getting dark earlier now and the fading light made Claudia want to hibernate at home. As she waited impatiently for the traffic light to turn so she could cross the street, a piece of paper taped to the lamppost caught Claudia's eye. A local man was advertising math GED classes at $20 a session. She paused at the flyer, reading it over a couple of times.

If she was going to make changes in her life, this was where Claudia had to start. Lucy and Jackson were getting older, and pretty soon Betsy wouldn't need a full-time nanny. Claudia knew she had to start building a new path, one that brought her closer to her dream of becoming a nurse. Ever since she was a child, Claudia had wanted to work in a hospital, but she gave up too easily when it came to her education. She always let life — a pregnancy, a broken heart, money she needed to earn and send back home — get in the way of her dreams.

Claudia didn't know how she could fit the class into her already busy schedule, but she pulled the flyer off the lamppost anyway. This time would be different, she convinced herself. She would make a decision and stick to it. She would finish what she started. Shoving the paper to the bottom of her bag, she could not get the idea out of her head. If she could pull it off, taking this class might just be the first time Claudia did something for herself simply because she felt like it.

TWO

DOMINICA, THE COUNTRY Claudia referred to almost daily as "back home," is one of the poorest and smallest islands in the Caribbean. Twenty-nine miles long, sixteen miles wide, it has a population of about seventy thousand. It is known in the United States as a nontouristy tourist destination, a place for nature lovers and scuba divers. It has rocky, black sand beaches and subsists mostly by exporting bananas. Rain forests, cloud forests, rivers, waterfalls, hot springs, and the world's second-largest boiling lake all make Dominica an exceptionally beautiful country. When tourists did pass through Claudia's town, they threw candies from their open-air jeeps, a trail of kids chasing them for the treats.

"I would never eat their candy, though," Claudia said in typical laconic fashion. "I don't know what's in it. Suppose it's laxatives."

In her darker moments, when she felt defeated and homesick, when she was broke and worried about how to feed her daughter, Claudia wondered if she would have been better off staying in Dominica. Claudia hadn't just left her home country for good. She also left her baby boy behind for her mother and sisters to raise. Over the years, Claudia had questioned that decision countless times. She ached for her son after she left him when he was three months old. Unable to go home once she was living in the United States, Claudia did not see her son for years. He was fourteen years old and felt like a stranger to her when they were reunited. To this day she feels so guilty about leaving her son, she barely speaks his name: Dexter. "I love my son," she said painfully. "But I don't know my son."

Claudia had regrets, yet she knew she would have grown restless in Dominica. There were too many limitations, too few opportunities. If she wanted to feed and clothe her child, if she wanted him to have a bike and toys, she would have to find work somewhere else. If she wanted a better life for herself, Claudia needed to find it in New York.

Dominica was so insular and small that when Claudia was a child, her mother stopped calling her by her given name, Beverly, after she found out another child in her town had the same name. Instead, Beverly became Claudia. Two children with the same name in such tight quarters caused confusion. "If you step off the plane in Dominica and ask for my mother by name, they can tell you how to get to her house," Claudia said.

The slave trade brought Africans to Dominica in the 1700s, and the island's population today is descended from slaves, Caribs, and colonial masters. Since Dominica gained independence from England in 1978, the country has faced challenges. Hurricane David destroyed 75 percent of the island's homes in 1979 and decimated the banana crop when Claudia was a teenager. Unstable governments have had coups and corruption. In a country with little industry, an unemployment rate at 23 percent in 2000, and few buildings that even stretch above two floors, it has become common practice to leave in search of better fortunes elsewhere.

Claudia was one of those fortune seekers. She had been gone for two decades, but though she loved Brooklyn and had no plans to leave the United States, Dominica was her identity. Even Tanisha, who was born in New York and had the sass of a Brooklyn girl, thought of herself as Dominican first. No matter how far away the island was, Dominica was in Claudia's blood. It was in the soup she brewed with chicken, yams, plantains, and dumplings. It was in the music she listened to at parties, calypso and soca, and it was in the lilt of her voice, the rhythm of her language, the metaphors and similes that slid off her tongue like effortless lines of poetry. With her ironic sense of humor and eye for the absurd, she was more New Yorker than American and more Dominican than anything at all.

Claudia grew up in Marigot, a large village set along the island's east coast. Raised in a two-room house with her grandmother, mother, and nine siblings, Claudia didn't have much as a child, but she didn't mind — her village was full of families like hers. Surrounded by lush trees and flowers, a vegetable garden her mother planted, and some fowl wandering the land, Claudia's family lived modestly but adequately. They ate tomatoes, lettuce, cabbage, carrots, and spinach, all homegrown. Sometimes, when her mother wanted meat, she grabbed one of the chickens, wrung its neck, plucked its feathers, and cooked it up. At night, they slept where they found a spot: on the floor or in a bed with another sibling. Claudia owned two pairs of underwear; one she wore and the other she washed and hung out to dry on the back of the refrigerator.

The house had electricity, but the kitchen, a shower, and a pit toilet, were outside. Instead of glass windows, the house had large shutters that threw the interior into complete darkness when they were closed. When the family ran out of flour, bread, or other groceries, someone woke early, caught a 5:00 or 6:00 A.M. bus, and

rode to Portsmouth or Roseau for a day of shopping before returning to Marigot late in the evening. Often, the father of Claudia's sister Jill came by the house, although he never lived with
them. He brought her favorites — Shirley biscuits and Coke —
along with meat and fish for the entire family to eat. He called her
"Claudo," and he was the closest thing to a father she'd ever had.

School was far away, and sometimes Claudia grabbed a ride.
Usually, though, she made the long walk, dressed in her uniform, a
brown skirt with a single pleat and a yellow shirt. She was a quiet
girl, even then, especially in school, but she loved going. At home,
the few times Claudia did get in trouble, her mother, Agatine, used
a whip — a thin tree branch stripped bare — to get her back in line.
Claudia would take one look at that whip and scream so loudly the
entire neighborhood could hear her. Claudia jumped and spun
around until her mother called one of her brothers to hold her
down.

Agatine worked as a cook at a hospital, and Claudia spent as
much time there as she did in her own home, often sleeping over
with her mother. A nurse named Ruth took Claudia under her
wing, and the two became close friends. Claudia also became
friends with patients; she remembers combing the straight hair of
a Carib woman who was on bed rest while pregnant with twins.
After the woman gave birth, she named her two baby girls Claudia
and Claudine.

Perhaps this hospital put the idea of becoming a nurse into Claudia's head, but her childhood also trained her to be a caretaker in
general. As the oldest girl of ten children, Claudia took on every
chore she could to help her mother. She watched out for the
younger kids, cooked, swept floors, and cleaned. She was bred on
responsibility, and slowly, as she got older, the idea of helping her
mother became more important to her. There were a lot of children

to care for and feed. There was George, Sheldon, and Earl. There was Rawson, Robert, Kevin, Jill, Nadia, and Jonathan. And then there was Claudia, who slowly realized she could make a real difference to her family and have a better future for herself if she moved to the Virgin Islands or the United States, where jobs were plentiful, and sent a portion of her earnings home. She can't pinpoint exactly when the idea took hold, but Claudia grew determined to someday get herself to New York.

Claudia had come a long way from her childhood, but she did not always see it that way. She tried to tell herself that she was living better as an adult than she did growing up, that she kept her daughter decently dressed, well fed, and happy. Sometimes she just wished she could be honest with people in Dominica about how tough it really was to survive in New York, but they wouldn't believe the streets weren't paved with gold until they saw it for themselves. And if Claudia told them the truth, they would think she was lying, wanting to keep New York and all its riches to herself.

Instead of admitting her struggles, she put up a front. There was nothing else she could do. As an immigrant with an established life in Brooklyn, it was her duty to support family back home with money or a place to stay if one of them wanted to visit or make a go at a life of his or her own in New York. Over the years, Claudia had sent enough money back home for her mother to build a bigger house on the same piece of land as her childhood home. She had taken in relatives who sometimes stayed for months. And if she did plan a trip to Dominica, she automatically figured in the cost of a crate full of American clothes and shoes. If she couldn't afford the gifts, she didn't get on the plane. She couldn't come home empty-handed, appearing selfish and stingy.

On the trip home for her grandmother's funeral, Claudia arrived to discover none of the plans had been made yet for the burial. Her mother and siblings had kept her grandmother on ice at the funeral home until Claudia and her brother George, who lived in New Haven, Connecticut, arrived to pay the bill.

Claudia repeated to herself all the things she had done for her family, but deep down, she could not convince herself that she had done enough with her life. In her eyes, not much had changed since she was a child in her mother's home. She was still responsible for others, taking care of their daily physical needs. She was still putting their lives before hers.

The flyer Claudia pulled off the lamppost in early September was still at the bottom of her bag in October. She could not bring herself to ask the Halls to rearrange her schedule just so she could go to class. Nobody said anything to Claudia directly, but she could see that things were changing around the Hall household, and she didn't want to add to the stress. Since September, James was home regularly, but he was mostly on the phone or in front of the computer, slipping in and out for meetings. Betsy rushed around as she prepared for her first show at the gallery, checking in with Claudia about the kids but not staying still long enough for them to chat. Claudia spent her days watching James and Betsy for signs of a slowdown, waiting for their lives to get under control before she brought her own issues into the mix.

James had quit his job and was now out on his own, working as a consultant. Betsy had mentioned the change to Claudia in passing, but they never discussed it in detail. Claudia came to work prepared for anything. She might walk into a peaceful, dim apartment and relax with the kids while James was out at meetings. She might open the door to bright lights and James hunched over his desk in the corner of the living room, typing on the computer or talking on the phone. Claudia usually took the kids out of the house to avoid him. She did her best to spend the last warm days of fall at the playground before winter forced them inside.

The first couple of weeks after he appeared at home, Claudia worked around James, going ahead with play dates she had scheduled for Lucy with Cynthia and Kai, a cheerful, sweet child with a head of hay-colored curls who wore cargo pants and rocker T-shirts. Claudia saw Kai so often she felt as if he were one of her own charges. She wrapped him in her arms when he came running. Lucy and Kai were best friends, just as Claudia and Cynthia were best friends. When all four got together, it was effortless and entertaining. One afternoon, the children raced through the living room, laughing, yelling, erupting into fits of crying and then embracing each other in giggles all over again.

"Enough!" James screamed from his desk. "I can't even hear myself think!"

A look of fear spread across Kai's face as James fumed. The house went uncomfortably quiet, and soon afterward Kai and Cynthia left. A few days later Cynthia broke the news to Claudia. Kai had refused to return to Lucy's apartment if James was home.

"He told me, 'Lucy's daddy is mean,'" Cynthia said with a sigh. "He's scared to come over."

Claudia wasn't happy about the situation but she brushed it off easily. James didn't scare her. She knew he was sweet deep down. Instead of complaining, she made herself scarce, spending afternoons at the playground or arranging play dates in other people's homes. Sometimes it was exhausting, but Claudia reasoned that James couldn't possibly, after all these years out of the house, work from home forever.

Even with James's bad moods, Claudia knew her frustration at work had nothing to do with the Halls. It wasn't the job itself that got her down. It was something much deeper. She ached for more in life.

Claudia had left her newborn son when he was still breastfeeding. It was the hardest thing she would ever do, but at the time it had all made sense. If Claudia was going to have a bright future for herself and help her family at home, she had to leave her child behind and make a new life in New York. It was true that she had accomplished a lot and sent money home over the years, but was it enough? Did her life now — taking care of other people's children and working mostly off the books — justify the fact that she and Dexter never really knew each other? If Claudia had left her child behind, shouldn't she accomplish something big in return, shouldn't she be moving mountains? Did the life she lived now justify the fact that she had given up her son?

While James built his business at home, Betsy was under the most intense pressure of her adult life. She had put in many long, low-paying hours at several prominent galleries over the years, starting as an intern after she graduated from Vassar with an art history degree. Now she was taking the risk she had always dreamed of, creating her own space and her own vision. Claudia admired Betsy's success on the job and her ability to remain a good mother. She also worried about her. When her boss came in at night after a long day at her gallery, she didn't even take a minute to herself.

"Betsy must get tired," Claudia said. "She goes from work to home to be supermom."

In truth, it wasn't just concern for her boss that had Claudia watching Betsy so closely. Claudia was waiting patiently for things to calm down so she could choose just the right moment to bring up the math-prep class. Ever since Claudia had seen the GED flyer, she couldn't stop thinking about her future. Weeks went by, but Claudia didn't sense a good opening.

"With Betsy's busy schedule and James's busy schedule, it's kind of hard for me to tell her. Some people, when you come to work for them, they don't want you to go to school. I think if I explain to Betsy, she would try to make a way for me to go, but I don't want to see her long face. I don't want to see her unhappy. Betsy have a big project right now. She doesn't need pressure on top of pressure, so I'm just giving her time."

Claudia arrived at the Halls' apartment late on a Tuesday morning in October with Lucy in tow, barely noticing James was at home. She was in a bad mood when she got off the subway and a bad mood when she picked Lucy up at school. Now, she took her jacket off and tried to shake the depression. It was a relief to be at work today, away from Cap, who had just returned to Dominica after a short visit; away from Tanisha; and away from her sister Jill, who had come from the island just as Cap was leaving. Jill was contemplating a permanent move to the United States, but that would mean she could not go back home until she got her papers. Their mother was getting older, and Jill was afraid that she would get sick or die and that Jill would never see her again. For some reason, Tanisha had been rude to Jill since the day she arrived.

"I think she's upset about Cap," Jill had told Claudia, trying to explain Tanisha's moodiness.

"You're right," Claudia had answered, feeling guilty.

"I know I'm rude, Mommy," Tanisha had told her mother when they had talked about her behavior. "But a lot of parents wish they had a child like me. I don't hang out in the street with boys. I don't give you that kind of trouble."

Claudia smiled, remembering her daughter's words, and then turned her attention to Lucy, who was racing around the house while her father was trying to work. Claudia managed to keep Lucy away from James until it was time for her ballet class. The child flew around her room, a ball of energy, and Claudia reached out to grab her. She managed to hold Lucy down long enough to put a pair of light pink tights on her before the child was off again. When Lucy paused for a moment, leaning over her Angelina Ballerina board game, Claudia scooped the little girl up, popped her into a black leotard, and pulled a pair of green socks over her feet.

"Come on, we're going to be late," said Claudia as she pushed Lucy's stroller out the door.

Claudia turned left when she walked out of the apartment building and headed up Eighth Avenue. A block later she made a right turn onto Fourteenth Street, passing a pizza place and an old doughnut shop, the few dingy holdouts in a neighborhood now full of quaint, well-lit shops and sleek, trendy restaurants and windows featuring fall clothes in fabrics Claudia could never afford: cashmere, merino, silk. The Marc Jacobs and Ralph Lauren stores she passed on her way to the playground on Bleecker Street didn't mean much to Claudia, but she did sometimes like to take a walk to the Banana Republic in Chelsea to see if a pair of pants or a sweater or a shirt she might have spotted had now made its way to the sale rack. When she went into the clothing stores in Manhattan, Claudia knew she was being watched for shoplifting. Sometimes she pictured herself snapping at the salespeople, "My money is the same color as yours." Instead she kept shopping, pretending she didn't feel their stares.

People flew past Claudia and Lucy, darting by with coffee cups and briefcases in hand, newspapers folded under arms. They ran across streets when the walk sign was against them but the coast was clear. They caught crosstown buses and marched underground for subways. They hailed cabs, lifting long, confident arms into the air, and the cars stopped at their feet like magic. Everyone, it seemed, needed to get somewhere, and they needed to get there fast. Claudia did not mistake her life for theirs.

At the corner, Claudia waited patiently for the light as cars honked at aggressive pedestrians. Then she spotted a man up the street she would have done anything to avoid. But it was too late — she would have to pass him to get Lucy to class on time. Claudia did not know the man's name or why he always chose this particular street to camp out on. Breathing in, Claudia pushed Lucy forward and kept her eyes on a point off in the distance, pretending the man didn't exist. It didn't do any good. She could not will herself to disappear today.

"Nanny!" the man called out in a song, leaning in toward Claudia as she passed. He taunted Claudia, his voice as high and nasal as a kid's in a schoolyard. "Nanny, nanny, nanny!"

This crazy white man made Claudia's skin crawl. He was too well dressed to be homeless but too odd to hold down a job. She wanted to run him over with Lucy's stroller. Did he yell at the other nannies in the neighborhood and humiliate them? she wondered. But she never had the nerve to ask. For a while, she had thought about bringing it up to Betsy and James, but she was too embarrassed. One Friday over the summer, she had passed him with Jackson.

"Nanny, nanny, nanny, today is payday!" the man teased.

"Claudia, what's payday?" Jackson asked.

"It's when you get paid."

"Why is he saying that?"

"Oh, Jackson, I don't know," she said. "It started a long time ago."

Claudia walked quickly as the man, still close by, kept yelling at her back. She remained expressionless, but in her mind she looked straight at him and said, "You look sick to me." Then she choked the daylights out of him.

Lucy's ballet class was held in a building with an elevator so old Claudia had to pull open a door with an old brass handle in order to board it. The door was heavy and narrow, and there were always a few awkward minutes before class began as mothers and nannies and children tried to maneuver strollers inside. Upstairs, the studio was warm and bright, with exposed brick walls and gleaming wood floors. Whenever Claudia walked in, her eye immediately went to a poster of a young woman on the wall. Vermeer, she would think with a smile. She knew this painting well. It was on the cover of *Girl with a Pearl Earring,* a book Betsy had lent her a year ago. Claudia had loved it. She had recently tried to read a novel by Paula Fox, also from Betsy, but she eventually gave up.

"It wasn't the kind of book you couldn't put down," she said.

Claudia undressed Lucy and sent her down the hallway in her leotard and tights to class. She watched the child go with a grin on her face. Lucy had so much spirit, she kept Claudia smiling even on days like this. With Lucy gone, Claudia sat down to rest in the front room. It was empty, the other nannies milling around in the hallway. Claudia was alone with her thoughts.

When Cap had left for Dominica after his visit, Claudia hadn't bothered to give him a proper goodbye. He told her he'd be back for another visit soon, but Claudia had her doubts. She wasn't even sure she wanted him back in the apartment. He'd been officially gone for seven months now, not including his recent visit, taking most of their savings and leaving behind promises of a new house, but Claudia could imagine Cap using the money to play the big man with fat pockets in town, a whole bunch of desperate women hanging on his every word, boosting his ego. She did not have time for his nonsense.

Claudia had to think about herself now, about how she was going to pay the bills and keep Tanisha happy. She had to start her math class and stick to her plan to take the GED no matter what happened in her personal life. Claudia knew she wanted more out of life, but she also knew she had a tendency to give up as soon as things got tough. She was passive to the core, a trait she tried to fight but to which she usually gave in. The right thing to do at this point was divorce Cap and focus on her own education. But guilt about Tanisha kept getting in the way.

"How come you and Daddy don't sleep in the same bed?" Tanisha had asked her mother after her father left. "Aren't you married?"

At least Tanisha knew and had lived with her father most of her life so far, Claudia told herself. Cap looked out for Tanisha and showered her with affection. Claudia decided she couldn't turn Cap away when he wanted to visit. She knew what it was like to live without a father. There was a man in Marigot whom Claudia knew to be her own father and the father of a few of her siblings as well. One day she overheard him arguing with her mother. "Claudia is not my child!" he yelled. He admitted the other children were his and sometimes stopped by to see them, bringing treats with him. She couldn't figure out why he didn't acknowledge her as well. From that day on, Claudia rarely referred to the man again. She tried to deny his existence.

Daisy, who brought Violet to the dance class, stuck her head in the doorway. "We're all meeting for lunch tomorrow. You wanna come?" She walked into the room and took the empty seat next to Claudia.

"Oh yeah? What's the food?" Claudia asked. Both women kept their jackets zipped up. Daisy had a cap on her head.

"It might be Chinese. The food will be good. If I say it's good, it's good."

A father walked into the room and stood awkwardly, hands in the pockets of a pair of shorts.

"I had to move a bathtub today," he said, addressing no one in particular. His pale legs were out of place on a cold fall day. Maybe he was nervous when he dropped his daughter off at class, a single man in a group of nannies, but for whatever reason, he usually said something strange. He was another crazy white man, thought Claudia, but he was harmless enough.

"Oh yeah?" said Claudia politely, throwing Daisy a glance.

"Up an entire flight of stairs."

No one spoke. He walked back out of the room.

"I'm graduating in the spring. I have to start thinking about getting a job," Daisy said after the man was gone.

Daisy was almost finished with her undergraduate degree. It was a good thing to have, but Claudia wondered how Daisy would put it to use if she didn't have a green card. She'd have to get married to a citizen or find a sponsor. Claudia, meanwhile, had her green card but no college diploma.

James was on his way out of the apartment by the time Claudia returned at the end of the day with both kids. Lucy started begging for television, but Claudia didn't give in. James instructed Jackson to start his homework immediately, barking the order at his son in a way that made Claudia go stiff. He was too stern with his children these days. She didn't approve. In the past, Claudia had warned the kids that she would speak with their parents if she needed to get them in line. But recently, when Jackson was acting out and she had threatened to call his father, Jackson had looked at Claudia with an expression of fear that she had never before seen on the child's face. Silently, he began to shake.

"Mira can't come over anymore. It makes things too crazy in the afternoon," James told Claudia before he left.

"Okay," she answered, without looking him in the eye.

James was starting to cross the line now. Mira, a nanny from the fifth floor, had been stopping by every day at 4:30 P.M. with Max, a boy Lucy's age, for a quick half-hour play date so she could stay out of her boss's way. Claudia hated the thought of turning the woman down now. She had stopped having play dates at the apartment except with Mira, and now she would have to give that one up too. James was making Claudia's life more difficult, and there were no signs of him working out of the house again anytime soon.

While Lucy played and Jackson stared at his homework, Claudia went to her black bag sitting on the table. She stuck her hand down to the bottom and pulled out the flyer. She had delayed long enough. If she waited for everything to fall into place for the Halls, she'd be waiting forever. Claudia called the number on the flyer and found out there was a math prep class with open spots starting that night. After weeks of thinking and watching and holding back because she didn't want to make life more complicated for Betsy, Claudia picked up the phone again and dialed without giving it too much thought. She told Betsy about the class, and Betsy agreed to be home a little early that night.

"We'll figure out your hours once you know what the class schedule is," Betsy promised.

Betsy was almost relieved that Claudia was making plans. She worried about her nanny and what would happen to her when the job ended. School was a way out for both of them. "That for me would be ideal. She goes to school. The kids are going to school. She gets her degree, gets a job, with health insurance and benefits," sighed Betsy. "Then when I only need someone three hours a day, I hire a college student. Or spend one day with the kids, they have afterschool programs and then a babysitter a couple of days. But Claudia will be off to a brighter future."

Without skipping a beat, Claudia dialed the phone again to leave a message for Tanisha and Jill, telling them where she would be that night. If Jill was out, Tanisha could go over to Royette's to eat dinner. In the living room, Lucy hugged a pile of pillows she had pulled off the couch and arranged on the floor. From the kitchen, she looked like a tiny creature lost in a sea of white, one pink leg sticking into the air, her thin blond hair a trail of yellow against the stark couch pillows.

"We have to run back out to the supermarket," Claudia called out to the kids.

After a few minutes of back and forth and a quick cleanup in case James came back, Claudia maneuvered Lucy into her stroller again. Jackson walked alongside his sister, unhappy at being dragged around. Claudia looked exactly the same now as she had earlier in the day, the colors of her clothes a dour black and gray. But inside, she felt the buzz of something new. She wouldn't even care if she saw the crazy man up the street again. Let him tease her. His words would roll right off her now.

Claudia had gone through many of the biggest moments of her life alone. She had stood alone, hiding in the bushes when her father claimed she wasn't his, and kept the secret to herself. She had given birth to Tanisha alone while the rest of her family was at a wedding and Cap was betraying her with another woman in Brooklyn. Alone, she had made the decision to send her son to live with her mother, leaving him behind forever. She had arrived in this country alone. She was alone when Cap flew back to an island full of women twelve years later, betraying her again. And climbing the stairs out of the Church Street subway stop, Claudia never expected to be anything but alone when she walked into her first math class.

She walked past the token booth, dodging the people making their way into the station, and pushed through the doors onto the street. Standing before her was a cluster of women, her daughter, her sister, and her best friend, waiting patiently for her to arrive. They had come to escort Claudia, instinctively knowing that Claudia kept quiet when things meant the most to her. She didn't tell them how excited she was and she didn't have to. They already knew.

All four women headed to Albemarle Road, a quiet residential street. The noise of the shops and the subway drifted away until there was only the occasional holler from a building courtyard. When Claudia found the address, Tanisha, Royette, and Jill followed her upstairs, right into her first math class.

A handsome Haitian man led all of the women inside his apartment, which he had divided into classrooms. They sat together as though they were all taking the class. When the teacher began, Claudia sharpened her focus. She had never been good at math, but she was determined to learn now. The fractions, numbers, and symbols in front of her were practically shining. Claudia was in math heaven.

After class, Claudia stayed behind to talk to the teacher, and he told her that the women who had accompanied her would have to stay home next time unless they wanted to take the class themselves. She explained that she had a problem with math. It was her biggest obstacle to passing the GED.

"If you do your homework and hang with me," he promised, "you will pass the test."

"That will be the happiest day of my life," she said, and then she walked home with her family.

THREE

VIVIAN McCORMICK LIVED in a building called the Bentley that wasn't as grand as its name. A squat four-story brick structure, it faced a busy road and a small strip mall lined with a deli, a Laundromat, and a tanning salon. A large sign on the front patch of lawn proudly announced the building, but inside there were water stains on the walls and piles of junk mail on the floor that sometimes blocked the front door. The stairs were dusty and the sounds of neighbors drifted into the hall. Some people didn't understand why Vivian, who seemed so together for a twenty-eight-year-old and made a decent salary of $40,000 a year caring for twin boys, would live there. Vivian laughed at her friends' assumption that she would live someplace fancier. She was comfortable at the Bentley and, in a way, the building mirrored Vivian's personality. It had a bit of pretense, but it was still rough around the edges. A steady stream of traffic passed three flights below her apartment in a constant hum of noise, yet it was also possible to look through the windows and catch an unobstructed view of pure sky.

This apartment was a shrine to Vivian's profession. Framed photos of Devan and David Pritchard, the four-year-old boys in her care, were scattered around, along with one prized picture of Vivian sitting next to Lady Bird Johnson and her grandson. Vivian's former employer had recommended Vivian as a one-day nanny for the former First Lady's grandson when Mrs. Johnson had come to Boston to receive an honorary degree. Across from her couch, Vivian had set up an entire bookshelf for her large collection of books with "nanny" in the title, including *The Safe Nanny Handbook, The Professional Nanny, The Nanny World, The Nanny Textbook, The Nanny Book, The Good Nanny Book, The American Nanny, Complete Nanny Guide, Nanny Kit, The Unnatural History of the Nanny, The Nanny Diaries*, and *You'll Never Nanny in This Town Again*. Her desk area, where she did most of her nanny campaigning, was littered with newsletters and pieces she was writing about various aspects of the job.

Almost as prominent as the nanny theme was Vivian's commitment to Christianity: Three wooden crosses were tacked up, one on the front door, one in the hallway leading to Vivian's bedroom, and one on a wall. A framed copy of the Lord's Prayer hung in her living room. And on her other bookshelf she had placed copies of *Foundations of Pentecostal Theology, Intimacy with God,* and *Being God's Best Friend*. Raised in a Baptist church, Vivian had a deep belief in God and a strong commitment to her Christian faith.

The furnishings were casual and cozy. Vivian loved the oil painting in her living room of a garden in the morning light, the candles scattered around the apartment, and the expensive scented soap in her bathroom. Her bedroom, taken up almost entirely by a large wooden bed covered with a homey quilt, was her refuge.

One of the best things about the Bentley, besides the fact that Vivian truly felt comfortable there, was its close proximity to the

Pritchard family in Wellesley. The town of Framingham, or at least the part she lived in, wasn't much, but Vivian loved the convenience of the place. She was close to the Mass Pike as well as a few favorite restaurants. And if the Pritchard twins ever needed her, she could be at their door in fifteen minutes.

Vivian didn't think it was possible that she could love her four-year-old boys even an ounce more than she already did. On weekends, when they were apart for only two days, she called to check in on them. If they went away on vacation for an entire week, she cried just thinking about them. Vivian would climb mountains, cross deserts, and swim across seas if that's what it took to keep the boys safe. "I would take a bullet for them. I would kill for them," she said with absolute conviction.

Standing five feet eight inches tall and weighing just under three hundred pounds, with thick round shoulders and black eyes, Vivian was a bear protecting her cubs. When she first started working for the Pritchards, Devan and David were ten days old. For four straight years, she held them, dressed them, snuggled with them, and watched them grow up. Devan and David were as connected to her as her own arms and legs. They were in her bones. She could wake with a start in the middle of the night and know instantly that one of her boys was sick.

"I've gone to work in the morning knowing that one of them has an ear infection," she explained. "I have that much intuition and instinct with them."

At times, her love for the boys could be uncomfortable to those who didn't understand the strength of the bond between a nanny and her charges. Vivian ran the show completely while her bosses were at work, and had no qualms about voicing her opinion about the boys' care even after her ten-hour workday was over. When she discovered that Devan and David's mother, Catherine, had called Pinch Sitters for a babysitter on a Saturday night, Vivian heatedly lectured her on the dangers of hiring a stranger, and demanded that she be asked to work the extra hours instead. Later, Vivian told the story to her friends, portraying her boss as reckless.

Things in Vivian's world were done methodically, on a carefully planned timeline, and she had full control in the Pritchard house when it came to childcare. A pacifier was thrown out at three months. Food tossed from a highchair was never returned, and there were no choices at meals except to eat what was served or go hungry. Potties were placed in the family room right along with the boys' toys at twelve months so they could get comfortable with them before being trained a year later. Juice was not allowed until age four.

The results of Vivian's rules were impressive. Devan and David were very well trained. They sat quietly for long periods of time, always said please and thank you, and regularly told Vivian they loved her on command. Sometimes, Vivian liked to joke, they were just like the "Stepford children."

Vivian was an expert, and unwavering in her beliefs about child rearing: She believed in strong discipline and the Ferber method of sleep training. She believed the boys should clean up after themselves, always be polite, and never, ever have more control than she. Within the boundaries of her strictly followed rules, Vivian wove in fun time. She created "Fabulous Fridays," taking the boys on weekly field trips into Boston. She assembled an arts and crafts box and filled it with pipe cleaners, cotton balls, and confetti. She praised the boys' artwork and taped it on the walls of the Pritchards' home. And she threw the best birthday parties around. Vivian's rules also allowed for downtime: at the end of her day with the boys, she often curled up with them on the couch to snuggle.

• • •

Vivian's journey into the nanny world began when she was a young teenager, babysitting a group of eleven children at her Baptist church on Sundays. She went on to work her way through college as a nanny for a family who never let her leave the house with the children. In her senior year, Vivian realized she had to make a choice. The first person in her family to earn a college diploma, Vivian had always felt she owed it to herself and her family to find work outside of domestic care. When it came time to look for a job that related to her degree in math, she realized her passion was really for children. She decided to become a nanny. Two years after graduation, she got the validation she needed when she learned about the International Nanny Association (INA), a national non-profit educational organization of nannies and nanny agencies. That year, for the first time, Vivian saw that she could do what she loved and still be considered a professional career woman.

She flew all the way to Chandler, Arizona, to attend the INA's annual conference. Looking around at the other women who dressed and talked like her, Vivian realized she was home. Within three months, she was not only a member of the group, she was an active member of the board. Still in her early twenties, Vivian had already found her calling. Four years later, she considered herself a major player in her field.

Vivian was not your everyday nanny. She was a born image maker and a public relations master, and she knew INA was lucky to have her on its board. With a natural instinct for marketing, a love of slogans, and a knack for organizing packets and pamphlets, she was a woman on a mission to create the perfect picture of an American professional nanny. She moved fast, talked fast, expected quick results. Her patience was limited and she had little tolerance for excuses. When she spoke, her words came out in a tumble, one on top of the other, and if the person she was talking to could not keep up, she huffed in frustration, rolled her eyes, and repeated herself *very* slowly.

Her goal was simple — educate the public on the importance of nannies and set standards for the industry — and she approached it with the passion and fervor of an evangelist. She preached to anyone who would listen, wrote articles for trade magazines, boosted her resumé with workshops and conferences. Besides serving on the board of the International Nanny Association, she also paid dues to the National Nanny Association (an organization that closed in 2007), participated in an online Christian nannies group, and, most important, started her own nonprofit nanny support group for the Boston area. She even offered herself as an expert to the local media outlets, appearing in several community newspapers and magazines to position herself as a symbol of what it means to be a true nanny.

"I engage in the coordinated model of nanny care, where my role is team player in raising emotionally and physically healthy, happy children," Vivian told one reporter, repeating her self-created sound bite verbatim.

"I can't think of anything more important to do with my life than have an impact on children's lives. The world should know what nannies have to offer," she remarked to another.

If Vivian were a scientist, she would win the Nobel Prize. If she were a politician, she would be the first woman president. If she were an athlete, she'd take the gold at the Olympics. Vivian could barely keep her ambition under control. She plotted her rise to the top of the nanny world with precision and boundless energy.

She woke early in the morning and dressed quickly for her ten-hour workday with Devan and David. When it ended, she returned home, sat in the small corner of the living room she liked to call her office, and began working on the computer. Typing away, she e-mailed advice to younger nannies, updated her website, and laid out her monthly newsletter. When Vivian took a rare night off, she played basketball in a local women's league or grabbed a bite at 99 Restaurant and Pub, a New England chain that was her favorite dining spot.

Unlike many women her age, Vivian didn't party on the weekends or try out different jobs to see what fit. She already knew exactly what she wanted. She would be recognized as America's top nanny, fight for regulation, and educate the public on the importance of quality childcare. If the government didn't set standards for nannies, the way it did for daycare centers and nurses, Vivian would set her own. If the public wanted to call babysitters and au pairs nannies, Vivian would prove to them that there was a difference. She even dreamed of someday having a nanny-recognition week established in Massachusetts, founding a museum dedicated to the history of her profession, and getting a "nanny makeover" show on *Oprah*.

"I'm an ambitious nanny," Vivian said, raising a perfectly arched eyebrow with an ironic glint in her eye and a half smile across her lips. She was playful but serious, seemingly aware of the fact that many Americans viewed ambition and being a nanny as mutually exclusive. The best way to prove to everyone — her friends, her families, the American public — that she was the best of the best was to eventually be elected INA's Nanny of the Year.

On a cool spring evening at the end of April, Vivian rushed around her apartment, packing for her third International Nanny Association conference. This year's conference was dubbed "A Wild Time" on the International Nanny Association's website and in its brochures because it included a trip to the San Diego Zoo. Vivian thought the zoo angle was lame, but she was still as excited as a kid on her way to summer camp. She would attend a few workshops, compare notes with friends, and make a strong push with the INA board to have the next conference in her hometown of Boston.

Vivian pulled out her green suitcase and began to expertly fill it. Hyper-organized, she stayed on top of everything despite all she had going on in her life. This trip made her think back nostalgically on the years she had spent with Devan and David, how tiny they were when she first met them and how big and independent they had become. These days she was prepping the boys and herself for preschool in the fall. Vivian was nervous about the transition. She did not do well with change when she was not in a position to control the outcome.

Her boys were going into a situation she didn't know from a hole in the wall. How would the teachers treat the boys? Vivian wondered. Would they be loving and nurturing? Would the boys' needs be met? Would they be treated like a matching set of twins or like the distinct individuals she so clearly knew them as? It wasn't the specific preschool that put Vivian on edge; it was the idea of preschool itself. All of a sudden, Devan and David would be in the hands of someone else, dropped off in an unsupervised environment with new teachers and new kids.

"The teachers get paid eight dollars an hour," Vivian said to herself. "Why are they there? Are they there because they want to be or because they have to be? Do they love what they do or do they hate what they do?"

Preschool wouldn't start until September, still months away, and the boys would only go from 9:00 A.M. to 12:00 P.M., but Vivian already felt pangs of empty-nest syndrome. She had no idea how she would spend those three extra hours a day, and she was also concerned that Catherine would question keeping her at the same salary. She worried as well about the year after preschool, when the boys would start kindergarten. Her vote was for the local public school, which had a great reputation, but she suspected that Catherine's husband, Trevor, preferred that the boys attend private school.

"I don't want them to be raised thinking they're entitled to everything, and be rich, stuck-up snobs," she said, explaining her resistance to private school. "I want them to have an education that becomes what you make of it. A real-world approach, not this Harry Potter school shit with kids running around with a BMW."

Vivian laid her clothes in her suitcase. She chose five Lane Bryant suits, flats and pumps, and a bathing suit. She also packed her brag book, a collection of photos of the boys she planned to show off to her friends and colleagues. Retrieving ten strawberry and chocolate Atkins diet shakes from the kitchen, Vivian placed the cans in around her clothes. Technically obese, Vivian did not feel defined by her weight, but it was something she was determined to change. So far, Atkins had worked wonders. Its strict rules appealed to Vivian's sense of order, and she was quickly heading to her goal weight of 180 pounds. Studying three travel toiletry bags, she debated whether to bring the weeklong, weekend, or overnight size, and then went with the middle choice. She threw in some makeup, knowing she would probably never wear it.

By the time Vivian walked out her front door for work the next morning, her entire apartment was spotless, pillows fluffed, bed made, papers put away, kitchen counter bare, refrigerator buzzing and empty.

"Every good nanny has a touch of OCD," she joked when she went into an organizing and cleaning fit.

Vivian carried her suitcase out of the house, climbed into her blue Toyota Corolla, and headed to the Pritchard house in Wellesley. From her first day with the Pritchards, Vivian had been a full-charge nanny, meaning she was in charge of everything when it came to the boys. Trevor, a marketing executive, spent much of his time traveling, while Catherine, who was a grant writer for a nonprofit organization, was easy to work for. Vivian believed that Catherine had an innate understanding that handing over fifty hours a week of childcare to another woman meant handing over much of the control. Her first nanny jobs had had more restrictions, and she had sometimes felt like a babysitter.

Vivian was hired by the Pritchards as a professional nanny with experience and expertise, and the job had gone well from the start. She took her freedom on the job and ran with it. She was the CEO of childcare for the Pritchard family, organizing toy areas, buying clothes, making play dates, arranging field trips. She felt she had full decision-making power when it came to every aspect of discipline, from whether the boys made their own beds to how they acted when eating out in a restaurant. Catherine wasn't always as hard-line with the boys as Vivian, preferring to spend her few hours a day having fun instead of enforcing rules, but she usually backed Vivian up. Vivian didn't just consider herself a happy employee in the Pritchard house. She basked in the power of being a third parent.

Vivian parked her car on the street, leaving her suitcase in the trunk. The Pritchard house, built in the 1920s, had a long brick pathway and a pillared front portico that gave it a presidential air. Large but understated, with spots of peeling paint, it was simultaneously intimidating and welcoming. The back room on the main floor, where Vivian always entered, had a set of French doors leading straight to the deck and a casual, child-friendly feel. The front rooms of the house, which Vivian almost never entered, held traditional American furniture, antiques, winged upholstered chairs, uncomfortable couches, and Oriental rugs. This was the museum, the showplace, the untouchable part of the house. But in the back, where it was safe to spill and leave toys on the floor, Vivian ruled.

It was a typical morning when Vivian stepped inside. Catherine rushed around the living room, throwing her wallet, car keys, and cell phone into her bag. Devan and David gave Vivian her morning hug and then she sat on the floor with them to distract them from their mother. As usual, Trevor wasn't in the kitchen. Vivian assumed he was at an early meeting or away on business.

"I'll be home in time for you to catch your plane," Catherine said after she hugged her kids. They clung to her for a minute before heading back to their toys in the family room.

"Don't be late," Vivian called out, already concerned about missing her flight.

When Catherine closed the door, Vivian turned her gaze to Devan and David. It would be a quick and easy day. She would read them books, let them run around outside, and show them on their map exactly where she would be flying that weekend. It was never too early to teach them about all the states in America. Vivian relaxed. The Pritchard house was hers.

When Vivian first saw the house, she knew it was expensive, but she didn't spend much time assessing the quality of the furniture or the number of rooms or the art hanging on the walls. None of that mattered to her. While she never had much as a child, Vivian had always lived in upper-middle-class towns. During these years, nobody ever knew Vivian's family received public assistance or that her designer clothes were from consignment shops or that the apartment her mother rented wasn't really an entire house owned by her family. After a childhood spent around others who had more than she did, Vivian was not overly impressed with wealth.

Instead, her eyes had gone straight to the family room off the kitchen, where she immediately spotted couches that were potential hazards and tables with sharp edges. In her mind, she baby-proofed the entire room. And over the years, Vivian had become the gate-keeper to this part of the house, a place constantly in flux as the boys grew older and their needs changed. The room morphed slowly, guided by David and Devan's developmental milestones.

When talking about the boys, Vivian's voice softened, her tone grew wistful, and the corners of her mouth turned up in a half smile. Love flooded out of her as she compared her boys to the colors of the rainbow. David was yellow, his moods falling into the middle spectrum, steady and predictable, always the lovable class clown. Devan was the entire rainbow, his moods swinging from the brightest colors to the softest. Vivian lived for the challenge of working with twins — in fact in her short career she had cared only for twins, even in her earliest days as a nanny while going to college, carving out a niche for herself — and liked to tell people she rose to the task by fulfilling the needs of one child without sacrificing the needs of the other. She treated her current charges like individual boys with distinctive personalities, and she loved them equally but differently. In their quieter moments, Vivian sang each child a private song softly in his ear. Devan's was "Going on a Bear Hunt," and David's was "Jesus Loves the Little Children," a song she loved from church.

Vivian thought through the cause and effect of every situation with the boys. Even now, with the end of her job nowhere in sight, she took care to prep the twins for her eventual departure when they got older. "I always say, 'I'm not your mom, I'm your nanny. Mommy and Daddy are going to work and that's why they chose a nanny,'" she said. "'You could be like the other kids and go to an afterschool program all day.'" While she felt she did the bulk of the work of raising them, she acknowledged that Catherine and Trevor came first and said without a trace of regret that she knew the boys loved Catherine more than her.

"Let's get the day started," Vivian said to Devan and David in the family room. "We don't have a lot of time today."

After a few hours of playing at home, feeding the boys, and running a few errands, Vivian's workday was over early. She handed the kids over to Catherine, hugging them as she headed out the door. Before she boarded the plane, she called her mother to check in as usual and say goodbye. An hour later, Vivian turned off her phone and sat back as the plane took off, flying over the country toward the West Coast.

The weather in San Diego was cool and overcast. Thick clouds hung in the air. If not for the palm trees, Vivian could still have been in New England. She took a cab to the Town and Country resort, a hotel and conference center with an English garden theme that faced Interstate 8. With a trellis courtyard, rose garden, poolside gazebo, and meeting rooms named Sheffield, Hampton, and Windsor, the resort was British-themed. But its Royal Palm Drive, Royal Palm Tower, and San Diego, California, and Pacific Ballrooms, along with the roar of passing cars on the highway, made it all-American.

Vivian made her way up Royal Palm Drive and found her room in Royal Palm Tower, an aging building set back on the property with views of the Fashion Valley Mall. After unpacking her bag, she headed straight into four days of workshops and meetings with a group of ninety other nannies, agency owners, and agency employees. This was Vivian's life away from the Pritchards, a world of planning committees and welcoming committees and membership committees, a world that gave her number one passion in life, working with children, the validation she needed.

FOUR

VIVIAN KNEW EXACTLY why the nannies at the INA conference looked alike. Many of them were fat. These women, like Vivian, had traveled from almost every state in the country, but they could have been born in the same exact hometown, related through one big extended family. They were all white American women with fresh-scrubbed faces and little makeup. Their clothes were impossible to date, just as unstylish that year as they would have been in 1983, oversized suits with long skirts and boxy jackets, button-down shirts made of polyester blends. As individuals, they could melt into any crowd, fit in with any family, and that was the point. They were told by their agencies not to attract too much attention, to dress like their bosses would dress for work on casual Fridays.

Even at the Nanny of the Year luncheon, the forty nannies assembled in the Pacific Ballroom made a striking sight for exactly the same reason. They packed their best outfits for the professional nanny conference, yet they were still surprisingly plain, with simple haircuts and modest jewelry. Among the children they cared for, they were sparkling and beloved. In the adult world, they didn't make much of an impression.

As the other women at her table speared chef salads, spread butter on rolls, and dug into slices of chocolate cake, Vivian ignored the lunch she was served and took an Atkins strawberry shake out of her purse, popped the can, and poured it into a glass. Her willpower made her feel stronger than any woman in the ballroom. Looking around, she assessed the crowd. An insider, Vivian could easily separate the room into two groups: nannies, and agency owners and employees. The agency women were thin. They had styled hair, painted lips, and cute suits from stores like Ann Taylor. They wore tailored pants or perfectly ironed skirts and pumps with sweet little heels. Many of the nannies were washed out in comparison, faces less vibrant, colors faded, the lines of their clothes loose, straight and sexless, bodies wide. Thinking back to the conference months later, Vivian would describe the women as "fat and unkempt. There was a lot of grooming issues. Hairy lips."

Vivian's observations were nonjudgmental. She simply acknowledged the fact in her usual, to-the-point style. And having once hit an all-time high of 336 pounds herself, Vivian was proud to sit with these women. They were her peers, her colleagues, her friends. Some were morbidly obese, others just a bit overweight, a few had grown larger from one year to the next, their shirts a little bigger, pants baggier, dresses longer, covering what was probably now a bulging belly or thicker thighs. Vivian could even point out a few of the thinner women rumored to have had gastric bypass surgery or the few she suspected had, like her, polycystic ovarian syndrome, an endocrine disorder that, among other things, could cause obesity. Yet there was no place in the world Vivian wanted to be more than in this room full of nannies.

Vivian had struggled with weight her entire life, but this latest diet wasn't nearly as difficult as she had imagined. She had made the decision to do it, set a goal weight, and then stuck with the regimen no matter how badly she wanted to stray. There were no excuses. There was no cheating. She planned her meals, laid down all the no-carb rules, and followed them like a set of perfectly outlined instructions she might have given her boys. Vivian had had a rock-bottom moment that became an epiphany. In March, she had taken Devan and David to their kickball class and heard a group of kids referring to her as Ursula the Sea Witch — the overweight, purple cartoon villainess from the animated film *The Little Mermaid* who was modeled after a drag queen. Vivian was shocked into revelation. She could certainly endure fat jokes — she had for her entire life — but she could not bear the thought of Devan and David being teased on her account. She went on a diet almost immediately.

"That cake looks awful," Vivian commented with a devilish grin as she took a sip of her own pink drink. "This shake is so much better."

"How come they have fake flowers on the tables when there are so many real roses all over the property?" asked another woman at the table of six caregivers.

"My goal is to have a nanny car by July," said another, ignoring the flower debate.

It was the usual conference small talk among INA nannies. Friendly, innocent, benign. These were, after all, the nannies a family would be lucky to hire — if they could afford on-the-books salaries, paid vacations, overtime, and health benefits. While they have to pay a premium for an INA nanny, the families who hire them are not typically the superrich. According to INA president Pat Cascio, the families employing INA caregivers are often two working professionals who value education, who appreciate the professionalism of their childcare workers, and who look for individuals who are passionate about their jobs, because they know that these qualities will benefit their children.

Of the nannies attending the conference, many were college educated. They had extensive experience as live-ins and live-outs. But most of all, they loved their work. The everyday, down-in-the-trenches domestic rituals of raising children that were mind-numbing to some people were challenging and fascinating to them.

They had tricks up their sleeves for teething, tantrums, bad behavior, and just plain fun. They shared views on child rearing at their local support groups; wrote articles, as Vivian did, for trade newsletters; and mentored younger nannies just starting out in the profession. Swapping advice, they sounded like new, highly focused stay-at-home mothers: Are your kids heading to school for the first time? Establish a special goodbye routine, like giving them a kiss and saying "See ya later, alligator" with a big smile. Dealing with chronic ear infections? Try grapefruit-seed extract or mullein before antibiotics. Taking a long road trip? Don't forget your nanny survival kit, complete with boredom busters like books and games and emergency snacks.

The Nanny of the Year luncheon was one of the most important events of the four-day conference. A formal, catered affair with white tablecloths, it was one of the few times during the conference that nannies and agency employees gathered together. During the bulk of the conference, they sat in separate workshops geared toward their particular needs. The previous year's workshops had touched on difficult subjects like "The Disengaged Parent," "Agency War Stories," and "I'll Just Call My Lawyer: Liability Issues." This year's lineup included "The Magical World of Nannies" and "Activities to Grow On." The INA nanny didn't travel this far for the workshops alone. She came to stand among those she viewed as the elite in her field, the cream of the crop, the true professional nannies.

Standing highest among these choice nannies was the Nanny of the Year, a woman introduced as the best of the best by a special INA committee of nannies and agency owners. Vivian sat at her table, took a sip of her Atkins shake, and watched as Amy Lynn made her way to the front of the ballroom, taking her place behind a podium, her speech in hand. The thirty-four-year-old nanny from Minneapolis wore a long flowered skirt with a matching flowered jacket and a pair of flats. She had brown, kind eyes and a Buster Brown haircut that would have suited a child just as well. This ten-minute speech was the moment of a lifetime, and every nanny in the room knew it. Some of them, like Vivian, dreamed of winning the honor themselves but had never been nominated, others had been nominated in the past but passed over, and a select few were past winners.

Amy's was an emotional speech, the ultimate underdog moment, and she ran through the years of her life, from her struggles with dyslexia as a child who was mistakenly labeled stupid to her college graduation against all odds to her life-changing realization, not unlike Vivian's, that being a nanny was her true calling. Amy paid special tribute to her mother, who had supported her and believed in her when her own teachers wrote her off.

While others gave in to the sentimental moment, Vivian dissected Amy's speech like a political pundit assessing the State of the Union address. "Drama," she thought to herself. "This isn't professionalism." She had strong feelings about the Nanny of the Year award. It bothered her when nannies got up on the stage and cried, going on about their personal lives. It bothered her when the Nanny of the Year was a great nanny on the job but did nothing to improve the nanny industry as a whole. In Vivian's opinion, the Nanny of the Year should not only be the best nanny, she should be working to change the entire nanny landscape in America.

"I think to be Nanny of the Year," she said, "you should be involved in the profession and the industry, not just a boring presence year after year, thirteen conferences, just existing. Do something. What have you done?"

Vivian could have told a story as heartrending as Amy Lynn's, but what would be the point? Raised by a single mother, in housing subsidized by the government, Vivian was not the type to let the past get in the way of her future. She mostly kept the details of her childhood to herself, unless she was singing her mother's praises, but when she talked about her father, it was hard to imagine he did not have an impact on her. She described him as a sometimes violent alcoholic who had disappointed her throughout her life. After he moved out of her mother's house, Vivian and her brother sat in the window waiting for him to appear on his visiting days, but he often never showed up. Even now, as Vivian struggled to sever all ties with her boyfriend, Reed, who had repeatedly hit her when they lived together, Vivian brushed off her childhood as unimportant. She had better things to do and too much to accomplish to dwell on a father who drank and a boyfriend who took advantage of her insecurity around men.

The crowd sat enthralled, chins held high, eyes focused on Amy as she wept openly, her voice shaking. Vivian remained expressionless.

"I would also like to thank Oprah for bringing back her book club," Amy joked before she finished her speech.

Vivian watched Amy leave the stage, but in her mind she was the one walking away with the award. One year from now, Vivian decided, she would be the next INA Nanny of the Year. There wasn't a single doubt in her mind. Vivian quietly finished her drink, but her mind was racing. She was already making plans.

"When I'm up there," Vivian thought to herself, "I will present myself as a professional, not as an emotional mess."

• • •

Except for the zoo outing, the attendees didn't see much of San Diego. Their schedules jam-packed with workshops, the nannies didn't venture into the city, and it was too cold to spend much time lying by the pool. Vivian never got to use the bathing suit she had carefully packed. The INA website had promised a sunny time in Southern California, but the sheets of clouds that greeted the nannies never lifted and the air remained surprisingly damp. The organizers might not have realized their mistake. They had booked a city known for its seaside location and its warm weather, but they set the date on a weekend between April and May, the city's cloudiest and gloomiest time of year.

The nannies bundled up and headed out to workshops with pens and pads, heading in small groups and pairs into Royal Palm Salon 4, where most of the presentations were held. For three straight days, they sat in this double-sized room, shades drawn, stale air blasting through vents, complaining about parents' inability to discipline their children, giving pep talks to each other on how to negotiate a more lucrative contract, and confessing a lack of self-esteem. The workshops were equal parts group therapy, child-development refresher, and career counseling for a group of women who admitted they were sometimes passive about their lives.

One workshop, "Positive Communications/Negotiations without Ulcers," quickly disintegrated into personal confession as a few nannies described their childhoods, blaming those early experiences for their inability to demand better contracts from their employers. Raised in poverty or in working-class homes, several nannies said they were accustomed to disappointment. Others expressed guilt at putting a dollar sign on a job that had, as its top requirement, love for a child. If they demanded more money for the hours they put in, did it mean their love was not authentic? Did it mean it was not real?

INA took great care in sculpting the image of its nannies as dynamic women who perfectly navigated the unique terrain of working in someone else's home. The INA nanny loved her children like they were her own but recognized and respected the limitations of that relationship. She kept her mouth shut when she saw a first step or heard a first word, leaving her employers with the illusion that they had witnessed the baby's milestones. This nanny consistently reminded children that their parents came first. Meanwhile, she gracefully did much of the hard work, taking care of her charges' physical needs and instilling them with confidence and a clear sense of right and wrong.

But within the walls of Salon 4, the INA image slowly disappeared, leaving some of these nannies exposed. They weren't supernannies, after all. They were flawed human beings. They belonged to a group that identified them as the best nannies in the country, but that status didn't always translate into self-worth. Whether it was asking for more money or demanding more communication and respect, some of these women had trouble articulating their needs. Instead, they quietly waited for their employers to offer words of praise or raises on merit. When recognition or higher pay didn't come, these nannies grew resentful, feeling that their hard work was going unappreciated. The INA conference was the place to work out this frustration and learn to speak up. Vivian acknowledged that even the INA nanny could feel exploited on the job, especially if she was just starting out in the field.

"They do feel they are underpaid or they have too many domestic tasks. But usually nannies like that, it takes one job to cure them," Vivian said, explaining why networking was so important for nannies. "A parent's worst nightmare is having their nanny get connected with another professional nanny."

Sometimes, Pat Cascio said, these empowerment workshops

worked against the nannies. Pushed too hard to negotiate, the women could come across as aggressive in interviews, forgetting to highlight their experience and love for the work. She described one woman who had trouble landing a job because she went straight to discussing the financial terms, putting families off.

The tone shifted dramatically in the room over the four days of the conference, illuminating just how complicated, emotionally draining, and rewarding raising other people's children can be. The nannies expressed sadness for the children who saw their parents just a few hours a day. But they also knew that these children were lucky to have them, the best nannies in the country, stepping in to fill the void. It was a heady mix of emotions in a bland hotel conference room: sadness and happiness, resentment and contentment, insecurity and confidence. And after just a few hours of workshops, it was clear. This INA conference was less an educational setting than a meeting place for women who didn't normally socialize with other nannies while at work, a place where these caregivers could convene in a group to share the ups and downs and frustrations and joys of raising children who were not their own.

Many had battle scars from jobs gone bad and children they had to leave. Some were engaged in conflicts with the families they worked for. But all expressed a commitment to their work and a belief, even as their jobs did not command respect in the larger society, that the long hours they put in made a difference in a child's life.

Vivian popped in and out of the workshops, staying only when something struck her interest. As a board member, she had other responsibilities. But she made the time to attend one of the most engaging workshops of the conference, a two-part lecture held on Friday morning that was innocently titled "Nurturing the Child."

Madelyn Swift, an author and expert on discipline, family dynamics, and personal communication, was the speaker. Dressed in a modest navy suit, with glasses perched on her nose and a short, moppy haircut, Swift immediately grabbed everyone's attention.

"How many of you work for dysfunctional families?" she asked coyly, leaning back as she took in the rows of nodding heads and smiles. She was speaking their language, acknowledging the many women who worked for parents who were afraid of setting limits and, as a result, relinquished control.

A great number of the women in the room said parents had instructed them, directly or indirectly, not to say no to their children. This was a familiar parenting style, and Vivian had mentally ended interviews once she saw the writing on the wall. "We don't say no. We distract," one mother told Vivian, who shook her head, thinking back on the interview. The Pritchards never shied away from no.

Instead of acting like parents, Swift and the nannies agreed, their employers tended to treat their children like friends, giving them whatever they wanted so they didn't have to face tantrums or rejection in the little free time they had together. One nanny described her nine-year-old charge as so spoiled, she asked to be paid for the simple act of turning on the dishwasher. Another complained that her six-year-old charge had a weekly massage appointment.

"With regard to children in this country, we have been blowing it big-time," Swift declared to a rapt audience. She painted a picture of America in crisis, with children calling the shots at home only to suffer later when they brought that same level of entitlement into the outside world.

"Parents think their child is baby Jesus," Swift railed, insisting that children should never be treated as special but rather told they are unique.

"That's why I never let the kids win at Candy Land!" Vivian said, laughing at her own determination to teach her boys how to fail. "But what do you do with a wealthy family where the children get whatever they want?" asked a nanny whose business card featured a stenciled picture of Mary Poppins's carpetbag. As much time as these women spent with their charges, they couldn't completely control how the children were raised. Swift made a strong argument for her views on child rearing, and all of the nannies seemed to agree with her theories. But putting her techniques into practice with someone else's children could be a real challenge.

"Sometimes parents are so detached, but they feel guilty," said another woman, explaining why even families who weren't wealthy spoiled their children.

"But then parents are letting themselves off the hook by saying, 'I'm not there but I do feel guilty so it's okay that I'm not there,'" Swift shot back.

Stories poured from the nannies, a catalog of anecdotes about parents who threw gifts at their kids but rarely gave them their time. One nanny had watched, heartbroken, as her charge marched up to her mother, handed over all of the money from her piggy bank, and begged her to stay home, only to watch her walk out the door as usual. Another nanny had seen her charge role-playing as a nanny to her stuffed animals.

The nannies were heading toward a line that was not often crossed: judging the parents who hired them for needing their services in the first place. Nannies might be critical of parents for working long hours because they believed it hurt the children, but they generally kept those thoughts to themselves, to avoid negative consequences. "I don't think they'd ever admit it," Vivian explained later when asked whether nannies felt mothers should stay home with their children. "It's a Catch-22. If you say, 'You work too much,' then you're out of a job." Vivian also believed that Catherine was a better mother because she worked outside the home. "Part of your job is to facilitate that relationship," Vivian said, describing life with a working family. "Part of your job is to set up the transition when parents come home so they can have special time with them. You back up the parents."

Swift suggested that nannies stress the importance of parents spending more time with their children, encouraging them to have dinner as a family at least five times a week, and that discipline and limits were better than bribery. And as she spoke, in a conference room far away from the tangle of dysfunctional families, that goal seemed momentarily possible. Swift was a coach and her team was ready and willing. They felt sure that they could change the future for a generation of emotionally deprived, materially overindulged children and realign entire families' priorities.

"The nation is depending on you!" Swift shouted, closing in a gust of inspiration.

The nannies applauded enthusiastically, then got up from their seats and filed out into the hallway. Outside the walls of the INA conference, the empowerment spell was broken: cars raced by on Interstate 8, leading to the real world. And in that world, nannies didn't have the power of Jo Frost on *Supernanny* or Nanny Stella and Nanny Deb on *Nanny 911*. Swift had struck a chord with these women, but in the end, her advice was more wishful thinking than practical strategy. How could a nanny, hired by parents, turn around and tell those same people that they were doing a lousy job as parents?

There was no way to tell how the lessons learned in workshops would translate on the job, where boundaries were blurred and emotions often ruled, where love and guilt trumped standard-of-living raises and dental insurance. Taking care of children was the easy part; walking the line with parents was the challenge. Push too hard and risk angering a parent. Push too little and risk getting less than deserved. Say too much and put parents on the defensive. Say too little and watch a bad family dynamic solidify.

Switching gears from the intensity of the workshop, the nannies milled in the hallway, smiling, laughing, and making jokes. They were used to living in a world where they witnessed so many mistakes and stood powerless to stop them, keeping their mouths shut. In a job like this, it was one of the main challenges. Sure, there were things about the job that made them sad, but really it was nothing new.

"It's potty time!" one sang out as several women headed toward the bathroom.

As the conference progressed, it was difficult to pin down exactly what INA accomplished besides organizing an expensive, exclusive conference. The agencies viewed INA's role as educational, providing resources on its website for nannies, parents, agencies, and the media, as well as a mentoring program and newsletters. Some nannies wanted more, growing increasingly frustrated when they didn't see results. They thought INA should work to regulate the industry, weeding out bad agencies and nannies, a task Pat Cascio said was impossible.

Cascio acknowledged that there were underground agencies that fabricated papers for undocumented women; she described how an investigative report by a television news crew had found one Houston-based agency using the same reference for multiple nannies. That same agency charged the nannies, rather than the families, with the placement fee — taking up to a hundred dollars out of their salaries a week — and continued to draw nannies' salaries from families' accounts for weeks after the jobs were terminated.

"It would be nice to clean up the industry, but you'll never be able to clean it up," Cascio said in response to the charge that INA didn't do enough. "Those underground agencies will always be operating quietly. The bad will survive."

Vivian remained devoted to INA, but she also saw its shortcomings. Many ideas presented to the board were stalled by internal politics. "The mission of INA is never clearly defined," Vivian remarked. "Every year we spend hours and hours reevaluating the mission statement and no one can ever come to an agreement. Are we going to be a regulating body or an educational body?"

The only standard INA had created was an optional nanny credential exam. By 2008, only sixty nannies — including Vivian — had passed the test, an insubstantial number in a country where INA estimated that more than a million nannies worked. INA nannies like Vivian wanted higher requirements, like accreditation, set for the industry so they could distinguish themselves from individuals who entered the childcare profession as a short-term steppingstone or because they had no other choice. They wanted to be clearly set apart from au pairs, babysitters, and undocumented workers doing the job because they had to.

Vivian was not shy about voicing her opinions. Even if a woman had worked sixty hours a week caring for children for a decade, if she was undocumented and paid off the books, Vivian refused to grant her the title "nanny." Vivian wanted clear-cut government regulation distinguishing as nannies only educated American citizens working on the books.

"They steal our jobs because they'll work at a lower rate," she said, explaining her position. "We come into this with education, with knowledge, knowing our worth. We believe in what we do because we could do anything. I could be a lawyer. I could be an architect. I could be a journalist. I could do whatever I want to do, but I choose to be a nanny because I love it. A lot of these women that are here illegally can't go into an office building and get a job. Their only option is domestic help. So not only are they stealing our jobs, but they're putting our children in jeopardy. Do you think they would call 911 if there was a problem? No. They're too afraid of getting deported."

Other nannies besides Vivian, past and present INA members, also felt that they weren't given enough support by the board. Elizabeth Benavides, an undocumented nanny from Scotland, lobbied the United States Department of Labor aggressively for years to change the classification of nanny from unskilled laborer to professional, which would make the immigration process smoother. When she became an INA member, she couldn't understand why an organization that was supposed to represent nannies wasn't already working to change this label. Some of the board members were supportive of her efforts, but others argued against her, saying that putting nannies into the professional category would mean taking away their right to overtime pay. Benavides didn't agree with that argument, but she did point out that after the classification was changed in 2005, her green card was fast-tracked.

Another former INA member, Lora Brawley, said she joined INA ready to jump in and work to set industry-wide standards for care. She quickly grew discouraged when she saw that the agencies, not the nannies, had most of the control over the group. She also believed its membership and conference fees automatically excluded average nannies who couldn't afford the rates. Brawley went on to become a founding member of the National Association for Nanny Care (NANC). In 2008, she said this group was in the final development stage of a three-tiered credential program — unlike INA's one-level credential exam — that would offer qualifications for all levels of nannies in the United States, not just professionals.

Cascio was aware of NANC's three-tier program but said she "scratched her head" over it because she didn't see it having much of an impact — just as INA's own exam had little impact. In her opinion, parents didn't see the exam as important and were unconcerned about whether or not the nannies they hired passed the test. The exam was more about nanny pride. She also pointed out that INA was developing its own much easier exam — to be available online — which would focus on basic skills like CPR, home safety, and age-appropriate activities.

Still, Brawley felt that some of INA's members set themselves too far above the other nannies working across the country, and wondered if her credential program was being ignored because it would be open to all kinds of nannies — young college students, immigrants, and professional nannies — if they were inclined to take it.

"Some nannies can be very nasty," Brawley said, describing her efforts to be more inclusive. "They are very segregated. They're very cliquish. There are nannies who feel they are 'professional' nannies, which is a word I have come to hate in this industry. What that means is that if you're not like us, then we don't consider you a real nanny."

Until INA embraced all nannies working in the United States, experienced and inexperienced, American-born and undocumented, Brawley didn't believe the organization would have much impact. In fact, she felt it was the type of nanny who did not belong to INA who was most in need of its help. As a nanny in New Jersey, she was shocked to see how other women were treated on the job.

"I was the only American nanny in the play group we had, because all my employer's friends had foreign nannies. And I was a foreign thing to them. They were like, 'You don't do anything.' I don't cook. I don't clean. I didn't even do the child's laundry. And then what happened was, I would say, 'You guys shouldn't be doing this either.' They were providing their own transportation. They were cooking and cleaning and ironing and weeding the garden, if necessary. These employers would leave a list for them. And I was being paid literally five times as much as them. They were being totally abused."

In Vivian's perfect world, INA would have been a unified, action-oriented group, but even with its flaws, she still saw the benefits of membership and hoped that as a board member she could push the group to do more. She valued the friendships and working relationships she had developed with nannies and agencies. INA might not have been perfect, but Vivian still wanted to win its highest honor. Being named Nanny of the Year would legitimize her choice to be a caregiver for life and crown her as the best of the best. She would not only be a nanny, but the ultimate nanny, and if she won, she would make sure everybody knew it.

The conference finished off with a poolside Mexican fiesta, featuring an open bar almost none of the nannies approached. A chill hung in the air and many of the women who had saved their best summer dresses for this night had to turn to warmer clothes. Others braved the cold, goose bumps covering their arms and legs. Perhaps it was the weather or just the natural vibe of the evening, but the event took on a subdued tone as old-timers reminisced about conferences past, when raucous nannies broke out with impromptu games of limbo and dancing. The mood lifted as the annual raffle began, the women sitting on the edges of their seats, clutching tickets.

"This is cutthroat," they joked as they all eyed the best prizes: a Buzz Lightyear doll and a Winnie the Pooh suitcase.

When it was all over the next morning and most of the nannies had rolled their suitcases out of the hotel lobby, Vivian was one of the few who stayed behind. As a board member, she had one final meeting to attend, to evaluate the success of the event and make plans for the following year. Heading into yet another air-conditioned conference room, Vivian was even more determined than ever to get INA to Boston. She had daydreamed about winning Nanny of the Year all weekend, envisioning her mother, her grand-mother, Catherine, and the boys all sitting in the audience as she gave her speech. Her mind was already made up. Nothing would stop Vivian from getting the next conference to her hometown.

Vivian opened the door to the Terrace Salon, surveyed the room, and chose the "power seat" directly across from Pat Cascio. Before long, the bickering began. On the outside, it had seemed like the nannies were happy at the conference, catching up with old friends and taking part in workshops, but Vivian felt there was an underlying negativity because the nannies were increasingly irri-tated that INA wasn't all it could be. "People get frustrated," Vivian said later. "Every year it comes to a head at conference because every year people want an update of what's happened, and nothing happened."

Several women had pointed out that while the number of nan-nies working across the country had increased, the number of nannies attending the INA conference had decreased. Including airfare, food, hotel, and a hefty $300 attendance fee, the conference could easily cost over $1,000, a large sum for a group of women working at low- to average-paying jobs. INA's solution to the high cost was to suggest passing it on to employers, an impractical move considering so many of the nannies that weekend had admitted they had trouble asking for cost-of-living raises, let alone all-expenses-paid trips.

"If we have the conference in Boston next year, I can bring in a large number of nannies," Vivian stated when the conversation shifted to poor attendance. "I guarantee we'll have a bigger conference."

Vivian did not get the answer she was hoping for. The board resisted her suggestion, saying the city would be too expensive for a conference, the fees for nannies too high. Vivian later remarked that INA was being shortsighted, that it was overlooking her proven ability to get things done.

"I can help with the numbers. I can bring in every member of my support group. I can do it. I'm telling you, I can do it. If you're not going to do it, then I'm going to do it," Vivian said, knowing her words would be taken as a threat. The conversation continued, a sharp back-and-forth until things got a bit too heated. Recalling the exchange with a laugh, back in her apartment in Framingham, Vivian said that she had been so pushy, Pat Cascio threatened to kick her out of the room if she didn't stop talking about Boston.

Vivian did not let the meeting deter her. She had never let anything get in the way of her goals. At three years old, in preschool, Vivian had been named Most Likely to Succeed. Not much had changed since then. As she packed her bag at the end of the conference, put her toiletries in Ziplocs, and tucked her brag book inside her purse, she wasn't rattled at all.

The plane took off for Boston, the city where Vivian resolved the next INA conference would be held. She ran the board meeting through her head and thought, "Don't they know me at all? Don't they know if I say I'm going to do it, then I'm going to do it?" She decided to launch her own conference, a free conference that offered better speakers, made a real impact on the industry, inspired INA to have its own event in Boston, and, most important, paved the way for Vivian's Nanny of the Year triumph.

If the board members refused to listen, Vivian vowed on that plane ride home, she would prove to them just what she could do on her own. She would hand them a success that they could not deny. By next spring, Vivian told herself with steely determination, she would stand before a crowd in her home state, a hundred pounds lighter from strict dieting, as she accepted the Nanny of the Year award. She was, after all, a professional American nanny with an entire career still ahead of her. This was Vivian's year to climb.

FIVE

THERE ARE COUNTLESS stories of nannies mistreated by their employers. These are tales told on street corners and playgrounds, in libraries and bookstores and all over the Internet, whispered over children's heads, away from parents' ears. Dawn left her job on Long Island after her abusive boss sent the housekeeper out in a storm to buy sanitary napkins. The housekeeper returned, soaking wet, and the mother threw the box at her head, accusing her of stealing the change. Krista, a nanny in Brooklyn, opened the refrigerator at her job and discovered that all of the food had been labeled with Post-its, specifying what she could and could not eat. Pam, a New Jersey live-in, cared for three children while their mother stayed in bed all day drinking on the top floor of the house.

Kimberley Falls didn't have that kind of horror story to share. In her twenty years working as a nanny, she had been through ups and downs with families and been involved in plenty of their drama, but she had never felt disrespected on the job. Work had always been the one place where her confidence never faltered, where she felt most at home. It was her personal life that was a mess.

At forty years old, Kim had been through so much, it was hard to imagine her tiny body could hold it all. She was stronger than she looked. A wisp of a woman, five feet three inches tall and 110 pounds, she had the fragile quality of a bird with hollow bones. Breathe too hard on her and she just might tip over. Yell too loud and she might crumble. Shoot her a look and immediately she might wonder, "What did I do wrong?" She wanted to be liked and loved; she wanted a simple life in a quiet, peaceful place where she could spend her days with her children and her nights with her husband. A cozy life, a manageable life. But so far, no matter how hard she tried and no matter how often she wished for it, this was not the life she had been able to pull together.

Kim was facing a second divorce, and with nowhere else to go, she was heading back into a job as a live-in nanny. As the hours passed on a sunny July morning, she found herself marveling at all she was about to lose. This had been her last weekend in Georgetown, Texas, a town just outside Austin. She stood in the house she had decorated with her husband, Sam, taking note of all the little things she had done there over the past three years. The claw-foot tub in the bathroom she had found and restored. The central air conditioning they had finally installed. The walls they had painted, the floors they had covered, the addition they had added so Sam's daughters, Amber and Jessica, had a larger room to share. She had loved this house with all her heart, and it showed.

Kim could not believe she was about to go through another divorce. After their several attempts to have a child, Sam had suddenly refused to keep trying. He didn't want more children. When Kim tried to discuss the issue with him, he shut her down, saying he wasn't going to change his mind. Depressed and heartbroken, Kim stopped eating, her already tiny frame shrinking down to bone. Sam never said a word, and it wasn't until a friend who hadn't seen her in months expressed alarm at her appearance that Kim grew angry. Her own husband wasn't concerned about her health. Kim stayed in the marriage anyway, hoping it would get better, even hanging on for months after Sam sighed one day and mumbled, "This isn't working anymore."

Now Sam barely spoke to her; her stepdaughters only grunted. All three had escaped to her mother-in-law's house for the weekend, leaving Kim alone to pack her things. While she and Sam had been married only a few years, they had known each other since childhood. He was her best friend, and after her first misguided attempt in her early twenties at a marriage, she thought he was the man she was truly meant to spend the rest of her life with.

The Thursday night before her family left, Kim felt almost as if nothing had changed. When the evening came to a close, she padded into the girls' room. Standing in their doorway, she spoke, knowing they were listening even though they didn't make eye contact with her. Jessica, who was nine, sat quietly on her bed. Amber, fifteen years old, typed away on the computer, probably instant messaging with her friends.

"You're leaving tomorrow," Kim said, trying to keep her voice steady. Wisps of her brown hair fell into her eyes. "I probably won't see you anymore."

It was an awful, awkward moment. Kim had always thought of the girls as her own, even referring to them as her daughters in public, unless their actual mother was around. She attended cheerleading practice and concerts. She bought birthday presents and clothes and looked forward to seeing them off to their first proms. It was impossible for Kim to imagine walking away from all that now. Amber continued staring at her computer screen, stone-faced, but Jessica's chin dropped slightly and her eyes closed as she held on tightly to her emotions.

The next morning, Kim was surprised when both girls appeared at her bedside. Leaning down, they gave her hugs before they left for school, exactly as they had done on every ordinary school day. Then they were gone.

"I'm not coming home tonight either," Sam had said, knowing Kim would be in the house until Sunday. "I'm going to stay at my mother's, too."

"You're chicken," Kim spat back.

She spent the rest of the weekend alone. When she wasn't packing, she was crying. She cried over the sink and the light fixtures she had picked out. She cried sitting on the couch she loved and in the kitchen she had kept stocked with food. At night, she cried herself to sleep. By late Sunday afternoon, the nanny car — a Honda Accord her new employers had given her for the job — was packed with her belongings. Kim was all cried out. She breathed in deep as she climbed inside and drove toward Austin.

Kim loved living in Texas because it was so different. She had grown up in New Hampshire, with mountains all around her house. The mountains at home were lush and green in the summer, on fire in the fall, and covered in snow the rest of the year. In Austin, the winters were mild, the hills gentle and low. She felt relaxed living in a college town, and although it was hard to be away from her family, sometimes she appreciated the distance. Not a day had passed when she lived with Sam that she hadn't taken a moment to appreciate the Victorian storefronts in Georgetown, laughing at the thought that this New England girl was now living in Texas. She took one last look at the beautiful town she had called home and said goodbye.

After a long, lonely weekend, Kim was ready to turn herself over to a new life, even if it was someone else's.

At the end of a winding road in Westlake, behind a large wrought iron gate, tucked away from view by shrubs and trees, Brian and Holly Porter lived in what seemed like a perfect home from the outside. Inside, it was a constantly evolving construction site, an obstacle course of gutted interiors and completed rooms that never seemed to end. Eventually, they had told Kim, this parcel of land would rival all the other plots on the road inside and out, with cutting-edge appliances, intricate tile work, updated fixtures, newly landscaped pool and waterfall and outdoor fireplace. Up on this hill, there was a view of downtown: the University of Texas Tower, the state capitol, and about a dozen high-rise buildings. The traffic on the interstate, the people rushing to and from work, the bustling restaurants and cafés — all were far removed from this quiet gated residence.

Kim's heart pounded as she drove slowly through traffic on Interstate 35 toward Westlake. She didn't mind living so close to an urban center like Austin, but she preferred life in places like Georgetown, small towns like the place she grew up in. As a child, Kim had fished with her brothers in the brook behind her house. She attended the same Catholic church her father's entire family was married in, and after services on Sundays she marched into the store on Maple Street with her cousins to pick out penny candy. That same pack of children then spent the afternoon at Kim's uncle's house, where they ran wild in the backyard, popping inside just long enough to eat a piece of her Aunt Josephine's fried dough.

When she talked about her early childhood, the time before her parents divorced, Kim tended to edit heavily. She remembered the boisterous family and the food, the five pregnant women who lived on her street, four of whom had girls named Kim. She remembered all of her elementary school teachers and her first date at the town pool. As she talked, layers of nostalgia built one upon the next until it became clear that her memories of girlhood were intertwined with her unfulfilled dreams for herself as an adult. The life she described having as a young child was the exact life that had eluded her all these years. She still didn't have a family of her own.

By the time she arrived at the Porters' gate, she had passed countless houses of the wealthy. She would be living among them, but Kim wasn't that impressed. She had worked for the rich long enough to know that the old cliché was true: money does not buy happiness. Walking toward the front door, leaving all her suitcases behind in the car, Kim breathed in deeply. This was it: after marrying Sam and having her own home for three years while she worked as a part-time nanny, she was about to go backwards and work as a full-time live-in nanny again. She had decided to arrive on a Sunday night, three weeks before Holly Porter was due to give birth to her first child, so that she would have a chance to get settled in the new house and organize the place for the baby.

Ringing the front doorbell, Kim didn't feel nervous or excited. She was numb. Reality had hit her, but it didn't make much of an impact. For now, at least, Kim was a little dead inside. Brian opened the door, smiled, and led her into the living room. Holly, busy at a laptop computer, shouted a hello from the adjacent room she and her husband were using as an office until their individual workrooms were ready. Brian struck Kim differently than he had at their interview, and she realized her first impression of him had been wrong. In her mind, Brian had been tall, handsome, and athletic. The first thing that had popped into her head the last time he opened the front door was *GQ*. Yet as he stood before her today, his wheat-colored hair combed down awkwardly, his skin pale and shiny, he was more computer geek than men's magazine. He had the same air of confidence and entitlement she had seen countless times before in the upper middle class and wealthy, but she also sensed an intensity and insecurity she hadn't noticed in the interview.

"We have movers coming tomorrow to move the furniture upstairs," Brian said, pointing to the bedroom downstairs, where he and Holly were currently sleeping. "But if you could get all our clothes moved up tonight to get things started, that would be great."

Kim looked at Brian in shock. It was five thirty on a Sunday night. Her first official workday wouldn't start until the next morning, so she didn't consider herself on the clock. And this wasn't the plan they had come up with before she had arrived. They had all agreed that until the house was finished, and a private apartment was made ready for Kim, she would live in the first-floor bedroom, which had a semiprivate bath that would be available to her employers only during the day, when Brian and Holly were in their home office. Meanwhile, Brian and Holly would sleep upstairs, where they had their own bathroom and a tiny room they could use as a nursery.

Kim had assumed that the room they had discussed would be empty and ready for her upon her arrival. Now she wasn't sure where she would be sleeping that night. All she wanted to do was unpack her suitcases, set up her toiletries in the bathroom, and climb into bed to watch television. She wanted a few minutes alone to get comfortable and contemplate the enormous life change she had made that day. But instead, Kim did as she was told. She turned on her heels, headed into Brian and Holly's room, and got to work packing for the second time that day.

• • •

Entering a new live-in job was a lot like agreeing to an arranged marriage. Kim always hoped for the best but couldn't be sure how any of it would turn out once she moved in. She operated on instinct, and she usually knew from just one interview if a job was a good fit. In the past, working as a live-in had come naturally to Kim. She preferred being with a family, even if it wasn't hers, to living on her own with a roommate. When all the personalities worked in sync, when all the pieces came together organically, Kim considered living-in a "sweet deal." All of her expenses covered, she could save her salary and not have to worry about things like cars and rent and utilities and health insurance.

A homebody by nature, Kim didn't mind the isolation of her live-in work and actually took pride in the fact that she gave the children one-on-one attention instead of distracting herself with a network of nanny friends. She e-mailed her friends and sometimes saw them after work or on the weekends, but she did not integrate them into her workday. For Kim, the best time to talk to other nannies had been at the handful of nanny conferences she was able to attend over the years. She loved the camaraderie of the events and the boost she always felt seeing her professional peers. Beyond that, Kim did not socialize on the job. If her charges had play dates, it was for their benefit, not hers. Many nannies Kim knew who tried living-in vowed never to do it again once they got out, citing the long hours and the lack of boundaries.

Kim also agreed that there was a downside to working as a live-in. Live-in nannies got wrapped up in the families they worked for, forgetting themselves in the process. "Nannies have put their lives on hold. They've delayed marriages and children," Kim explained, describing some of her friends in the field. "But it's a vicious circle, because then the families treat them like they don't have a life, especially for live-ins."

So far, she had been lucky with her work families. She loved all the parents and children she had been with, whether live-in or live-out, and had kept in touch with many of them. At only nine years old, Kim got her first babysitting job for her neighbor's five-year-old twins. As an adult, she had worked in stores and offices, but nothing stuck until she fell into a job caring for the two-year-old son of a divorced woman. She loved the work and came to the gradual realization that she was meant to be a nanny. Kim was still in touch with that family and knew she would be invited to her first charge's wedding. She laughed when she talked about this now-grown man, describing how he still called her "Miss Kim." It was exactly this connection that made the job so satisfying for Kim and why she was so committed to it.

Other people might not appreciate the importance of being a nanny, but Kim always carried herself with pride and even showed a hint of defiance when she told certain people what she did for a living, perhaps anticipating their condescension. It bothered her that some people looked down on her career choice, but she couldn't imagine doing anything else. There was no way to describe the joy she felt witnessing a child grow from newborn to toddler to school age and beyond, knowing she had a hand in that miraculous transformation.

The interview with the Porters had gone well enough, if not perfectly. Now Kim wondered if her impression of the interview was as wrong as her first impression of Brian. As she packed up their belongings and listened to them pound away in silence on their laptops, she ran that interview through her mind again, realizing she had sensed something under the surface, a tiny, nagging intuition she wouldn't have ignored if she really felt she had a choice. At the time, instead of listening to her gut, she had chosen to sweep her instincts aside. She needed the job. "I liked them," she said, trying to explain why she accepted the position even though she had mild misgivings. "But I wouldn't pick them as friends."

Kim had rung the Porters' front doorbell for her interview wearing a loose brown corduroy jumper that hung almost to her ankles, with a long-sleeve turtleneck underneath. Her chin-length hair was blown out, stick straight and perfectly neat, with a part carved straight down the middle. It was an absolutely sexless choice of clothing without an ounce of trendiness, but it was one hundred percent Kimberley: modest and professional for the parents, yet comfortable enough that she could get down on the floor and play with a child. As she always did on interviews, she carried her resumé and a small stack of written references. Over the years, as Kim had gone through many personal ups and downs, from rocky relationships to three miscarriages to depression and an eating disorder, not one of those problems had been evident when she was at work. Work was her refuge, the place where she forgot about her own problems and focused on a family's needs.

Kimberley was a nanny's nanny. Kind, calm, loving, focused, and smart, she could handle all aspects of the job, from helping parents deal with tantrums and the emotional upheaval of toddlerhood to the smaller details of picking out the best swaddling blanket on the market. Even away from work, Kim had the classic nanny traits. Keenly aware of other people's feelings and emotions, she appeared utterly approachable and safe. Without children of her own, she was still maternal to the core. It wasn't arrogance: she knew she was one of the best nannies in Texas and that her nanny agency told all prospective employers this. It was simple fact. Kim was college-educated, experienced, passionate, and dedicated to her work. What family wouldn't want those traits in their caregiver?

The first thing Kim noticed when she walked into the Porters' house was the clutter. Brian and Holly had moved into the house knowing they were going to renovate it, so they'd never really made it a home. Kim sat on their sectional, holding her glass of water through the entire interview because she couldn't find a free space on the coffee table. Her eyes wandered around the room to the half-empty packing boxes and the piles of books and stacks of paper. She liked to walk into a house and get a vibe, but it was impossible to sense anything about the Porters with certainty because they were living in a state of flux.

Holly and Brian sat side by side, eyes wide, as they began the conversation. Holly wasn't at all the kind of woman Kim had imagined would be a corporate lawyer with a handsome husband and a baby on the way. Instead, Holly was plain: an average woman wearing unfashionable glasses, white sneakers, and a loose T-shirt. Her thin brown hair was pulled back in a rubber band, a few stray wisps framing her eyes. Compared to her husband, with his bright blue eyes, crisp pants, and collar-up polo shirt, Holly was forgettable. "These two do not fit together," Kim thought at the time. And then she spotted Holly's wedding ring. Flashing in the light, it was a three-carat rock, highlighted by a thick, diamond-studded wedding band that looked almost painful. This ring was as out of place on Holly as the man sitting next to her. Kim looked down at her own ring. She still couldn't bear to take it off. Kim loved the ring, though it was a fraction of the size of Holly's.

"We have no idea what to ask you," Holly said with a nervous smile.

"What do people ask you?" Brian echoed.

Kimberley smiled to herself. Most first-time parents, especially the ones looking to hire a nanny of her caliber, had a long list of questions gathered from friends or off the Internet. These two were absolutely clueless. Their living room was full of history, business, and science books, and they both had master's degrees from Ivy League colleges. Kim immediately categorized them as the types who got all their information from books but didn't do so well with the everyday. Looking at their eager faces, she decided to run the interview herself.

"Well," she began softly. "You would ask, 'What are your theories on discipline?' And I would answer that as a nanny I don't believe in corporal punishment and as a nanny I'm not allowed to hit your child. So if I'm ever with a family that says, 'We spank our child,' I can't do that. As children get older, I tend to use time-outs. But more than putting a child in time-out, I tend to put things in time-out. If they can't play correctly with something, then that thing goes into time-out."

Brian and Holly sat, taking in Kimberley's question-and-answer session. Kim asked herself about her experience and the way she would handle an emergency and how she communicated when problems came up with her employers. She described some of her past jobs and told the story of how she first became a nanny and how she knew this was what she wanted to do for life. Then she turned the interview around, directing some of her most important questions to them.

"Are there any guns in the house?" she asked. After her last live-in job, this was her most important question.

"No. We don't have any guns," they answered.

"Do you have a regular housekeeper?" she asked, knowing that they probably did.

"We do," said Brian. "And a gardener."

Housework on this job would be the same as for all her other positions, Kim was promised. Her responsibilities would be limited to the baby's toys and laundry, with minor straightening. She would not be expected to do any major cleaning, and the line between nanny and maid would be clear. She had higher status.

"When the baby is napping," she asked, to set the rules straight ahead of time, "if I have everything else done as far as the laundry, the dishes, and the bottles prepared, do you have any problem with me watching television or going online or reading a book?"

"Well," answered Brian, "you can go online and you can read, but we don't want the television on during the day, even if the baby is napping."

"What's the difference," Kim wondered silently, "between watching television and going on the Internet?" When Kim was on the job, she was highly focused and committed, but when she was off, she loved catching up on her soaps and other shows. Over the years, her favorite dramas had been *Thirtysomething, Sisters,* and *Once and Again.* Her current favorite was *The Amazing Race.* It didn't matter that much to her. She'd adjust and watch her soaps at night on video, but this was the kind of nonsensical rule that had to be followed when you worked in someone else's home.

"I see you still have your wedding ring on, but we know you're getting divorced," Brian said gingerly. "Is that absolutely definite? What if we hire you and then you reconcile? Is there any chance you and your husband will stay together?"

"No," Kim said. "The truth is I don't want the divorce, but if I accept a job and make a year commitment it doesn't matter what happens in my personal life. I'm committed for a year."

"We'll also be hiring a baby nurse for nighttime," Brian explained. Kim had taken a liking to Holly, who was easygoing and relaxed when she did speak. Brian seemed manageable, if a bit controlling.

"Really? You would be the first family I ever worked for that had a night nurse."

"But how do the mothers heal?" Brian asked, mystified. "Everyone told me that you can only get two hours of sleep at once, and then you won't heal."

"That's true," Kim said. "But every mother gets two hours of sleep at a time because the baby needs to be fed every two hours."

"Well, this way Holly won't have to get up to go to the nursery," Brian explained, and Kim kept a straight face while she chuckled to herself. "The night nurse can bring the baby to Holly so she doesn't have to get out of bed."

"That's your job!" Kim finally said, laughing.

"Well then how am I supposed to get any sleep?"

"Welcome to being a father," she answered with a smile, and then she changed the subject. "When do you want someone to start?"

"Well, let's see," began Brian, once again speaking before Holly. "The baby will be born in July, so we were thinking you could start in August."

"No," Kim said sternly. These people really were clueless, she thought to herself, once again taking control. "This is your first child. You've never even babysat. You've got this house under construction, a baby nursery to set up. Holly, you're working right up to your due date. Don't you think you're going to need someone to start before the baby gets here or at least within the first week after the baby is born?"

"Well, maybe you're right," Holly said, looking at Brian. Kim remained silent as the couple made eye contact and nodded their heads. She could see their minds were made up.

"We think you're fabulous," said Brian. "We knew on paper that you looked incredible and in person you're even better. Will you take the job?"

"No," Kim said, and they stared at her blankly. "All of your friends and family will tell you that you're absolutely crazy. You've got to interview more people to know that you've made the right decision. You may still come back to me, but you've got to do this first."

Before she left, Brian offered to take Kim on a tour of the house so that she would have a sense of where she would be living when the renovation project was complete. When it was done, Brian told Kim excitedly, the house would have bigger windows, a full nursery suite, and an open family room. The stairs were covered with sheets of brown paper and tools, but Brian insisted Kim climb up to see out the upstairs windows, explaining that they would all be replaced with a bigger set to enhance the view. Brian sent Holly up the stairs first and told Kim to follow his wife. Standing behind her, Brian pushed Kim gently forward, guiding her up.

Kim felt Brian's hands rest softly on her hips as she began to climb, navigating her past the tools. It was an intimate touch from a stranger, and for the five seconds it took her to get to the top, Kim was uneasy. A little voice went off inside her head. "This is wrong," it said. "Things aren't right here." By the time she'd walked back down the stairs, Kim had shaken the feeling off, telling herself those two hands on her hips were just an innocent gesture, something she had misread and nothing to worry about.

Of course, the Porters came back to her and, of course, Kim took the job. She had to get out of Sam's house as soon as possible, and besides the Porters, the only job the agency had for her was with a special-needs child. The phone interview for that job, with a very harried mother, had been brief. In the middle of the conversation, the mother had suddenly dropped the phone. Kimberley had listened to a muffled struggle.

"I'm sorry," the mother said apologetically when she returned to the phone. "My son was chewing a hole in the bar stools."

"That's okay," Kim said. She had a sinking feeling.

"So," the mother continued, describing her child. "He's in therapy and he doesn't like to be touched. If you are going to touch him, you have to hug him hard."

Kimberley knew immediately there was no point in meeting this family. She wasn't the right nanny for the job. "I can't have a child I can't touch," she thought to herself. That left her with the Porters. It seemed, on paper, like the perfect situation. While she wouldn't have her own space in the beginning, eventually they would build her a separate apartment with a private entrance, a detail she considered nonnegotiable as she got older. Along with the apartment, Kim would receive $2,200 a month before taxes for up to sixty hours a week of work, full access to a nanny car, health insurance, and car insurance. Her wireless network and cable television would also be covered. It was everything she would need when she walked out of Sam's house for good, Kim told herself when she accepted the position.

Now, an hour into her new job, Kim already knew more about the Porters than she had learned in her entire interview. Brian was not only controlling but anal, and Holly wasn't just plain and modest, she was almost selfless. Brian's side of the closet was packed with clothes meticulously organized according to style and color, right down to his socks and underwear: white socks, casual socks, business socks, athletic socks, boxers, briefs. His shirts were also labeled: polo shirts, old shirts, new shirts, long-sleeve shirts, turtlenecks. Holly's side of the closet held half the amount of clothes, although she was the one with the full-time job as a lawyer. Brian, as far as Kim had gathered, had owned a startup company that he sold; he was now an executive coach, working mostly from home. He also sat on the boards of several companies. Kim emptied out Holly's few drawers and ran her hands along the single bar holding a row of her unremarkable jackets and skirts.

Brian sat in the living room, reclined on the couch in front of his laptop. Holly, who popped in for a brief hello while Kim was working, spent the evening on the phone or typing away on her own laptop in the office. Kim took in everything around her. It was an outdated house compared with the brand-new houses in the area, despite its size and view, and she could see why they were remodeling. Off the jam-packed living room was a temporary kitchen, long and narrow with a buzzing old refrigerator, almost no counter space, a microwave, and no dishwasher. Kim saw everything before her, but she didn't interrupt her task to think about her situation. She didn't dwell on how awful it felt to have her own home one hour while she was living in someone else's the next. Standing with Brian's underwear in one hand and his socks in the other, she still did not panic.

Instead, Kim moved. She climbed, bent, stacked, and stuffed. Arching her back, standing on the tips of her toes, she grabbed things from the higher shelves. Dropping to her knees, she cleared the lower shelves. She filled garbage bag after garbage bag and one by one carried those bags up the stairs to the Porters' new bedroom, where she dropped them on the floor. The closet almost empty, Kim spotted a patch of water damage on the wall and called Brian in to take a look.

"We have a water problem!" Brian yelled when he saw the damage, surprising Kim. She didn't see any point in jumping to conclusions. "We're going to have to tear the entire closet out now. And you'll have to wash all of our clothes and refold them before they go into the upstairs closet."

Once again, Kim stared at her new boss in shock. It was now past nine and she hadn't taken a single suitcase out of the car. She knew the way she was being treated was wrong. She had been hired as a professional nanny, not a housekeeper. They had agreed on that in the interview.

But, she rationalized, the Porters had hired her because of her impressive recommendations, her experience, and her talent as a nanny. Right now there was no baby to take care of and it was her job to get them organized. She sucked it up and started a load of laundry. When the buzzer went off, she moved the wet clothes to the dryer and started a new load; when the dryer was finished, Kim began to fold.

By ten thirty, she could barely stand.

"I can't do anymore tonight," she said, peering into the office at Brian and Holly, who were still on their laptops.

"Okay, we'll get the air mattress," answered Holly. Until their furniture was moved the following morning, Holly and Brian would sleep downstairs. Kim would spend her first night in the empty bedroom upstairs.

The Porters didn't have an extra set of sheets, so Kim dug into the boxes in her car and pulled out her own set, along with a thin cotton blanket, toiletries, and clothes for the night. Leaving the rest of her belongings in the car, Kim headed back inside. Upstairs, Kim immediately took in the view, twinkling lights against the black sky.

"Good night," Holly and Brian said. "The movers will be here early."

Kim closed the door behind them and felt a tremendous sense of relief. She was finally alone, in a private room with her own bathroom. She opened all the windows to breathe the night air for a moment and paused to look at the view again, gazing in the direction of Austin. Her family was probably back home for the night in Georgetown, Amber on the computer, Jessica waiting for her sister to turn out the light. Sam was no doubt already in their bed, about to drift off to sleep.

She heard a storm building in the distance and closed the windows. It came on fast, the lightning flashing through the windows, rain pounding the glass as the house rattled. Thunderstorms did not hit this hard in Georgetown, and suddenly Kim felt very far from home.

The song *Somewhere Out There* popped into her head and as she hummed it to herself, Kim thought of Sam. She was all cried out by now, but she still felt so much love for him, and she wondered, as the light flashed in the darkness before her, what Sam was thinking and feeling. What had this awful day been like for him?

Her body already ached from all the lifting and climbing, and suddenly the numb feeling faded and she was filled with anger. She wasn't angry at Brian and Holly for not making her feel more at home or even giving her a blanket to sleep with. She was furious at Sam for throwing away what could have been such a good life. Rage and frustration rushed through her. Then, when she could not think anymore, Kim pulled on her pajamas and a pair of socks.

The Porters had their thermostat well below what she was used to at night, and Kim was freezing. She lay down on the air mattress, on top of her Winnie the Pooh sheets, under her thin blanket. As her eyes adjusted to the dark, she made out the shadows of black garbage bags all around her. Kim pushed Sam and the Porters out of her mind. She closed her eyes and shivered in the dark.

SIX

CLAUDIA'S FIRST JOB in the United States was in a beautiful house on a bucolic street in Westchester, New York. To most people, this place was the American dream, a leafy green affluent suburb with excellent schools and spacious homes tucked away from the road. To Claudia, it was no better than living up in the bush in Dominica.

Loneliness hit Claudia hard and deep. The intense quiet of the suburbs hummed in her head. Inexperienced as a nanny, she had to figure out how to live with a family while not being a member of the group. It was inside this black-shuttered house that Claudia first learned that reading kept her alive. It was also there that Claudia made herself disappear for the first time, and there that she honed her skill.

Desperate for a job, Claudia arrived in the United States with only a few hundred dollars in her pocket. She laughed just thinking about it decades later, about her shock when she landed on American soil and saw that the streets were not really paved with gold. Within minutes of getting off the plane, Claudia was dizzy from the lights and the people running around. Carrying directions to an apartment in the Bronx where two friends from Dominica had been living for two years, she found her way to the closest subway stop. When the train started to move, she was so nervous, she swore it was going backwards.

The first word that popped into Claudia's head when she arrived at her apartment was "Oops." This was her new home? She had expected a big house or a grand apartment, not this one-bedroom place overflowing with five other people sleeping and eating in shifts. As she tried to get to sleep that first night, Claudia realized she was far away from home, with no return date. The springs in the living room sofa bed poked her back, and she heard the breathing of strangers around her, but she told herself something she would repeat countless times: no matter what happened, she would stick it out.

"I want to come here and work and help my mother," Claudia explained, remembering that scary first night, "to come here and help them, give them stuff, to give them money so they could eat."

Within a few weeks, through a friend of a friend, Claudia got the Westchester job, in the home of Richard and Lisa Mann, a working couple with two girls, one-year-old Natalie and three-year-old Abby. Every day, Claudia woke early in the morning before Richard and Lisa went to work. When the house was all hers, she took the girls into the backyard to play. Claudia didn't know how to drive, and there was no car for her to drive anyway. There were no other nannies in the neighborhood. To break the monotony, she took the girls for walks to the nearby tennis courts, where they collected balls for fun.

Claudia slept in a room in the basement with a tiny window and a broken-down television. At night, the boiler clicked on and off, but she slept with her door open because she was terrified the house would catch on fire and she would get stuck in her room and burn to death. Just outside her door was a bathroom, with a toilet and tiny sink and Lisa's StairMaster.

"Claudia, where do you get your patience from?" Lisa would ask her on days when the girls were acting up. "You're so easy, so cool, so calm. I'm so huffy puffy."

Lisa had no idea that Claudia was going nuts. Every day she gave her affection to two girls while her own son was thousands of miles away. She washed them and dressed them, read to them and took them out back to play on the swings. She laughed with them and let them have a little piece of her heart. All the while she felt weighed down by a bottomless sadness, a constant longing for her son.

"I know he's angry, but he doesn't say anything. He may say it someday," Claudia said, looking down at her hands as she recalled the first time she had seen Dexter after many years. "He was looking at me like, 'Who is this lady?' He was fourteen."

Dexter did not know that he haunted his mother as she cared for those two girls. She thought about everything she could not do for him. She could not wash his hair and hold him tight before he went to bed. She could not teach him how to feed himself or hear him say his first word.

Over the years, Claudia sent Dexter money, clothes, and letters, and they talked on the phone. One year he mailed her a handmade Valentine's Day card she still had tucked away in her apartment. But as much as she did from a distance, Claudia could not get around the cold hard fact: she was not raising her own child; she was raising someone else's.

Claudia couldn't articulate her loss eloquently. Words failed her when she talked about her son. She looked at a wall, at her hands. If she said her son's name too often, the memories would come back and she might not be able to face them. To the Manns, Claudia was a live-in nanny, but mostly, during those early years in the United States, she was a mother grieving for her child. She passed many days sitting in the house, staring out the window at the trees, wishing she could blink and be back home for just a minute to hold her child, wrap him up tight, and inhale the scent of his still-soft head.

The drama at the Manns began when Christopher showed up. Claudia initially had the house to herself with the girls while both parents were off at work. Soon Lisa started taking midday "coffee breaks," inviting her old friend Christopher over to share the box of doughnuts he always brought with him. Christopher was a nice enough man — he always offered Claudia a doughnut — but Claudia was no fool. After a few minutes, he and Lisa would walk upstairs to the bedroom as though Claudia hadn't seen a thing, as if she didn't exist at all.

Claudia assumed that the woman she worked for, the woman who had hired her to take care of her children, thought she was too dumb to put two and two together. "I don't think she ever even suspect that I knew something was going on. Maybe she just felt I was stupid. It was not my business, but Richard, her husband, he was a big teddy bear, and he would come and sit down and eat, and she'd have her fling, and he doesn't know nothing. In my mind I'm thinking, 'Poor you.'"

Lisa never kissed Christopher in front of Claudia, but she would follow him outside to his car. Claudia once ran up the stairs to Lisa's bedroom and peered out the window. There, below her in the driveway, Lisa and Christopher kissed passionately. After Christopher drove away and the family was together that evening, Claudia put her blank face on and went about her business as though nothing had happened.

The next line Lisa crossed infuriated Claudia, but she remained silent about it to the end. Every weekend Claudia went home to the city for a break from the Manns. For the first six months she stayed at the Bronx apartment, but eventually living with all those people around became too complicated. She was ready for her privacy. "It was too hard to sleep in when someone wanted to be up making breakfast and your bed is in the living room."

Claudia rented her first apartment in Flatbush after her hand came up in a susu. In Dominica, susus are a common way to raise and save money. A group of close friends or relatives join together, select a leader, and agree to contribute a certain amount of money for a certain amount of time. The members hand over their share to the leader, and each week a different member gets a "hand," meaning they get the lump sum for the week. Susus have been used as a means to start businesses, to secure a down payment for a home, or, as in Claudia's case, simply to provide the structure and motivation to save. Over the years, Claudia had participated in several susus, and this one, which she joined while she was working with the Manns, helped her get first and last month's rent for her first apartment in Brooklyn. She lived for her weekends in Brooklyn, her break from the Mann family.

The weekly routine at the Manns' was simple. Lisa paid Claudia on Fridays. Claudia took some of her pay home with her on the weekends to spend and add to the susu, leaving the rest in her room at the Manns'. The first time some of her money went missing, Claudia figured it was a mistake. The next weekend, she came up $40 short again. And then it dawned on her.

The next weekend, Claudia counted her money several times before she left it in her room at the Manns' as usual. As she expected, when she came back the following week, some of the money was gone. Lisa, the only person in the house besides Claudia who used the basement, was stealing her salary. Claudia thought hard about what to do. She wanted to scream and threaten. She wanted Lisa to know that while she seemed calm and easygoing, she was no idiot.

But then reality stopped her. "In those days, you are alone and it's hard to get a job. You need experience and she hired me without that, and you have a kid back home you have to take care of. You don't have money. You don't have papers. You don't have nothing. What are you going to say?" Claudia reflected, explaining her predicament. For the sake of survival, Claudia kept quiet. She also hid her money.

Finally, after two years with the Manns, all of the anger and resentment Claudia had held inside boiled over. She sat in her apartment as Sunday evening approached, but she could not get herself to return to Westchester. The few possessions she had in the house, she could easily leave behind. She would never return to the house or see Natalie and Abby again. Lisa called, demanding an explanation for her absence. Claudia only gave her this: "I'm not coming back."

Claudia still felt affection for Natalie and Abby and regretted never seeing the girls again. Lisa Mann, on the other hand, represented a dark period in Claudia's nanny life. She had felt disrespected on other jobs since — one woman she worked weekends for would take off her sweaty sneakers after running and demand that Claudia carry them to the closet — but the Manns had made the biggest impact because they were her first nanny job and she'd felt so trapped. It was a rite of passage in the nanny world: suffer through one terrible job and then never put up with that kind of treatment again.

The circumstances and locations varied when Claudia and her friends talked about their worst jobs, but the theme was always the same: the powerful abuse the powerless, the big man stomps on the little man, the First World takes advantage of the Third World. Domestic Workers United (DWU), a Bronx, New York–based grassroots organization, collected these kinds of stories in a survey to demonstrate just how bad nannies' conditions were and to fight for their rights. The group canvassed local parks, stopped nannies on streets, and handed out pamphlets. It also provided a nanny training course and English classes geared toward helping workers communicate with employers.

It held marches and press conferences and highlighted women's stories of abuse. In November 2005, DWU announced a federal civil rights lawsuit seeking $350,000 on behalf of Cindy Carter, an undocumented nanny from Barbados who had cared for the three children of Fontaine and Donald Sheridan on Long Island. DWU held a press conference outside Donald Sheridan's Manhattan office, accusing Fontaine Sheridan of discrimination, physical abuse, and harassment. Carter said Sheridan beat her, threatened to have her deported, and used racial slurs. Sheridan was arrested after one altercation and pled guilty to second-degree harassment; she was sentenced to fifty hours of community service and ordered to attend an anger-management class and to pay for Carter's medical expenses. In 2008, Carter and the Sheridans settled the nanny's federal lawsuit and a defamation case the couple filed against her.

Besides bringing domestic-worker abuse to light in the media, DWU had success helping to win passage of reform legislation. In May 2003, the group successfully lobbied the New York City Council to approve a bill that required employment agencies to inform domestic workers in writing of their basic rights and to get families that hired them to sign statements outlining those rights and the employer's responsibilities. Under the legislation, employers who hire nannies, housekeepers, companions, or caregivers for the elderly through employment agencies are required to sign statements saying they are aware of workers' rights, including minimum wage, overtime, and Social Security.

The group also urged members of the New York State Senate and Assembly to pass a Domestic Workers' Bill of Rights that provides for paid holidays, paid vacations, standard overtime guidelines, and a minimum wage of $14 per hour, but by 2008 the bill had not been approved. In June of that year, DWU was an organizer of the first National Domestic Workers Congress, a four-day event held at Barnard College, to continue its fight for the Bill of Rights and encourage nationwide activism and campaigning.

Claudia was pleased when she first saw nanny activists canvassing in her local park. "I think it's a good thing that we have a voice, someone to speak for us. I thought about it a long time ago. Why can't we have a union? Why nannies can't have a union?" Claudia had seen countless violations against fellow nannies over the years: women fired without severance, forced to work extra hours without compensation, given no salary at all when employers went on vacations. "They never pay them. They just exploit them. If they have somebody to talk for us, that would be good. There's a whole other thing going on out there. You would never believe," she said, shaking her head.

The last light of day disappeared as Claudia walked into Royette's building, just a few blocks from her own apartment. She had just finished a math class and she couldn't keep the grin off her face. Claudia was going to class regularly, thanks to Betsy, who had reduced her hours and kept her at the same salary. Betsy couldn't have been more different from Lisa Mann, and in many ways Claudia felt she was lucky to have a boss like Betsy Hall. She never treated Claudia as if she were stupid. They talked about Claudia's future, and Betsy had encouraged her to go to school so she could eventually apply to nursing programs.

Claudia now began her workday around noon, while Lucy was in school, giving Claudia extra time to study or take a morning class. Otherwise, her job hadn't changed much over the past month — James was still home and unpredictable, Betsy was still working hard — but none of it really mattered. Claudia no longer tensed her shoulders and stared straight ahead, willing problems to roll off her back. They slid off naturally now. Her mood was too good to dampen.

These days her bag was as heavy as Betsy's, bursting with notebooks and workbooks. She ran fractions through her head, and when Tanisha complained that she was having trouble with her own schoolwork, Claudia counseled her cheerfully, "You've got to put yourself in a math state of mind."

Tanisha had gone over to Royette's while Claudia was in class to hang out with Royette's daughter, Ava, and Monique, a twelve-year-old girl who lived across the hall from Claudia with her mother, Grace. The three girls were as tight as sisters and fought just as often. They were getting ready for the annual Halloween party in Claudia's lobby. Each year, the kids in Claudia's building dressed up in costumes and ran around the courtyard.

Royette's stairway was dimly lit. Music and voices from other apartments echoed off the walls. Inside, Royette's home was bright and cozy. Her two-bedroom apartment was bigger than Claudia's but also more cramped, because two women from back home were living with her until they found jobs and affordable places to live. They stood in the kitchen chatting with a younger woman they knew who was going to Brooklyn College.

In the living room, over the music blasting out of the CD player, Royette and Claudia talked about Royette's latest job prospects. The apartment was carefully decorated with red and white curtains, a giant vase holding fake flowers, and a colorful bowl of ceramic fruit identical to the one Claudia had on her own kitchen table.

Royette, Claudia's closest friend, had grown up in St. Martin and Curaçao, but she was originally from Dominica. In many ways, their friendship was like a marriage. They watched each other's children as though they were their own; they bantered and joked with ease; they listened to each other when they had problems at work or worried about things like paying the rent and keeping their daughters out of trouble. Although they weren't blood relations — Royette's and Cap's mothers were sisters — Claudia called Royette her cousin because she could rely on her like blood. Claudia didn't tell anyone everything about herself, but she told Royette more than most.

Royette was struggling to find work as a nanny after her most recent family had moved to Long Island. There was a lot more stress in Royette's house these days than at Claudia's. While their two daughters giggled in a back room with Monique and dressed for the Halloween party, Claudia talked to Royette about her latest job interviews.

"Excuse me, honey, can I wear my belt?" Tanisha interrupted Royette and her mother. She managed to use the word "honey" as a term of true affection and a way of mocking her mother simultaneously. Standing in a pink tracksuit, her hair in pigtails, Tanisha still looked like a little girl. But there was no mistaking the gleam in her eye and the way she prodded her mother: she was becoming a teenager.

"You know you cannot wear that belt!" answered Claudia, shooing her daughter away. After Tanisha went back into Ava's room, Claudia rolled her eyes at Royette.

Claudia's sister Jill had gone home just a few days before. Her latest trip to Brooklyn hadn't gone as well as it should have. Tanisha had insisted on fighting with her, acting out in jealousy and anger. As punishment, Claudia put Tanisha's favorite belt off-limits and demanded that she write an apology letter to Jill. Meanwhile, Jill continued to speculate that Tanisha's behavior was a direct result of Claudia's problems with Cap, feeding into Claudia's fear that divorcing Cap would devastate Tanisha and erode the girl's self-esteem.

"This February my rent is going up to eight hundred and fifty dollars. I don't know what I'm going to do. I'll need at least six hundred a week to survive," Royette sighed.

Claudia didn't say a word, but she knew it would be tough for Royette to find a job at that salary, not that she didn't deserve it. She had been living on savings, part-time work with the family who moved to Long Island, and a little bit of help from her boyfriend, who was married. If she didn't find new work soon, Claudia didn't know what would happen to Royette.

If Royette had it to do over again, she wouldn't have come to the United States at all. The first problem was employment. She had been a nanny for years and the jobs had gone sour more often than not. Like Claudia, she had been a live-in. One of her jobs had been in Nyack, where she worked alone while Ava was being cared for back home by family. Nyack was a nice town, but Royette had been bored. "You're living their life, not your own," she said, dismissing live-in work.

The family tried to be nice to her and even insisted she have dinner with them. What they didn't understand was that, even though she wanted to be asked to dinner, she didn't actually want to join them.

In the end, they hadn't turned out so nice. When Royette asked for time off because Ava was coming for a visit, the family agreed. On her weekend off in Brooklyn, Royette received several calls from them, but they never actually connected. That Sunday evening, she arrived at the train station and the father was there to pick her up as usual. Within seconds, Royette saw that he had packed all of her belongings in his car.

"I was taking care of your child. The least you can do is give me notice," she cried. "You're treating me worse than your dog."

Ultimately, the family gave her a small severance and Royette returned to Brooklyn, eventually finding work again. She later heard from the family's neighbor that they hadn't planned on giving her any money at all until the neighbor persuaded them that it was the right thing to do. Royette had been furious, but this kind of treatment didn't surprise her. She had also worked for a family who played dumb when she told them their nine-year-old son hit her. They claimed it was an accident and didn't do a thing. Royette wished she could hit the boy right back. Hours before this family fired her, they all ate dinner as if it were any other night. Then the father came downstairs to Royette's room. After telling her to pack, he dropped her off at the station on a freezing cold winter night. Her next job, in Riverdale, ended when the mother owed her $700 and decided she needed someone cheaper.

After working in Riverdale, Royette found a job with a family on Central Park West who had an eight-year-old brat of a child. "Whatever Stephanie wanted to do, that's what Royette did," Royette said, describing life on that job.

Once she overheard a friend of Stephanie's ask her, "Why are you so mean to Royette?" In the end, it was Stephanie who got Royette fired. Recalling how she lost her job because a spoiled child didn't like her, Royette laughed bitterly.

On top of the difficulties Royette had with work, she worried about her young daughter being on the streets in a place like Brooklyn. She second-guessed herself all the time, wondering if the girl would have been better off at school in St. Martin or Dominica, where the children have to wear uniforms to school and show respect.

Claudia and Royette agreed: back home, discipline was a much bigger priority. You could discipline each other's daughters if you saw one of them acting out in public. And at school, children had to show that their nails and teeth were clean. The schools in Brooklyn seemed big, unruly, and scary to Royette. Even with a babysitter to watch her daughter when she was at work, and knowing Claudia and Grace were also keeping an eye out, Royette was anxious.

Saying goodbye to Royette, Claudia grabbed her black shoulder bag. Her papers and math workbooks poked out of the top, making it awkward to slip her arm under the strap. She left her daughter with her two friends to catch some time for herself at home.

Claudia's building was a six-floor, Tudor-style structure with an arched tunnel that led straight to an open courtyard. It was easy to imagine the courtyard in its glory days, filled with grass and flowers, a tiny piece of nature greeting the people who lived there. But tonight the yard was in its usual dismal shape — a large mound of bare dirt surrounded by a peeling iron fence. Claudia didn't notice, because the place was swarming with kids running, eating candy, laughing, talking, and dancing. The lobby echoed with music, and a few adults stood around. The children ran in and out of apartments, around the lobby, through the courtyard, and back again. Some wore handmade costumes, some store-bought outfits, and others dressed as if it were any other day.

Claudia made her way up the stairs and into her one-bedroom apartment, where she closed her door on the sound of children enjoying Halloween and the blasting music. It was time for her to relax. Before long, Tanisha would appear with her friends, needing attention or money or just to give her a hard time. Claudia lay down on her bed in the room she shared with Tanisha and picked up a *Star* magazine. Just when she was getting comfortable, the phone rang.

"Tanisha's outside without her coat on again," Grace, Monique's mother from across the hall, informed her.

"What am I gonna do with that child?" asked Claudia.

Claudia hung up the phone and picked up the magazine again. Then she put it down with a sigh and thought about her daughter. When Tanisha was just Lucy's age, she might put up a fight about getting dressed, but she always did what Claudia said. Things were harder now that Tanisha was following her own mind. Claudia worried Tanisha would be even more difficult to control now that her father wasn't around. The next time Cap came home, Claudia would have to let him stay in the apartment again. For tonight, though, Claudia was on her own. She geared herself up for yet another talk with Tanisha about the importance of keeping warm.

Cap did come home again in December for about a week, and Claudia went through the motions of being a wife. She let him stay in the apartment and encouraged him and Tanisha to spend time together. She was civil, talking to him about who was making dinner, what Tanisha was up to, and the usual small talk that makes up a day. She did not let Cap back in her heart, though. And he never made it to her bed. It would have taken a grand gesture to break through Claudia's anger, but Cap did nothing out of the ordinary.

Claudia was sad at work and it showed. Betsy noticed that she was quieter, withdrawn and distracted. Things ended up in the wrong places. Lucy's socks were sometimes mismatched. The only time Betsy saw Claudia animated was when they talked about her math class. No matter how depressed Claudia seemed, she was still determined to take the GED.

"Are you okay?" Betsy had finally asked Claudia on a day when she seemed particularly down.

"It's Cap," Claudia answered.

"You let me know when you're ready to do something and I'll help you," Betsy told her after hearing from Claudia about Cap's various misdeeds. So far no one had been all that supportive of Claudia's getting out of the marriage. Claudia's mother had called from Dominica, stressing the importance of staying with Cap for the child's sake. But how could Claudia sit back and let her husband go off with other women as though she didn't exist at all? What kind of example would that set for her daughter?

"He's gone again," Tanisha had complained after her father had left for Dominica. "And it's all your fault that I don't have a father here anymore. You drove him away."

Tanisha's words echoed in Claudia's head as she made her way to Manhattan on a cold December morning just before Christmas. So did Betsy's offer to help. Claudia was damned if she did and damned if she didn't. Staying with Cap would set an example for Tanisha that men could walk all over you. But if she listened to Betsy and kicked Cap out, Tanisha would blame Claudia for leaving her fatherless. Underneath all her worries about Tanisha was the worst thought of all: Cap had been the love of Claudia's life and now she was losing him.

Jackson trailed Claudia as she walked into the Citibank a few blocks from the Halls' apartment. He had grown up fast, but she could still remember him as a little baby, blond, blue-eyed, and good-natured. Now his moods could be just as unpredictable as his father's. He was smart and sweet, if a little difficult at times, sometimes acting younger than his age. She knew Betsy worried about his social skills and was pained when his friends excluded him, but Claudia didn't worry about Jackson at all. Boys will be boys, she thought, and besides, these kinds of things happened between kids all the time. Lately, Tanisha, Ava, and Monique had had their share of squabbles, and they seemed to be growing apart.

Claudia pushed the numbers on the screen of the ATM to access her checking account. She was hoping for a nice Christmas bonus this year. When all the nannies in the neighborhood returned from the holidays, the streets buzzed with numbers. Nannies either showed off their bonuses with smug smiles or complained they hadn't been paid enough. They came together, compared and contrasted their bonuses, and then went back to work feeling content — or angry and ashamed.

It was a question Claudia dreaded, an invasion of privacy: "How much did you get this year?" Her finances were nobody's business. As far as Claudia was concerned, those who asked were no better than all the kids at Tanisha's school who bragged about their Christmas gifts — brand-name clothes or sneakers way out of Claudia's price range. It would be tough for Claudia to make ends meet this Christmas season, let alone buy Tanisha what she wanted.

Jackson dawdled behind Claudia as she touched the screen for a cash withdrawal. The money slid out, and her new balance flashed on the screen. The amount displayed took Claudia's breath away. She felt like throwing up. Shaking and queasy, Claudia wrapped the cash around her bank card and rushed Jackson out of the building and back onto the cold streets. What was she going to do now? What the hell was she going to do now?

Later that day, Claudia realized she'd been so distracted at the bank that she'd actually put the money and her card into a pocket of Jackson's backpack that had a hole in it. Now her cash and her card were both gone. It was a stupid and embarrassing thing to have done. She wouldn't tell anyone about it. Far worse, far, far worse, was seeing the balance that had flashed across the ATM screen: her account was almost empty. Cap had stolen her money to buy his last plane ticket home. Claudia was flat broke.

SEVEN

FOUR MONTHS AFTER her trip to San Diego, Vivian had long since put away her conference suits for full nanny gear: an oversize white T-shirt, fleece zip up, and jeans a few sizes too big. Driving the Pritchards' nanny car, a silver Chevy Tahoe, she passed the rows of houses built in the 1920s lining the streets of the Pritchards' neighborhood, as well as the occasional jogger or cyclist. Devan and David sat quietly in the back, worn out after a busy day at their new preschool and, after that, kickball class.

Vivian pulled into the driveway of the Pritchard house, stopping the vehicle neatly in the space reserved for the nanny car. Vivian knew that if she parked the Tahoe too far to the right, Catherine would have a hard time getting her own car in, sparking one of their harmless spats. When Catherine first made the request, Vivian was irritated because the car was so close to the side of the house it left her little room to get the boys out of their car seats. Years later, she still begrudgingly followed Catherine's instructions. Walking up the back steps with the boys in tow, Vivian opened the door as she did every working day and marched into her world.

David and Devan followed Vivian into the house and began to play with their toys while she started their dinner. The open kitchen overlooked the family room, and Vivian watched the boys while she cooked. The walls were covered with their paintings and a recent set of pictures of apples they had put together in honor of fall.

"When a child shows you a drawing, never ask, 'What's this?' Say, 'Tell me about this drawing,'" Vivian said, looking over the art on the walls.

Devan sat on the Thomas the Tank Engine rug while David lounged on a worn blue slipcovered couch. Toys were stacked against the back wall of the playroom, along with countless books and a set of Brio trains that drove Vivian nuts because the pieces always came apart. A television, used in limited amounts, sat on the floor directly across from the couch.

Calling the boys to the table, Vivian put their dinner of chicken, rice and beans, and buttered peas in front of them. They ate without complaint as Vivian cleaned the pots she had used. When the dishes were put away, the boys' table was cleared, and all three were relaxing in the family room, Catherine opened the side door and stepped inside.

"Mommy!" the boys yelled, running into her arms.

Catherine leaned down, hugging Devan and David. She smiled broadly as the boys enveloped her, balancing herself on one knee, her pocketbook strap slipping off her shoulder. Vivian kept her eye on the boys, knowing they would act out a bit now that their mother was home.

It was part of Vivian's job to let the boys be rowdy around their mother, but it was also her job to maintain order when Catherine was gone. One evening, after Vivian made the boys kielbasa on the grill for dinner, Catherine came home in the middle of the meal.

The boys immediately began complaining about the food being too spicy. Vivian stood silent as she watched them manipulate their mother, knowing that the moment Vivian stepped out the door, Catherine would cook them something else. Vivian believed it was important that the boys eat what she served them, without complaint, so the next morning, she opened the refrigerator, pulled out the leftover kielbasa, and whipped it up into an omelet she fed the boys for breakfast.

Vivian smiled now as she watched the boys with their mother. Eventually they detached themselves from her and went back to playing, while Vivian stood up to chat with Catherine at the kitchen counter before she headed out for the evening.

Now that the boys were settled in preschool, Vivian had really started to worry about the following year, when they would enter kindergarten. She knew that choosing a private school would soon require the Pritchards to do research and take tours, not to mention interviews and applications. Vivian was eager to voice her opinion on the matter; she thought the boys would be better off in the local public school, which she felt offered a great education and a more diverse group of students. Knowing Catherine as well as she did, Vivian also believed that Trevor was the one pushing private school. Vivian launched into her pitch for public school, but Catherine caught her by surprise, cutting her off almost immediately.

"This is a personal decision," Catherine said, shuffling papers on the counter without making eye contact with her nanny. "I don't want to talk about it with you."

Catherine, a pretty woman with the same black hair and green eyes as her boys, had always been laid-back and approachable. She loved her job and never expressed guilt about leaving the boys to go to work, which made it very easy for Vivian to deal with her.

Quiet and reserved, Catherine's personality was the opposite of Vivian's, and Vivian knew that that was why their relationship had been so smooth. They balanced each other out. They read each other's minds. They had the same views on discipline, and even when they disagreed, they faced the issue head-on, clashing openly and honestly and clearing the air immediately. Vivian had always felt like family. But now her boss had shut her down so completely that Vivian wasn't sure of anything.

She absorbed Catherine's words, her mind going into overdrive. If Catherine didn't want to hear her thoughts on the subject, it must mean she didn't really appreciate all the things that Vivian had done over the years, all the love she had showered on the boys, all the thought she had put into helping raise them to be polite, confident children. "Now, after I've been raising your kids for four years," she said, her voice shaking slightly, "you're telling me it's a personal decision, that anything related to them is a personal decision, that my input doesn't matter?"

Catherine remained silent, continuing to busy herself with the papers on the countertop.

"But I'm the only person who has seen the boys interact in a classroom setting," Vivian pressed, her eyes brimming with tears. "Don't you want to know what I think is the right fit?"

The two women stood not two feet apart, but they could have been on opposite sides of the house. Vivian held herself together. Catherine remained silent. Finally Vivian shook her head in frustration and disbelief. She collected her things, grabbed her bag, and gave the boys a hug goodbye the same way she did every day. Then she walked out the side door, past the Chevy Tahoe in the driveway to her own car parked on the street. Vivian closed the car door and started the engine, her hands shaking. She was devastated. It was a minute-long conversation — if you could even call it that — yet she felt sure that nothing would ever be the same between her and Catherine again.

Over the years, Vivian and Catherine had had plenty of disagreements over little things like how to properly load the dishwasher — Vivian didn't rinse and Catherine did — or the way the car was parked or why Vivian had once assumed an entire baked ziti Catherine made was garbage and threw it away. They got on each other's nerves and sometimes argued heatedly, but the issues they disagreed about were rarely substantial. Through all their petty arguments, Vivian had always believed her opinion was valued. She had never felt disrespected.

In some ways, while Vivian cared for Devan and David as attentively as a mother, she in turn considered Catherine a mother figure; someone she went to for advice, someone she could trust. Like the day Vivian showed up at work with a broken hand after a night of fighting with her boyfriend, Reed.

Two years into their relationship, he had already hit her on several occasions. This time, drunk and angry, Reed had tried to leave the house with the car keys. Vivian blocked the door, refusing to let him out. He grabbed her hand, crushing it inside his fist until the bones snapped. She did not go to the hospital. She went to bed and then she got up and went to work as usual. When the day was over, she finally drove herself to the doctor's.

The next morning she arrived at work with her hand in a cast and sat down with Catherine to discuss the boys' upcoming birthday party. Catherine immediately noticed Vivian's hand.

"What happened?" her boss asked.

"I got it caught in a door," Vivian lied, but then she broke down and told the truth.

"Well," Catherine said calmly and decisively. "You need to move out, and I'll help you. Trevor will say you need to move out. He won't let you work here unless you move out. You can't see Reed anymore."

Vivian lived alone and safely now at the Bentley, thanks to the Pritchards' help with her first and last months' rent. She told Catherine that she had left Reed for good, but she still saw him occasionally and took his calls, hoping to wean herself off of him gradually. The image that Vivian publicly put forward didn't always reflect the reality. Behind the bravado, behind the speed-talking and continual list-making, Vivian was just a girl finding her way in the world. Vivian's need for control was almost out of control, and her intensity and emotions sometimes got the better of her when things did not go exactly as planned.

Catherine and Trevor, who never had much to say about the boys' lives in the past, were beginning to have opinions as their sons got older. By cutting off the discussion about where the boys would go to school, Catherine was sending Vivian a signal that Vivian was unwilling to accept. Trevor, whom Vivian hadn't had to deal with much over the past four years, since he traveled several times a month, had lately been spending more time at home. For the first time since she'd taken the job with the Pritchards, a crucial decision about the boys' future would be made between husband and wife instead of wife and nanny, and Vivian would have no input. Change was coming, Vivian realized. She had a sick feeling in the pit of her stomach. If there was one thing Vivian hated, it was change.

On a cloudless Monday a week later, Vivian was back at work as usual. Still feeling bruised from her conversation with Catherine, she was too busy now to dwell on it. Driving up Central Street in the Chevy Tahoe, Vivian turned into Wellesley's downtown, heading for Chipmunks preschool to pick up Devan. David sat quietly in the back seat, sick that day with a fever, and Vivian glanced at him in her rearview mirror every few minutes to see how he was doing. Vivian was happy to have David with her. They had had a quiet morning, just the two of them, drinking lemonade and playing Yahtzee. It was a few stolen hours now that the boys were so heavily scheduled with school and activities.

Over the weekend, Vivian had pulled off the biggest achievement of her professional life, the perfect distraction from the uneasiness she now felt at work. Undeterred by the INA board, Vivian had spearheaded a free, one-day nanny conference in Boston. It had been an undeniable success, pulling in more than twice the number of nannies as had attended the last INA conference. Over the summer, Vivian had worked with several local nanny agencies to get funding for the event. She had even recruited her mother to cater the lunch. As usual, Vivian had used the stress as motivation, growing cranky and impatient just before the event, and now, two days later as she headed to pick up Devan, swinging from self-congratulation to doubt about how well she had run it.

The Dr. Seuss seminar room at the Boston Children's Museum had been the perfect setting for the conference. One by one and in small groups, attendees had crossed the museum's pedestrian bridge leading to the conference room, seagulls squawking overhead in the salty breeze, for a day of lectures and workshops. The mood was friendly; the nannies were excited and grateful. Even Catherine had shown up with the boys. The event had been such a smash, the INA had informed Vivian the very next day that the decision had been made to hold the next conference in Boston. So far, everything was going just as Vivian had planned after the San Diego conference. Vivian knew that INA would now be hardpressed to find a better choice for Nanny of the Year.

When Vivian was on a mission, dressed in a suit, answering cell phone calls, shooting off e-mails, and laying out plans for her next campaign as she preached the virtues of professional nannies and the importance of the nanny industry, it was difficult to imagine her as a childcare worker. She was more lobbyist than nanny. Her intensity could be overbearing, her New England accent harsh. Her impatience with adults could make her seem unapproachable and gruff. But in the presence of her boys, Vivian's focus shifted, her energy was redirected, and it became unquestioningly clear: Vivian had a passion for children. She presented a combination of care-giver traits. She was fun, loving, consistent, and in control, part teacher, part role model.

Vivian brought David with her into the local Starbucks for her daily Mocha Frappuccino Light and cinnamon twist. Since the INA conference, Vivian had lost seventy pounds and had switched from the Atkins diet to Weight Watchers. Every time she put a piece of food in her mouth, she added up the Weight Watchers points to make sure she wasn't exceeding her calorie limit. With the weight loss, Vivian looked years younger. As she shed excess pounds, her face became more defined, revealing surprisingly del-icate, finely chiseled features. All her life Vivian had heard, "You have such a pretty face," and she understood that the statements re-flected people's discomfort with her weight. Now she took those words as a compliment.

Walking toward the preschool gate, Vivian glanced at the activ-ities board posted there to see what book Devan read that day and to check for any special reminders. When the boys had started at the school a few weeks before, Vivian had arrived early to pick them up. She'd looked into windows and peered into the yard, making sure her boys weren't mistreated or abused. She'd spied on the teachers from a distance. Did they sit around drinking coffee instead of interacting with the kids? Did they break up obvious cliques? Did they intervene when one child hit another or stole a toy?

In general, Vivian was happy with what she saw. The classrooms were well organized, the teachers were warm and attentive, and the overall atmosphere of the place was cheerful. She had quickly become an old-timer at the school: Vivian knew the schedule of events and the names of all the teachers and children, and she had a sense of each child's personality.

Opening the gate, Vivian stepped into the yard, David right behind her. Children darted here and there, teachers and parents milled about. Cindy, a nanny friend, waved hello and Vivian nodded in return. Vivian had spent almost every workday of her first three years on the job with Cindy and her charge, Gideon. They had rearranged the Pritchards' entire family room, pushing the couch to the side, making a baby pit with soft foam letters on the floor, a colorful gate, and lots of toys inside. It was a safe place for the children to move freely and explore while the two nannies hung out together.

A year after they met, Cindy had confessed to Vivian that she was a lesbian. Vivian was shocked and appalled — according to her religious beliefs, homosexuality was a sin. She'd found it somewhat amusing that Cindy's employers had bought her a dozen roses when Cindy came out to them. But Vivian was not so accepting.

"I think you're going to hell," she finally told Cindy after a long talk.

Eventually the two women agreed to disagree. It was a very different falling-out that eroded their friendship for good. Cindy — always a bit unstable in Vivian's opinion — had become convinced that Vivian was jealous of her because she didn't start work until noon, while Vivian's day began at 8:00 A.M. When Vivian denied being envious, Cindy accused her of lying. Their disagreement suddenly erupted into a major fight in the Pritchards' living room — with all three children standing in the middle.

"You cunt!" Cindy screamed at Vivian, throwing a plate through the air.

Vivian told her to leave, but Cindy refused to move, so Vivian ushered the children upstairs and threatened to call the police.

"Get the hell out of this house!" she yelled.

When the fight was over and both women had calmed down, Cindy made several attempts to reach Vivian on her cell phone, but Vivian refused to answer when Cindy's name popped up on the screen. Then Cindy called Catherine, infuriating Vivian even more by involving her boss. The two nannies finally talked things through for the sake of the children, who had been friends since birth, but the easy camaraderie was gone forever, and the two women scheduled only an occasional play date now. Vivian kept her distance from Cindy. She didn't want any drama.

Vivian spotted Devan immediately and a smile spread across her face. As she moved toward her charge, the September sun shone on her dark hair. It had been thinning rapidly over the last few months, but Vivian didn't think the hair loss was related to her weight loss. Her mother had the same problem. Someday Vivian planned on getting hair extensions to fill it in again.

Just before Vivian got to Devan, Sylvia, the one Chipmunks teacher Vivian did not feel comfortable with, cut across her path. From the beginning, Vivian had been wary of the woman because she seemed to single out Devan and David, accusing them of acting out when Vivian knew they were just being boys. She had expressed her reservations about the teacher to Catherine, who brushed off her concerns, telling Vivian she was being paranoid. After Vivian met Sylvia's son, she was even more convinced that there was bias.

"Sylvia has a son who is clearly either really feminist or really gay. He had tight, tight jeans rolled up to his calves," she said after she met the boy, confident her instincts about Sylvia had been validated. "All I can think of is she didn't raise an aggressive, typical boy, so now the boys are labeled as aggressive boys when they are just boys. And I see a clear distinction between how the boys are treated and how the girls are treated."

"Devan got hit by a swing today," Sylvia said, handing Vivian a sheet of paper. "It was nothing serious, but I have an accident report."

Vivian took the report, then marched over to Devan and held up his chin for inspection. The boy looked perfectly fine. Within ten minutes the twins were in the car, buckling themselves into their booster seats. Vivian listened for the click of the seat belts, leaned back to make sure the belts were secure, and then started the engine as she pulled out her cell phone.

"Devan got hit by a swing but he's fine. I have an accident report," she told Catherine. Steering the wheel confidently with one hand, she glanced at the boys in the mirror. "David's doing good," she reported. "His fever is down. He said, 'I'm glad I stayed home with you.'"

The boys sat quietly, each looking out the window. They were not identical twins, but it was sometimes difficult to tell them apart from a distance, their height and coloring exactly the same. Up close, their differences were evident. David had sharp, defined features to Devan's soft, round looks and long, curved eyelashes. With jet-black hair, striking green eyes, and rosy cheeks, they looked like future members of the popular crowd, natural selections for the Ivy League. Sometimes Vivian worried they would end up spoiled, with a sense of entitlement like that of their father; Trevor seemed to have a new expensive hobby every other week. It was one of the reasons Vivian felt so strongly about public school.

Vivian ended her phone call with Catherine as she drove down Central Street to Chandler Lane, where the Pritchards lived. The farther she traveled from town, the larger the houses grew. Brick homes with white pillars, shingled mini-mansions painted traditional gray or white or yellow. This classic New England town, with its thick old maple trees and charming, character-filled houses, was rooted in history, a suburb close enough to Boston to be a short train ride home, but far enough away to feel like a peaceful, safe bubble. It was the kind of town that made for picture-perfect Christmases, with white sparkling lights on real fir Christmas trees, red-bowed wreaths on front doors, and starlit skies glowing over snow-covered streets.

"I missed you, Devan. Tell me about your day," Vivian said, breaking the silence. Her little boy smiled, his eyes lit up, and he began to tell her how he got hit by the swing. Vivian loved car time with the boys. She never let them have toys in the back seat. Instead she had chats with them about their days, prepped them for events they were heading to, and drilled them on important safety rules.

"Boys!" she would exclaim, getting their attention. "What's my phone number? What's your name? What's your parents' name? Where do they work? Where do I live? Where do you live? Who is the neighbor? What do you do in case of a fire? What do you do if a stranger talks to you?"

She'd repeat the drill over and over again until they got all the answers right. She was preparing her boys for any emergency. She was preparing them for life.

Once home, the boys put their bags down in their designated spot by the door while Vivian went straight to work making lunch as they played. When her cell phone rang, she flipped it open to take a quick call from Reed, who was checking in to see how the weekend went. Vivian spoke softly into the phone for a few minutes, laughing out loud a few times before hanging up.

The sun poured in from the backyard, hitting the Thomas the Tank Engine rug and the worn couch. Vivian put a pan on the stove and threw a load of laundry into the washing machine, mixing her own bra and underwear with the boys' clothes. She stood quietly at the counter for a moment, surveying the scene before her. Everything was as it should be. The counters were clean, the food slowly simmering on the stove, the boys obediently playing on the floor. Days like this gave Vivian a deep sense of calm. Life made sense.

Vivian knew that there were many parents who wouldn't have been able to handle her level of involvement on the job. She also knew she could never work for someone who would offer her fifty hours a week of childcare and not acknowledge the power that came with spending so much time with a child. From the beginning, Catherine had respected Vivian's opinion, and that was the main reason the job had worked out so well. Vivian had felt vital to the Pritchards. Every morning, she had come to work knowing she was valued. Until recently.

Her love for the boys had not wavered, but their parents were getting tougher to navigate. Trevor was in and out of the house more often, and Vivian found herself completely mute in his presence. Meanwhile, he ignored her altogether, rude behavior Vivian wouldn't normally tolerate. She still felt close to Catherine, but she was also starting to understand the limitations of their relationship when Trevor was around.

Vivian couldn't help it. She missed the way things were when she and Catherine ruled the house together. And she hated how tongue-tied and meek she became around Trevor. It was like her self-assurance just disappeared in his presence. She abhorred the way he treated Devan and David, constantly pressuring them to do better at sports, undermining their confidence. Vivian knew she should stand up to him. Her issues with her own father, her inability to break away from Reed, and her intimidation around Trevor were all linked. While Vivian was a powerhouse when it came to her job, she often felt powerless around men.

"I've had self-esteem issues with men," she said, explaining her lack of confidence around Trevor. "Trevor is a self-esteem issue. I feel beaten down with men."

The boys dutifully ate their lunch and then carried their plates to the dishwasher before heading back to their toys. Vivian sighed. They had one hour at home together and then they had to hop back in the car for the boys' afterschool activity. She had almost no time alone with them anymore and worried that she was becoming more chauffeur than nanny. Besides preschool from nine to noon, David and Devan had kickball on Monday, swimming on Tuesday, hockey on Wednesday, story time on Thursday, and Rhymes, Rhythm, and Reading on Friday. On top of that, thanks to Trevor's obsession with sports, they had more hockey on Saturday and Sunday. As far as Vivian was concerned, hockey was a ridiculous activity for two four-year-old boys who didn't even know how to ice-skate, especially three times a week.

Vivian got down on the floor with the boys to maximize the time she had left with them. Pulling out a family scrapbook she had put together, she sat with the twins, flipping pages, talking about all the fun things they had done together over the years, from the regular playgroup that Vivian and Cindy had organized, to birthday parties, to a family picnic during the Boston Marathon. Photos of Vivian were scarce, not because she wanted to keep herself out of the family album, but because she was usually the one taking the pictures. Putting the book back on its shelf, Vivian pulled out a laminated map of the United States.

"Where do you live?" she asked David, resting her cheek on his head.

"In Colorado."

"No, that's where you go skiing. Where do you *live?*" she asked patiently.

David paused, his finger hanging over the map. A smile burst across his face as he pointed to Massachusetts. Vivian relaxed; David knew exactly where he was.

By November, as Vivian raced around Wellesley running errands, the leaves on the trees were long gone. The sky had turned a heavy, metallic gray, and Vivian felt the small shifts in her job turn into serious cracks. It was shaping up to be the toughest year yet with the Pritchards. And for the first time, to her great surprise, she considered leaving the job. Trevor was driving her crazy. Lately he'd been showing up in the family room on a whim, interrupting her time with the boys and disturbing their preset schedule, raising their hopes of spending time with him only to abruptly walk out the door and leave Vivian to pick up the pieces. The night before, Trevor had burst in just as Vivian was about to head out, suggesting they play baseball in the backyard. Vivian relented and they all went outside. After about two minutes, the phone rang.

"I'll be right back," Trevor told the boys as he stepped inside to take the call.

"Daddy tried to play with you, but he can't right now," Vivian explained to Devan and David as she picked up the ball to play with them herself. It broke her heart to see their fallen faces.

Sometimes when Vivian saw that Trevor was having trouble rallying the boys or getting their attention, Vivian intervened to get the twins in line. She knew Trevor seethed with frustration when they behaved for her but not him; it was obvious to her that he resented her influence and her existence.

"Just because you're the dad doesn't mean you know the kids

when you've been gone all this time," Vivian said, describing the struggles in the house that month. "It's like my dad," she explained. "He was never really in my life and then I was going to prom and he was like, 'You can't go.' Who the hell are you? You haven't been around for three years."

Many times that fall, Vivian might be in the middle of playing a game with the boys, getting them ready for bed or a bath, but if Trevor appeared, she had to drop everything and let him take over for as long as he decided to stick around.

"We used to have a structure to our days, and now all of a sudden he's home and if he has time he wants to play with them, take them outside," Vivian said. "It throws everything off. Now I'm in a situation where I don't know what's going to happen, when he's going to be home."

The boys no longer knew what to expect in a day, and neither did Vivian. She also continued to struggle with the boys' jam-packed schedule, constantly worrying that Catherine resented the fact that she was now paying her nanny the same salary for fewer childcare hours. The following year, when the boys headed to kindergarten, could be an even bigger problem because they would be away from her even longer.

On the one hand, she worried that the Pritchards would fire her and hire in her place an afterschool babysitter. On the other hand, she worried they would keep her on but that her responsibilities would be more and more curtailed until she was nothing but an overpaid babysitter. She felt she was in a no-win situation. Leaving the boys was unthinkable, but staying meant sacrificing her career.

"That's what's different about me," she explained. "I want to know exactly what you expect of me so I can live up to that expectation. I have a hard time dealing with undefined roles and undefined expectations because then I don't feel like I'm doing my best."

For now, instead of leaving the Pritchards, Vivian made the most of her time with the boys. For Halloween, she'd thrown a huge party, inviting more than twenty of the twins' friends and preschool classmates. The kids decorated trick-or-treat bags, searched for plastic bones that Vivian had hidden in the backyard, and bobbed for doughnuts on a string. She invited a music teacher to conduct a program of Halloween songs. Vivian's good friend Laura, also a nanny, did a Gary the Ghost flannel board story. When the activities were over, the children feasted on candy-corn pizza, skeleton calzone, spooky Jell-O jigglers, and fruits and vegetables. Then they decorated homemade sugar cookies.

The party had reinvigorated Vivian, and on this November morning, she contentedly drove around Wellesley, taking care of the family errands, stocking up on groceries. Trying to adjust to the changes in the household, Vivian shopped and planned and did her best to keep things organized. She was not a roll-with-the-punches type of girl.

The groceries put away, Vivian once again left the house, climbed into the Tahoe, and headed to pick the twins up at school, expertly navigating the Wellesley streets. She was dressed in her comfortable nanny clothes, her weight loss even more dramatic now. Her jeans were even bigger.

"Well, you're halfway there," Trevor had remarked about her weight recently, in one of the rare moments when he deigned to acknowledge her. She wanted to punch him for being so rude and condescending, but she remained silent.

"I'm going to leave you for a fat girl," Reed had joked. He was almost as bad as Trevor.

It was a cool, gray day but the serious winter chill still hadn't settled in. There was no snow on the ground, no hats on kids' heads in the schoolyard. Pausing outside the yard at the preschool,

Vivian scanned the activities board. That day the class had read *Arthur Goes to the Library* and made Thanksgiving cards.

"Give me a hug and a kiss and tell me three things you did today," Vivian said after spotting David.

"We're working on a new word today called 'disruptive,'" Sylvia said before David could respond, ticking off several examples of the boys' misbehavior.

Vivian was not happy. She loaded the boys into the car in silence, got into the driver's seat, then ripped into David and Devan. She listened to what they had to say in their defense, then took out her cell phone to call their mother. The boys sat in the back seat, eyes focused on the floor, as she gave Catherine an account of what Sylvia had said.

"David told me he was being silly. Devan told me he was saying 'Hamburger, hamburger,'" she explained to Catherine, glancing into the rearview mirror.

"I don't want any more bad reports," she announced to them in the middle of her conversation with their mother. "If you get a bad report, then Devan, no *Cat in the Hat*. And David, no Rescue Hero."

The boys' chins dropped even lower as Vivian returned to her phone call with Catherine. She reiterated her distrust of Sylvia. Not only was she overly focused on the boys, Vivian believed, but her response when they did act out was ineffective, off the mark.

"Am I happy, boys?" Vivian asked, shooting them an intense stare in the mirror.

"No," they responded meekly.

"Are you going to be on best behavior the rest of the day?"

"Yes, Vivvy," they whispered in unison.

Her jaw set in a frown, Vivian pulled into the Pritchards' driveway, passing her own red Pontiac parked on the street. A tractor stood on the front lawn, and a group of men milled about, working on the shrubs. The front door opened and the cleaning lady slipped out. Vivian waved hello to the crew and inspected the lawn.

"The yard looks good," she said casually to Catherine, who was still on the line.

They went back to their discussion about the boys, who continued to sit in silence. The women agreed to address the boys' behavioral issues together, before they got worse.

"Are you gonna give it to them good? Give it to them good," Vivian said, laughing as she handed the phone to the boys in the back seat.

When the boys misbehaved in her presence, Vivian acted in a flash, and she came down hard. While other mothers might have recoiled at Vivian's tone of voice, Catherine supported her nanny's disciplinary style because she was always pleased with the end result.

Inside the house, the chastised boys were quiet and obedient as Vivian made their lunch. When it was ready, they dutifully put their toys away and washed their hands. While the boys ate peanut butter and jelly sandwiches with raspberries on the side, Vivian looked over her food diary, reviewing what she had already eaten for the day: yogurt (2 points), rice cake (1 point), butter (2 points), bread (1 point), orange juice (1 point), one-third cup baked beans (3 points), and cheese (1 point).

Back in the car again after lunch, as she drove the boys to their afternoon class, Vivian thought once again about leaving her job. She could start all over with a new family, a new set of twins, newborns ready to be raised and molded, two warm bundles she could hold in her arms. She thought of her snapshots of the boys' playgroup, one picture taken four years ago showing five babies barely able to sit up, and a more recent photo of the same group of children all grown up. It made her proud that the children had such a strong bond after all these years, and that that bond was due in large part to her efforts to maintain a social network. She had to admit, though, that that network was getting harder to hold together now that the kids were all so busy and her friendship with Cindy had fallen apart.

Pulling into the parking lot, Vivian opened the doors to the cool fall air. She breathed deep. The air was familiar, light and clean. No matter what happened in her life, Vivian felt calm and rooted living in this New England city, the place she had always called home. She would never live anywhere else.

Vivian led the boys into the building, ushering them inside an elevator that opened into a large gym. The class started and Vivian took her place on the sidelines. One mother stood just at the perimeter of the class, watching, but Vivian kept her distance. She didn't have to pay close attention to know what was going on. She recognized her boys' cries, their voices, and their laughter from the other side of the gym. A few minutes into class, Vivian heard David called out by the kickball coach for not listening to instructions. Vivian sighed deeply. She had no idea what was going on with the boys today, why they kept acting out, but she was not going to stand for it.

If Vivian were to list the three things she worked hardest to instill in her charges, those three things would be discipline, confidence, and love. Today, discipline was on her mind. A fan of Thomas Phelan's book 1-2-3 *Magic: Effective Discipline for Children 2–12*, Vivian strove to approach discipline in a consistent, unemotional way. But to an outsider, Vivian could appear a little bit harsh. One nanny had recently told her own boss that she didn't want to have any play dates with Vivian because she yelled too much, a story that made Vivian and Catherine laugh. They had watched other parents, in restaurants and on playgrounds, begging their children, in meek, deferential voices, to behave. Unlike other four-year-olds, Devan and David ate the food on their plates. They sat still in restaurants. They didn't interrupt conversations.

"The boys eat sushi. They eat everything. They'd eat anything I put in front of them," Vivian joked.

As soon as class ended, Vivian charged toward the boys, knelt down, and took David's chin in her hand. Looking him straight in the eye, she launched into another lecture about his behavior. Her voice grew loud, echoing off the gym walls, her gestures became hard and swift. Her tone was unyielding. A mother stood some distance away, observing the scene. Vivian was well aware of the woman's staring but didn't attempt to modify her behavior. It wasn't her job to make a good impression on other children's parents. It was her job to raise these boys properly.

"Now, Devan is going to get ice cream, but you're not getting any," Vivian said as David's face fell. He looked at the gym floor, his lower lip curling down in a pout, his shoulders slumped.

"I'm very sad," Vivian continued in the car on the way to the ice-cream parlor. "I don't understand this behavior. Is something hurting you? Did something bad happen over the weekend?"

For the next five minutes, Vivian continued her tirade as David apologized in a soft voice. Devan looked on silently. When they pulled up to the ice-cream parlor, Vivian was secretly relieved to see it was closed. She was off the hook. As big a show as she put on for the twins, she knew she would have probably spent that evening feeling awful for David if she really had had to deny him ice cream.

"I probably would have cried later and called and tried to explain why he couldn't have ice cream," she said. "It's harder for me than them sometimes. The whole time it's hard. You think I like to see them suffer and sitting in time-out and losing a privilege? But the difference between being a nanny and a parent is, I've seen it so many times, I know that the momentary defeat and sadness is worth it in the long run. It's worth it. I can give in but then my whole lesson is lost. I'm rewarding them for what I don't want to accept. It's hard but you have to. It's what's best for them."

The next time Vivian sent David off to school, hoping to avoid a repeat of the previous day, she made sure to arm him for good behavior. Vivian cut out a paper circle, punched holes at the edges, and tied pieces of orange, yellow, and red ribbon through the holes. Slipping it into David's pocket, Vivian told him to think about her even during the hours when she couldn't guide him directly. If he felt the urge to act out in circle time, he could reach inside his pocket and wrap a ribbon around his finger as a reminder that he needed to focus and pull himself together. If he felt fidgety, he could reach for red and then sit still. When he was tempted to speak out of turn, he could wrap a finger around orange and wait to be called on by his teacher.

"Viv," David said when Vivian picked him up from school a few days later. "We gotta talk about my bad behavior."

Vivian could only smile. Her hard work had paid off. The boys were confessing their misbehavior voluntarily. She had instilled a moral compass so they could guide themselves in the world. They were one step closer to being the responsible, caring adults she was raising them to become. She had read plenty of child-development books, but Vivian often worked on instinct, using her natural childcare gifts. When asked how she came up with the idea for the ribbon circle, she smiled, raised a perfectly arched eyebrow, and said, "I don't know. Probably God just told me. God tells me a lot of things."

Vivian believed she was a born nanny, and that this was the job God had chosen for her. Maybe God was also telling her that her work with the Pritchards was not over. For now, at least, Vivian knew deep down that David and Devan weren't ready for her to leave. Her job might not be as hands-on as it used to be, but she still had a responsibility to lead by example, to supervise from a distance. There was still work to be done.

EIGHT

KNOWING HOW HIGH Trevor's standards were, Vivian was surprised she'd been hired as David and Devan's nanny in the first place. She found it hard to believe that Trevor didn't immediately cross her off their list of candidates because of her weight, doubting her ability to chase after two young boys. Then again, her first impression of Trevor had been wrong. During the interview, she'd thought that he was friendly and mild. Other than a brief conversation about an acquaintance they had in common, he had remained quiet while she and Catherine talked. Vivian assumed that he was an involved father, concerned about the care of his children.

It was a bright spring day in May when Vivian first showed up at the Pritchards' door, feeling uncharacteristically nervous. She had worked part-time as a nanny for twins while she was in college, but now she was looking for the real deal: an on-the-books salary with full benefits. Her brief attempts after graduation to get a job outside of the childcare field had not gone well, and her heart was never in it anyway. She had endured an entire interview for a sales position only to be told to her face that she was too fat for the job. And after taking night classes for a year at a Bible college in the hopes of becoming a minister, her own pastor had crushed her dream. "You're too fat," he told her. "You're a poor reflection of the Lord."

Vivian had spent a lot of time picking out her clothes for the interview with the Pritchards, carefully choosing a red and black floral-print dress and a matching red jacket. It fit her like a tent, but she considered it her best, most professional outfit.

Outside the house, Vivian had buzzed with anticipation, worried about making a good impression. Inside, she was completely at ease. All of her interviews up to that point had been like dates with no chemistry. The mothers were too controlling or the family dynamic didn't suit her. One woman sent Vivian home when she appeared at the interview with a scratch on her lip, accusing her of having herpes. Another germ-phobic mother insisted that whomever she hired stay in the house all day long with the children. Then, of course, there were the parents who refused to say no to their kids, a parenting style Vivian shunned.

The Pritchards' family room was completely different back then, still untouched by Vivian's careful child-proofing efforts, with couches set up in the center of the room. The boys, tiny newborn bundles, slept through most of the interview. She held one of them, but to this day can't remember whether it was Devan or David. The baby had a soft, fuzzy head, old-man hands, a set of foggy, half-opened eyes.

"What do you think your method of discipline will be?" Vivian had asked.

"I don't know," Catherine said.

That small exchange would set the tone for their entire relationship. Vivian thought way ahead, planning and implementing her ideas. Catherine, laid-back and mellow, had no problem letting Vivian take the lead. The two women were totally different; but they clicked immediately.

"Believe me, I'm the best nanny you'll get," Vivian said to Catherine and Trevor as she walked out the door. "I hope you'll hire me."

And they did.

Five years later, Vivian woke up dreading the day ahead. It was an unfamiliar feeling for someone who had always looked forward to work. The boys had a school trip planned; Trevor was planning to go, and Catherine had insisted that Vivian accompany him.

That winter, as the New England chill settled in, Trevor's presence in the house continued to take its toll on Vivian. When he was home, she was tense or simply ignored him, just as he ignored her. Even when he wasn't there, she found herself anticipating his arrival. The things that Vivian had always loved about her job, caring for the boys and interacting with Catherine, were continually undermined by the uncertainty she felt at work; she was always questioning how much she was needed and whether Trevor wanted her there anymore.

"Trevor doesn't like me," she had recently remarked to Catherine.

"You're right. He probably doesn't," Catherine answered casually. The response was expected, but not at all reassuring.

When they were both in the house, Trevor would walk past her in the kitchen without saying a word and head straight for the stairs. He left the house in silence, the only signal of his departure being the slamming of the side door. He did not say hello and he did not say goodbye. He did not say when he was leaving and he did not say when he would return. If Trevor called the house and

Vivian answered, he always paused at the sound of her voice as if he had accidentally dialed the wrong number, asking, "Who is this?" Vivian felt like a nonentity, an unwanted presence, a necessary evil for Trevor because he had two little boys and a wife who worked.

February was a bleak month in Boston. Trees stood bare. The sky was a gray, heavy, impenetrable wall. Cold winds came in blasts as piles of old snow turned black with car exhaust at the sides of the roads. On days like this, it was impossible to imagine Vivian's long summers with the boys, running through sprinklers, eating ice cream, taking day trips to parks and lakes. Today, as Vivian parked on the street in front of the Pritchards' and braced herself for the cold, she could not shake the feeling that the school trip with Trevor was a bad idea.

It had already been a volatile week at work. As much as Vivian tried to keep her mouth shut, it just wasn't in her nature to stay silent where the boys were concerned. The more Trevor pushed Devan and David into sports, the more the anger built up inside her. On the one hand, Vivian was trying to accept that part of her job as a nanny was to let Catherine and Trevor make decisions on their own. On the other hand, she felt it was also her job to protect the boys and speak out on their behalf. As far as Vivian was concerned, Trevor had become obsessed with hockey, and it was starting to do real harm to David and Devan's self-esteem. Her face grew red and her eyes narrowed with anger as she recounted the many times that Trevor had acted like more of a child than his sons.

Vivian described a typical scene on a typical day when Trevor was at home: She stood outside, playing ball with David and Devan, hoping to build up their skills and confidence. They tossed the baseball casually, making jokes and laughing. As the boys jumped around in the cold, their smiles lit Vivian up too. Trevor was inside the house, hidden away, and Vivian had almost completely forgotten about him when he slid the glass door open, stepped onto the deck, and started to observe the boys as they passed the ball around. He paid particular attention to David, who was not athletic. Walking down the deck stairs, Trevor joined Vivian and the boys in the backyard.

"Come on, David! Catch the ball," he called out to his son. Vivian's defenses went up immediately.

When David dropped the ball, Vivian had no choice: she let the scene unfold.

"Come on, David! Catch the ball. Focus."

Trevor moved in to retrieve the ball, throwing it to Devan in a straight shot, and Devan caught it. Devan was a natural at the sport, pleasing his father effortlessly. David was the problem. And in general, while Devan worked to make his father happy, David kept his distance, gravitating toward his mother for affection. Vivian had watched over the years as these family dynamics developed and then solidified.

"Why can't you catch the ball, David? Your brother can catch the ball."

Eyes fixed to the ground, head bowed, David did not move. Jumping to action, Vivian picked up the ball.

"David, you can do it!" she said in a cheerful voice as she tried to distract him from his father. "Let's show Daddy you really know how to play."

She stood just two feet from the child, sending him an easy toss to get him motivated. He caught the ball without a problem and slowly Vivian stepped back, building up the distance one step at a time.

"Good catch, David! You can do it. I knew you could do it!" she yelled as a smile broke across David's face. Trevor turned and walked back into the house without a word.

When they were finished, Vivian put her arm around David, leaning in to him.

"Daddy's not happy with me, Viv," he said, looking at the ground.

"How does that make you feel?" Vivian asked.

"It makes me feel very sad."

"What are some things we can do when we feel sad?"

"We cry?"

"Yes, we cry." Vivian smiled. Love for this four-year-old boy rose up inside her. She couldn't fight his battles for him, but she could arm him. "But what can we say to Daddy?"

"You're mean."

"Well, you could say, 'Daddy, I'm trying very hard,'" she suggested.

Vivian opened the glass door, leading the boys back inside, where it was warm and the yellow light in the family room cast a bright, cozy glow. The boys continued playing, and Vivian wove herself in and out of their games as she straightened up and cleaned and took a cell phone call from her mother. Trevor did not come downstairs again until Vivian was gone.

Vivian walked through the side door of the Pritchard house, right into the middle of morning chaos. Catherine rushed around getting ready for work as the boys vied for her attention. Trevor stood sternly, a little awkward in the middle of it all. The school trip would take less than an hour: leaving from the preschool, they'd have a quick walk to the commuter rail station, where the children would ride the train just one stop. Catherine wanted Vivian to go as a chaperon for the kids in the class and to back up Trevor, who had never been to the school before.

Standing in the kitchen, Vivian gave Trevor directions to Chipmunks, feeling increasingly uneasy about the trip. She and Trevor had had a huge blowup that week, and while it had cleared the air, it hadn't made their relationship any more relaxed.

After several months of watching Trevor badger the boys about sports, Vivian had grown more and more incensed by his behavior; a confrontation was inevitable. Vivian particularly resented Trevor's insistence that the boys play hockey three times a week. She hated the layers of gear that took twenty minutes to pile on — long underwear, ski pants, shoulder pads and shirt, gloves, helmet, neckpiece, kneepads, elbow pads, and, finally, two sets of skates laced up just right. Vivian watched the boys head onto the ice, barely able to balance, bobbing back and forth like two little Frankensteins. It wasn't the game that had Vivian so worked up; it was the fact that David and Devan were the youngest ones out there on the ice, and that they tried so hard only to have to endure their father's disappointment. Vivian thought he rode them like a pro football coach, coming down hardest on David, just as he had the day they'd played ball together in the backyard.

Earlier in the week at the end of a long day, after tucking the boys into bed, Vivian had come downstairs, finding Trevor and Catherine sitting in the family room. So far Catherine had stayed out of the situation, although Vivian was sure she also felt that Trevor was pushing the boys too hard. "He's a stage parent," Vivian had fumed to Catherine more than once.

Vivian was getting ready to leave for the night when Trevor spoke up. "The boys need more ice time," he said. For Vivian, it was the last straw. Normally reticent and submissive around Trevor, she finally unleashed her strong, unstoppable, opinionated self.

"What do you mean they need more ice time?" she spat, frustration ripping through her. "They're already going three times a week and they're only four years old!"

Catherine sat in silence as the conversation escalated between her husband and her nanny.

"But they're the worst ones out there!" Trevor answered.

Vivian could barely bring herself to look at him. "They're the worst ones out there because they're only four years old in a league that starts at six years old!" she yelled. "All the research shows that teaching specialized sports this early is too much."

Her heart pounding, adrenaline rushing through her, her fear of Trevor vanished in the face of her own fierce determination to do right by the boys. Her hands in fists at her sides, her black eyes wide open, Vivian was in full mama-bear mode. There was no way her boys would be forced to play more hockey, not while Vivian was their nanny. Enough was enough. She looked at Catherine, who averted her gaze, still refusing to take a side. There was a time when Trevor wouldn't have even been a factor in a decision like this. Once again, Vivian realized the entire structure of her job had shifted under her. Vivian's partnership with Catherine was over. She was on her own.

"It's so intimidating to tell you that you're wrong," Vivian seethed, her eyes filling with tears. "You're supposed to be so intelligent. But you don't know shit about this. You're going to make them hate it. You're going to make them use steroids when they're older."

Now the tears were streaming down her face. As difficult as it was for her to stand up to Trevor, Vivian could not be stopped. It was her job to look out for the best interests of David and Devan. If she remained silent, what kind of nanny did that make her at the end of the day? Vivian grabbed her bag, her jacket, and her car keys and headed out the door, leaving Catherine and Trevor alone. Shaking, she drove a few blocks and then pulled over. She sat for a few moments before picking up her cell phone.

"I'm sorry I yelled at you. But this is really frustrating," she said when Trevor answered.

"It's all right," he said. "Calm down. It's not that big a deal."

"It is a big deal. It is a big deal. It's about the kids. You want them to be good at hockey. I want them to be emotionally healthy. You can't argue with me, because I have no ulterior motive."

"I understand that. I expect that," Trevor answered.

Later, when she replayed the argument to her friends, she disagreed with them when they suggested she was too involved in family issues. She might have a harder time separating herself from the boys than other nannies, she argued, but no matter how much she loved the twins, she knew her boundaries. This fight wasn't about being too attached; it was about protecting the boys from permanent psychological damage.

"They're not your kids," her nanny friends pointed out. "If they want their kids to play hockey, they should play hockey."

"No, that's not how it is," Vivian responded with conviction. "They hired me as a professional and an expert in raising their children. I am the children's advocate."

In the end, Trevor relented; the boys would continue to play hockey only three times a week. Vivian had won the battle, but she knew the war was far from over.

"It is, to be honest, hard to separate yourself and be like, you're not my kid, especially when you're right as far as their best interests," she admitted with a sigh.

Vivian prepped the boys for their field trip while she drove the Tahoe, explaining that they'd be taking a short train ride. Trevor would follow in his own car, meeting them in time for the trip. The fight with Trevor earlier in the week still fresh in her mind, Vivian hoped for the best. She pulled into a spot behind the school and made her way into Chipmunks with the boys. A water-stained cement building, Chipmunks was a relic from the 1970s that hadn't held up especially well over time. Inside, Devan and David strolled through surprisingly bright and cheerful rooms with Vivian right beside them.

By the time Trevor arrived, Devan and David were still in circle time. Vivian watched the boys' father, noting how awkward and out of place he looked in the casual atmosphere. Trevor didn't know a single child there but his own. He didn't know any of the parents or any of the teachers. Vivian, on the other hand, knew everyone. This was her turf. Walking over to Trevor, Vivian began introducing him to a few of the Chipmunks staff.

"You know what?" Trevor suddenly said to Vivian in a voice that was loud enough for others to hear. "You just need to leave. I can do this by myself. It's between me and the boys."

"But Catherine told me to come," Vivian replied quickly. "She said you might need a hand."

"Just go," Trevor said.

Vivian heard a roar in her ears, and her face turned hot. She felt like throwing up. Starting to walk out of the room, Vivian immediately thought of how confused David and Devan would be when they realized she had left without saying goodbye. But there was nothing she could do. She had to leave and she had to get out of the building fast, before anyone saw her cry.

"I'm sorry, I can't stay," Vivian mumbled to the school director on her way to the door.

"Why? You have to stay. We need you," the director answered, but Vivian was already gone.

She managed to get herself into the car before she fell apart. Tears streamed down her face as she shut the car door. In that moment, it felt like the most humiliating experience of her life. Hurt and demoralized, Vivian sat and sobbed.

Within a couple of minutes her cell phone rang and Catherine's name appeared on the screen. Vivian took a deep breath before answering. The two women had some of their most heated discussions when Vivian was in the car, after she dropped the boys off at school or at a class, because it was the best time for them to talk in private. Vivian's pain had given way to deep anger, and she knew she would not hold back now.

"Trevor just called me," Catherine started. "I don't know what the problem is."

"I don't know what *his* problem is!" Vivian yelled into the phone. Her public professional nanny face disappeared as she yelled at her boss. "I can't stand him! He's an arrogant ass. He's so arrogant and selfish. He wanted to play Superdad! He thought he could get away with it."

"I know," Catherine said with characteristic calm. "I don't know why he did that. I don't know what the problem is."

"What am I supposed to tell the boys when they ask why I left without saying goodbye?"

"Tell them Trevor asked you to leave," Catherine said, and then she sighed. "Look, Trevor is home more now. You two just don't know how to deal with each other."

Catherine tried to explain to Vivian that her husband was not a touchy-feely person, that he was a straight-to-the-point type of guy who could sometimes come off as cold. Her words didn't pacify Vivian. She knew that Catherine was just trying to defuse the situation, that her boss was in a difficult position, caught between a husband she lived with and a nanny she relied on.

When Vivian parked her car and walked into the Pritchards'

family room later that day, it didn't feel like her space anymore. The food in the refrigerator, the chewable vitamins on the counter, the hooks by the door for the boys' jackets were all there because of Vivian. But maybe, even with everything she did for this family, she didn't matter at all. Maybe it really was time for her to leave the boys behind and take on a set of newborns she could raise all over again. Maybe it was time for her to work for a family who appreciated her talents and recognized her commitment to the job.

Trevor came home after the field trip instead of going to his office, and Vivian walked right out of the house when he walked in. She picked the boys up and kept them busy downstairs until it was time to leave again for karate. Vivian tried to relax in the car, but she was still worked up.

"Why didn't you go on the field trip?" Devan asked, just as Vivian had predicted. "Where did you go? I was waiting for you."

"Daddy wanted it to be a Daddy and Devan and David day, so Viv went home," she explained.

"Oh," Devan answered, still sounding confused.

Later, Vivian played with the boys in the family room as the horrible day finally came to an end. When Trevor walked into the kitchen, ignoring everyone, Vivian kept quiet.

"Why did you send Viv home?" Devan asked his father suddenly.

"Just so you know," she said, looking right at Trevor, "the only reason I was there was because Catherine told me to go. I didn't really want to be there because I knew you were going."

"Yeah," he said, still avoiding eye contact. "It was a miscommunication."

Nothing felt normal anymore. Vivian knew things were never going to be the same. The ease of her early friendship with Catherine was gone. Trevor had come between them, and no matter how hard they tried, they couldn't regain their former footing.

Two days after the boys' field trip, Vivian felt slighted a second time when Trevor informed her that she was not welcome at the boys' hockey awards ceremony taking place later that afternoon. Vivian remained silent, but inside, she fumed.

The following week, Catherine asked Vivian to work late on Friday, and Vivian agreed, making plans to take the boys to the science museum in the city and to dinner afterward. If she was going to work late, she reasoned, she wanted to do something fun. That morning, the two women stood in the kitchen, running through the schedule as usual before the boys left for school. Devan and David stood nearby, already dressed and ready to go.

"I made a play date with this kid from school but I forgot I was going to be late tonight," Catherine said. She looked pretty as usual, her hair pulled back in a felt headband. Her green cardigan matched her eyes. "Do you want to go?"

"I'm going to go to the museum, remember?" Vivian said.

"Well . . ." Catherine began, filling up her bag for work.

"Can we have money for parking?"

"When are you going?"

"Probably at three thirty, and then we'll go out to dinner and be back here by seven," Vivian answered casually.

"But I want to come home after work and see the kids before I leave for the evening." Catherine paused and then dropped her wallet in her bag.

"Catherine," Vivian said, instantly irritated. "You're coming home for fifteen minutes to change for dinner."

"Yeah, but I want to see the kids."

"You're not going to have time to see the kids," Vivian argued, gritting her teeth.

"So I have to pay for you to go to the museum, and I'm not going to see my kids?" Catherine frowned. "Just take the money and go."

"This is ridiculous," Vivian huffed, irritated that Catherine was irritated.

Vivian was tired of how unpredictable her job had become. She didn't know where the boys were going to kindergarten in the fall and whether she would even get the same salary. She didn't know when Trevor would be home or how to deal with him when he was. She didn't know what Catherine's expectations were of her and whether she was fulfilling them. The job that had once been so effortless was now a constant hassle. There was no longer any communication, and Vivian couldn't take the uncertainty.

"I want to see the kids before they go to bed," Catherine said again.

"You know, you're coming home for five minutes and it's much easier if the kids aren't in the house."

"It will be dark out. You don't need to go to the city when it's dark anyway."

"Are you serious?" Vivian was stunned. "I've taken the kids where I want for the last four years and now all of a sudden I can't take the kids to the museum? Are you joking?"

"Well, usually you make an effort to have the kids here when I'm coming home for a few minutes."

"Catherine, I've worked late Wednesday, Thursday, and now Friday. I did it so I could have a special outing with the kids. I didn't do this so I could sit here all night."

"I'm sorry I ruined your plans," Catherine said sarcastically.

"Whatever. I need to get the kids to school," Vivian answered, ushering the boys out of the house.

"Listen, we need to talk about next year," Vivian told Catherine over her cell phone after she dropped the boys off at school. "This is absolutely ridiculous. The reason I didn't want the kids to be here when you came home is because it's not really fair to the kids to see you for two minutes when you have to rush out of the house."

"They're not like that," Catherine answered.

"Fine," Vivian said, agreeing to stay home.

In the past, Vivian had always prepped the boys when their mother would be making only a brief appearance before heading out again. She might say, "Boys, Mommy is going to come home, but she's only going to be here for a few minutes," hoping to avoid upsetting them. This time, Vivian didn't bring it up, letting Catherine handle the situation herself.

"Why are you leaving? Why are you leaving?" the boys cried, clinging to their mother as she tried to make her way back out the door later that evening.

Vivian sat and watched, letting the episode play out just as she predicted, without saying a word. She didn't have to. In her head, she'd been vindicated.

The month of February had dragged on interminably. Vivian was exhausted and strung out. Getting ready for work, she walked around her apartment, that shrine to her profession, the place where she worked on her Nanny of the Year portfolio and crafted her image. Even away from the Pritchards, who had made her ordered life so messy, things did not always fall perfectly into place. Hidden among the scores of professional nanny books and meditations on Christianity sat *Men Who Hate Women and the Women Who Love Them* and *Angry Men and the Women Who Love Them*, books she had bought to help her cut Reed out of her life for good. Her kitchen, impeccably clean at first sight, suddenly seemed barren and a little bit soulless, all food banned in an effort to keep herself from overeating. The only sign of life in the room was the constant buzzing of the empty refrigerator.

These days Vivian felt she was fighting an uphill battle. Her weight loss had leveled off, and she had seen Reed several times, against her better judgment. Just the thought of leaving David and Devan brought her to tears, but as February came to a close, she wondered if she had a choice. This month had left her feeling excluded, marginalized, and demoted.

Vivian went to work, dropped the boys at school, and then called Catherine on her cell phone. Sighing into the phone, she told Catherine everything she was feeling. She tried to be direct and logical, keeping her emotions out of the discussion.

"Look, your family's needs are changing," she began. "You and Trevor want to be more involved. And it's great. It's what's best for the kids and it's fabulous. But that means my role is decreasing and no one is talking about this. But you have to understand the effect of it all. All of a sudden, I can't go to the hockey thing and see them get their trophies. All of a sudden I'm not welcome because Trevor's going to be there. All of a sudden, I have to ask to do the slightest thing. Something is going on."

"Give me some examples," Catherine said calmly.

"When you discussed the school thing. You didn't ask my input. The hockey thing. No one thought to ask me if playing three times a week is too much. It was me and you and the kids before. Now Trevor wants to be involved and I'm being moved to second string. And that's great and that's how it should be, but we need to talk about it."

"Well, I'm not going to get in the middle of you and Trevor."

"Well, I've been here for almost five years and I really don't think I should have to ask permission to see the kids get their trophies."

"Well, you need to know, are you going as a nanny or a spectator? It's a public event. There's no reason you can't go," Catherine said.

"That's not being included and being a part of it. So I can go and stand on a separate side of the line?" Vivian was furious now. She had always planned on taking her own car to the event, attending on her own time.

"If Trevor's home and he wants to take them to hockey, you shouldn't want to take them to hockey anyway," explained Catherine.

"No kidding, Catherine!" Vivian said, her voice rising with anger. "You think I want to put pads on them for twenty-five minutes? I wanted to encourage them and be an additional supporter and an important part of their life watching them get their first trophy. I'm the one who has to deal with the question, 'Why didn't you want to be there?'"

The fight went on without coming to any resolution. Vivian sat in the car outside the house, so frustrated she could barely breathe.

"You need to start thinking about other childcare solutions," she finally said, the words spilling out before she could stop them. "This isn't working anymore."

NINE

KIM HEARD THE FIRST footfall at around 4:00 A.M. It was followed by a storm of stomping. Up the stairs, down the stairs, past her bedroom door, into the living room and then the study. Turning over on her air mattress, Kim opened her eyes to the dark, pulled her earplugs out, and listened more closely. She heard muted voices, drawers opening and closing, the thud of a suitcase hitting the floor. No one came to get her, but Kim knew exactly what was going on. The baby was coming.

Kim had continued to organize the Porters' house for the baby after she'd arrived that Sunday night. She had moved Brian and Holly upstairs on Monday and dragged her air mattress downstairs to the now empty room she was still hoping to make feel like home. During the day, she had followed Brian's orders and held her tongue when he talked to her like the help, silently reminding herself that it would all change once the baby arrived. Now, listening to the activity outside her door, Kim was thrilled. She stayed in her room, leaving her employers alone for their last few hours together as a childless couple, but inside she was singing. When the commotion outside her door finally ceased, Kim was sure they were on their way to the hospital. She breathed deep and smiled to herself. Soon the baby would come home and Kim could finally do the job she was hired for: she could be a nanny.

But after a brief moment of silence, Kim realized that the Porters hadn't yet left the house. A room away, she heard a now familiar noise: click, click, click. Less than a week into her job, Kim already understood her employers well enough to know exactly what they were doing. They were in their shared office, each hovering over a laptop, silently and furiously communicating with their other, bigger lives: work. Holly had a memo to finish for her firm and Kim pictured her diligently sending e-mails one after the other, pausing just long enough to let a contraction pass before she sent another one. Brian, Kim figured, had a list of his own things to attend to, although sometimes she suspected he created more work than actually existed.

Eventually the typing stopped, the laptops were closed, and Kim heard the front door slam for the last time. The silence that followed was like a small miracle. Alone in the house, Kim quietly celebrated. Nothing had improved since her first night. Holly was good-natured and easygoing but she was barely around. Brian, on the other hand, was relentless and controlling, and home all the time. Kim's emotions had swung wildly since she started the job, from delusional optimism that it would all get better when the baby arrived to the depths of despair as she tried to face the fact that she had made a huge mistake. For now, at least, she could simply turn over in peace and go back to sleep, knowing that no one would be there to manage her when she got up.

The morning after that first freezing night in the Porters' upstairs room, Kim had awoken, still shivering, black garbage bags scattered all around the room. Standing in the shower, she let the warm water wash over her until her shaking stopped. Her mind blank, still numb from all the work Brian had demanded the night before, she went through the motions of that first day without much reflection. If she had stopped for a moment to contemplate her situation, to really think about how dramatically her life had changed in the past twenty-four hours, she just might have dropped to her knees.

Within a few minutes of finishing her breakfast, Kim had the washing machine vibrating with Brian and Holly's already clean clothes and she folded everything left in the dryer the night before. When Brian walked into the room, she looked up and smiled. Carrying a set of keys and a cell phone, Brian handed them both to Kim. She followed him into the living room, where he introduced her to his personal assistant, who was sorting through a pile of mail on the table. A young guy in his twenties, Paul had large brown eyes, floppy hair, and a huge, infectious smile. Kim leaned forward to shake his hand, feeling relieved. Having another person in the house was just the buffer she was hoping for.

The three stood in the living room as Brian launched into a description of house rules. Kim was required to wear the cell phone at all times, and Brian asked her to communicate by text message as often as possible. Then Brian instructed Kim about his door-locking regimen. Besides the front door, many of the other doors in the house also had to be locked, even in the middle of the day. It was especially important that Kim keep the upstairs door locked because it would now lead to Brian and Holly's room and the baby nursery. Kim stared at her boss, taking in his request. Kim would be walking through the house with a key ring the size of a janitor's. Every time she went in and out of the baby's room, or ran upstairs to grab something, a door would have to be unlocked and locked again. As she glanced over at Paul, he shot her a grin and a slight eye roll. Right then Kim knew she had found an ally.

"Okay," Kim said to her boss. She held the keys tightly in her hand as Brian finished his speech.

"With all the contractors around, I don't want anything to get stolen," he explained.

Kim stared at her boss again. In her interview, she had told herself that Brian and Holly were good, nice people, even if they were a little too book smart for her taste and not exactly the type she chose as friends. Now, once again, she saw another layer to her boss. He was paranoid and mean-spirited. Why would he hire people he didn't trust? she wondered. Why did he assume the worst of people? Once again, she held her tongue. She sighed quietly to herself as she wrapped her fingers around the new set of keys.

"I had a dream about you last night," she said to Brian later that day when they were alone again, hoping to make things more friendly between them.

"What was it?" he asked.

"I dreamed that you came into my room in the middle of the night and told me it was time to go."

"I fired you?" Brian asked. He tilted his head to the side in confusion.

"No!" Kim laughed. "That it was time to go. That the baby was coming."

"God, don't say that!" he answered, abruptly walking out of the room.

Kim had expected a smile or a laugh, but Brian was impenetrable. She got back to work, folding, washing, dragging more black garbage bags upstairs. When the movers came, she had them bring her suitcases and boxes in from the car so she could finally set up her room. She would keep sleeping on the air mattress until a new bed arrived. The room didn't have a lamp or an overhead light, but luck-ily, she had her television and VCR, which she turned on at night so she could see. It was the first thing she set up, so that she wouldn't fall behind on *General Hospital,* a show she had taped for years while she was at work and watched in the evenings. Just as she was setting the timer, Brian walked back into the room, interrupting her.

"You know," he said, eyeing her VCR with disdain, "I could sell you my TiVo and then you wouldn't have to use a VCR."

"Thanks, but I'll stick with the VCR," said Kim. She already knew Brian was a believer in technology, but she wasn't impressed by new gadgets. If something worked for her, she stuck by it.

"I could give you a good price," he pressed. His hair was combed down, and he wore his jeans slightly high on his waist. Kim stiff-ened in his presence. She knew he was trying to be helpful, yet she also detected a condescending tone in his voice that set her on the defensive.

"I prefer the VCR. I know how to work it and I'm just fine with it."

"That is so *stupid!*" Brian said. He lifted a hand toward her face, pretending to slap her as a joke. Only it didn't feel like a joke. He stood just a few inches from her face, leaning down. It was hostile and intimate at the same time. Kim stood back.

"Brian," Kim answered sternly. "It's not your decision. It's my decision."

This time when he walked away, Kim felt sick to her stomach. How was she going to live with a man who was home all the time if every interaction was so full of tension, if every conversation felt forced and awkward? Brian, she realized, was the kind of person who believed he always knew the right way to do everything and made sure everything was done exactly as he said. It was the kind of arrogance she found tough to take from someone who was younger than she and had a lot less life experience. But here she was in his home with nowhere to go, and she had signed a one-year contract. She couldn't just walk away and break it now. She had to stick it out and hope for the best once the baby arrived.

The constant feeling that someone unhappy and demanding and disapproving was standing over her was gone, and she felt relaxed for the first time since she had arrived on the job. At 7:00 A.M. on the morning the Porters left for the hospital, Kim opened her eyes to an empty house. She enjoyed every moment of her freedom but she didn't slack off. Getting straight to work, hitting the pile of baby gear in the living room, she moved through the house easily now that the tension had lifted. While she worked, she called her friend and old boss Diane to fill her in on the new job so far. For the past year and a half, as her marriage slowly fell apart, Kim had worked part-time for Diane, a stay-at-home mother of two. They had clicked immediately when they met and Kim now considered Diane one of her closest friends.

Kim's interview with Diane couldn't have been more different from her interview with the Porters. Within minutes of meeting, they had established a connection, and both later described the other as a soul mate. They had cut right through the formalities of discipline and experience and headed straight to girl talk after Diane confessed she was pregnant with her second child but was nervous about telling anyone because of past miscarriages. Kim immediately told Diane that she had also lost pregnancies.

"How many miscarriages have you had?" Diane asked Kim.

"Three," she answered.

"What's your problem?" Diane asked immediately.

"Progesterone," Kim said.

"Me too!" exclaimed Diane.

Kim's first miscarriage took place when she was still in her twenties and married to her first husband. It was what she called a normal miscarriage with cramping and bleeding. She lost her second pregnancy when she was married to Sam, just twenty-four hours after saying their vows. The only explanation the doctors had was low progesterone levels. The third time she got pregnant, Kim took all the precautions she could. She started on progesterone suppositories before she was even pregnant and continued to take them once the baby was conceived. She lay down for an hour twice a day, scheduled an amniocentesis to make sure the baby was healthy, and had blood tests every week. She would never forget watching television the morning of Tuesday, September 11, 2001, and putting her hand on her stomach, instinctively protecting her baby from the horrors on the television. By the following Tuesday, just a few days shy of her twelfth week, she had lost the baby.

Diane's pregnancy went full-term and Kim was there from the start of Sophie's life. Kim held her, a tiny newborn bundle, in her arms, letting instinct take over as she gazed down at the child. As she took in the rosy cheeks, the half smile, and the heavy lids, Kim saw into the future.

"Oh boy, you've got trouble here," she had told Diane, predicting that Sophie would be a strong-willed child who knew her own mind. Diane had believed every word her nanny said. She knew Kim had a gift, a special instinct when it came to children.

"Oh my God! You've got to get out of there," Diane said immediately after hearing Kim's description of Brian and how she was treated her first night on the job.

They talked for over an hour, and Kim slowly felt better. Diane confirmed that Kim wasn't being overly sensitive, that there was something off about the Porters and that she wasn't being given the respect she deserved.

After she hung up with Diane, Kim dialed Nancy, another close friend and a fellow nanny, to get her take on the situation.

"You knew that was probably how it was going to be in the beginning," Nancy said, trying to see both sides of the situation. "Hopefully things will get better when you have the baby to focus on."

Kim took both of her friends' advice into account. It was a relief to have Diane on her side. But Kim also understood the particular role of a live-in nanny. All the lines were blurred when you lived with a family. A truly talented live-in nanny not only took care of children, she filled the role of wife and sometimes functioned as a secretary. She bought the children's clothes, she made the play dates, and she bought the groceries. She also subtly reminded a husband that his anniversary was a week away and might even offer to pick up the gift a wife had been hinting she wanted. A truly talented live-in nanny anticipated all the needs of a family and fulfilled them before they even knew something was amiss.

Kim wasn't ready to give up on the job yet, and now that the baby was coming home, things had to get better. Today would be a new day, she vowed. It was time to officially begin her job. When Paul walked into the house later that morning, Kim was full of energy and ready to go. She told him that Brian and Holly were at the hospital and ran down the list of things she needed to get done. Paul promised to stay at the house and help her navigate the area by cell phone when she ran her errands. Kim felt another boost having Paul around: they were already a team. The day before, Paul had proven her first instincts right, coming to her rescue when Brian, once again, addressed her with utter disrespect.

"I'm being bad and leaving my dishes in the sink," Brian had said, walking into the living room, where Kim and Paul sat getting acquainted.

"That's okay, they'll still be there for you later," she joked.

"No they won't," Brian answered sternly. His checks went red, eyes turning to slits. It was an expression Kim was already familiar with, a scowl that took over his face without warning. "Because you are going to do them."

Kim sat still on the couch, utterly stunned. She had never been directly asked — much less told — to wash an employer's dishes before, only the children's. Sure, she had done a family's dishes to be helpful and go the extra mile, but it had never been a requirement of the job. It was the kind of thing she did to show she cared. Clearly, it was also the kind of thing Brian simply felt entitled to. Kim could not allow this man to treat her like a maid. Paul took one look at Kim and Brian, taking in the standoff.

"I'll do them!" he volunteered cheerfully, breaking the tension.

Now, as she prepared for the baby's arrival, Kim was grateful for Paul's assistance. For someone so young, he seemed to grasp the subtleties of her working relationship with Brian. He did everything Brian asked of him, jumping as soon as he was called, but he recognized that Kim was being treated differently. Brian simply didn't lash out at him or demand as much as he did of Kim.

Kim explained to Paul that she only had a couple of days to get the baby's nursery ready now that Holly was in the hospital. She looked through the piles of things waiting to be set up and tried to imagine just how this particular mother might like her newborn child's nursery to look. All the basics were there — the crib bedding, blue with yellow stars, and a matching lamp. There was a mobile of rocket ships, a handful of stuffed animals, a rug, and a few posters that needed framing. The nursery furniture would arrive the next day and then Kim would put the entire room together.

Kim took a mental inventory of everything the Porters already had and came up with a list of missing essentials. They needed everything from cotton balls to a custom-fitted blackout shade for the nursery window. Telling Paul she'd call him from the road, Kim walked out of the house, climbed into the Honda Accord that the Porters had designated as the nanny car, and set out for the nearest Target.

The Texas sun shining down on her, the road in front of her, and Paul on the phone to give her directions, Kim navigated the local strip malls with ease. She was decisive and efficient, relieved to be accomplishing something so tangible. Holly had a long list, a typically exhaustive catalog of useless materials, as far as Kim was concerned. Kim already knew the Porters had bought many of the things on the list — a stroller, crib, bouncy seat, and glider — but they didn't have the tricks of the trade. Dreft laundry detergent, thin washcloths for tiny folds of skin, the best diapers, nail clippers, pacifiers, a bottle brush with a nipple brush, a waterproof mattress pad, piles of cloth diapers, baby socks and baby hats, and boxes of maxi pads for Holly's return from the hospital.

In Kim's experience, mothers always underestimated how many pads they would go through after childbirth. She made sure the house was stocked. Kim also used scores of basic cloth diapers, throwing them over her shoulder when she held babies, laying them down under their heads in the crib because they were softer on newborn skin than sheets and easier to clean if the baby spit up.

She and Paul were like two characters out of *The Matrix*. She was out on the street. He was back at the main base, navigating for her via the Internet. He told her exactly what store to go to and stayed on the phone with her while she found it. They worked well together, making jokes and getting a ton accomplished in a short time. It reminded her of what an effortless relationship was like and how fun it could be.

Back at the house, Kim didn't waste any time. Waving hello to the construction crew outside, she headed inside with her bags. It was a tiny nursery but she'd make it work. Standing in the empty room, she thought about the furniture that would arrive and where it would best fit. By the time she was through with it, this cramped room would be a gem. Later that afternoon, Brian walked through the front door.

"We have a Cooper," he said, and Kim smiled. She couldn't wait to meet the new baby boy.

The next day, Holly remained in the hospital with Cooper, but Brian spent nearly the entire day at home. Kim was nervous in Brian's presence but kept to herself upstairs, putting the finishing touches on the nursery, folding Cooper's clothes and blankets, getting the last of the laundry out of the way. After a couple of hours in the sanctuary of the baby nursery, Kim headed back downstairs. Brian was sitting on the couch as she descended the stairs, and the look on his face — a deep frown, eyes half closed but intense — told her she was in trouble.

"Where have you been?" he asked.

"Upstairs, getting Cooper's room ready. What's the matter?" she asked.

"Why didn't you have your cell phone with you? I've been calling you."

"I left it on the bed in my room. I didn't think I'd need it," she answered, honestly confused. She had been instructed to have the cell phone clipped to her at all times, but she didn't think that applied when they were both home. After all, it was a small house. "I turned it off so I wouldn't waste the battery."

"Well, I was calling you. I needed you," he said. Kim was floored. She had never worked for anyone who would call her on a cell phone while they were both in the house.

"What did you need?" she asked, trying to stay calm.

"I spilled something while I was making lunch and I need you to clean it up."

Kim looked around the room and saw the vacuum resting up against the wall, less than ten feet away from Brian. Staring her boss straight in the eye, she stood strong and breathed deep.

"Why didn't you get the vacuum cleaner yourself? It's right there."

"No! I'm eating!" he said.

Burning inside with anger and humiliation, Kim did as she was told. She vacuumed up Brian's crumbs while he sat on the couch. That night, alone in her room, she pulled out the diary she had bought to keep a record of her emotional progress after her divorce. So far, flipping through the first few pages, she saw more notes about her job than her personal life. She didn't have time to think about her own life because she was too busy trying to fit into the Porters'. That night, instead of looking out the window, wondering what Sam was doing that moment, Kim wrote these words in her diary: "I'm really worried about my role here." On the one hand, she had been hired for her expertise. On the other, it was clear to her that Brian had no real respect for her. He had hired her because she was considered the best, because her agency told him she was the best, but in his mind, she was still just household help.

What Kim did not write about in her journal was the fear that she also felt that night, lying in bed in the dark, knowing she was alone in the house with Brian. Of all the doors she was told to lock and unlock, hers was the only one that didn't have a lock. Anybody could walk in. She couldn't shake the feeling that she was vulnerable and alone, and that Brian could come in anytime he wanted. If pressed, she wouldn't have admitted it or even been able to put it into words, but she also had a suspicion that he might like her just a little bit too much.

Lying in bed now with Brian in the upstairs room, Kim felt the same unease pass through her that she'd felt during her interview, as he'd followed her up the stairs with his hands on her hips. She could not point to a specific behavior or anything Brian had said. It was a feeling she got from a glance he threw or the way he stood too close to her when he gave her orders.

As she slowly drifted off to sleep, Kim tried to forget that Brian was in the house. Instead she focused on Holly's homecoming and the newborn baby she would soon meet and grow to love. When everyone was in the house, when the schedules were set, maybe she'd discover she'd been wrong all along.

It was the moment she had been waiting for. Brian and Holly drove up in their Land Cruiser, the car seat securely fastened in the back. Kim sat upstairs in the nursery, waiting to meet Cooper. It was a makeshift room, barely the size of a closet, but Kim had transformed it. Crib bumpers tied on, sheet over the mattress, and a beautiful hand-stitched quilt draped over the back of a white wooden glider, the nursery was a perfect combination of yellows and blues.

Amid the chaos of stuff stacked into piles, the half-working kitchen, the torn-out bathrooms, and the construction project taking place all over the house, this tiny room was an oasis. Standing in the middle of the room, with the sun hitting the light blue walls and the smell of clean laundry in the air, Kim knew this would be her favorite room. She looked forward to pulling the baby out of his crib after a nap, resting his head on her shoulder.

Her own mattress had finally arrived and she had been able to set her own room up too. She still didn't have a lamp, but she couldn't wait to climb into her bed at the end of this day, after Brian and Holly and Cooper were settled. She would curl up in her own sheets, rest her head on her own pillows, and, lying under her comforter from home, she would catch up on *General Hospital*.

The car doors slammed and Kim heard them all pile into the house. Suddenly she felt nervous. From the beginning she'd had more interaction with Brian than with Holly, but she still wanted to please Holly. Going on her gut instinct for what Holly would like, Kim had arranged the room without any direct communication with her boss. Now she hoped she had made the right choices.

"Ohhhh," Holly said when she stepped into the room, carrying Cooper in her arms. "This is just how I pictured it."

Holly sat down on the glider with the baby, looking around, her eyes filling with tears. Kim sighed and reveled in the moment. It wasn't just Cooper's homecoming or finally getting to work as a nanny that made Kim happy, it was the idea that she had been able to make things easier for Holly. She had anticipated her needs and fulfilled them without having everything spelled out. It was a brief, perfect moment, the kind that came and went quickly for a nanny. And if Kim didn't take the time to appreciate it, she would miss out on all the satisfaction of the job. She knew that a nanny's triumphs often came in the quiet, private moments: A first word she kept to herself so the mother didn't know what she missed. The grateful look in a mother's eyes when Kim intervened to help but did not lecture. The warm, fuzzy head of a newborn up against her neck. The job was as difficult as motherhood itself and Kim was happy to take all of it — the grueling, repetitive work along with the fleeting moments of satisfaction and joy.

Holly shifted in her chair and pulled the baby up to her. Kim stood at a distance, taking the child in. Children were Kim's second language. She connected with them and read their thoughts. She considered this ability to understand children her number one talent. Cooper, a red-faced newborn with an oversize nose, spiky hair, and a cone head, was not an objectively pretty baby, but Kim saw him immediately through the eyes of a mother. She fell for him on the spot. Cooper wasn't attractive but he was a snuggly baby, a loving child.

Babies filled Kim up and made her feel at peace. She was drawn to them, even when she knew they were not her own.

"It's probably because I need so much love," Kim remarked with a laugh, trying to explain her passion for newborns. "And I just don't have any love in my life. And they're unconditional love."

Slowly, Cooper's eyes opened in his mother's arms. Kim stood back and let Holly get ready to feed him. Knowing Holly was a modest woman, she gave her some privacy as she maneuvered in the glider.

Kim looked up as Brian cleared his throat from the doorway; neither woman had heard him approach. "Did you wash your hands?" he asked his wife.

"Yes," Holly lied and Kim tensed up, knowing from the tone of his question that Brian knew she hadn't.

"You need to go right now and wash your hands," he said, walking into the room and leaning down to pull Cooper off of Holly's breast. Holly got up slowly and headed to the bathroom.

"And don't just rub your fingertips underneath a trickle of water," he instructed, like a father speaking to a child. "Soak them and scrub them in between and on top and use hot water."

The perfect homecoming moment slipped away as fast as it had arrived. Kim remained silent, but she wanted to scream at Brian, remind him that his wife had just given birth. Kim wanted to run out of the house and never come back. Here she was, stuck in another marriage that she knew would never work.

If Brian felt he could talk that way to his wife, who also happened to be a successful career woman, there would be no stopping him when it came to dealing with her, a mere nanny. He was a control freak, he was rude, and he was nasty, she thought. And then it hit her: things were not going to get any better. He would be home all the time, and she would be trapped here with him. Once again, she found herself wondering how in the world she had arrived at this place, living with this strange family, trying desperately to feel at home in someone else's life.

TEN

CLAUDIA KNEW HOW to live on air. It was her natural state of being. She took in $420 a week and paid her bills backwards, starting with the ones she had owed the longest, putting down the bare minimum. The thinner the envelope, the more likely she was to pay it. When a current bill arrived, it was thick, but when those same bills were reduced to reminders or threats, they were almost weightless. And that was when she paid, just enough to keep things going to the next month.

Being broke was second nature to Claudia. Her life had never been any other way. She'd worked out a budget a few times, but budgets left her feeling empty and depressed. There was no point in laying down a plan she could not keep. She didn't need to look at numbers written down on a piece of paper to know that she spent more money than she made. Claudia approached money on an instinctive level, without any clear system beyond damage control. She paid whatever was necessary to keep a roof over her head, the utilities on, and food in the refrigerator.

When things got tough and the bills became a mountain she

could not climb, she stopped opening the credit card bills altogether, dropping them in the trash can, unopened, with all the other junk mail. She did not think about the balances she owed or the late fees she would be charged or the interest rates that were growing exponentially. She threw the envelopes away with a little sigh and went about her day.

"I have to struggle. Four hundred twenty dollars is nothing. I have to know how to spend it, how to roll it around, how to stretch the daylights out of it," Claudia said, explaining how she got through every week. "I stretch it until I can't stretch it no more."

Sometimes she thought about finding another job, earning $500 or $600 like other girls she knew. Betsy and James had even encouraged her to look, explaining that they couldn't afford to pay her more. Between Claudia's weekly salary, her MetroCard for the subway, taxes, her Christmas bonus, and six weeks' paid vacation, Betsy and James spent about $25,000 a year on childcare, a small fortune for them. Claudia mulled over the idea of leaving but never considered it seriously. She was too attached to this family. She also knew her schedule would be more intense, a fifty-five-hour week instead of the thirty-five hours she typically worked now that Betsy had cut her hours.

Over the years, perhaps the most American thing Claudia did was supplement her income with credit cards. In the beginning, she couldn't believe her luck. When she wanted a cute shirt she saw in a store window, she bought it. When Tanisha begged for a new outfit, Claudia obliged. Claudia was amazed that she could buy things with money she did not have, and then she was amazed at how quickly the debt piled up. She told herself she'd catch up when things got better, once she had a few good months.

But things didn't get better. They stayed the same. Her salary leveled off, except for a few small raises, and every month there were unexpected expenses. Tanisha got sick, someone at home needed more money, there was a birthday to think about, or the season changed, bringing with it the need for new coats and boots. The day Claudia went to the bank and discovered that her checking account was nearly empty, she had no idea how much she actually owed on her credit cards. She didn't know how much of that money was for purchases she had made and how much was composed of fees tacked on by Citibank or Discover or MasterCard. For years, Claudia had been every credit card company's target customer, quickly adding to her balance but keeping up with the minimum payments. Now she was on their deadbeat list, her accounts sent to collection agencies that called and wrote but never saw a cent.

Collection agencies left messages at the Halls', but they never reached Claudia. In the evenings, Betsy took some of the calls and wondered briefly what was happening with Claudia's expenses, whether she was in trouble. Then she got distracted by the kids or involved with something at work, and the thought slipped away as quickly as it came. She had her own problems to worry about.

There was tension in the Hall house, and it all came down to milk. James and Betsy were at war over organic versus regular. There was the usual harmless bickering over disorganized drawers and cupboards, over the chaos and mess the children left in their paths, but the battles became heated when the subject turned to milk. James insisted they buy regular, while Betsy wanted her children to drink organic. She had read about the hormones, pesticides, and antibiotics in milk, and she thought it was worth it — an extra dollar per half gallon — to buy the best. As far as James was concerned, organic was a huge waste of money.

Betsy was irritated by her husband's typically cheap attitude, and James was frustrated with Betsy's total disregard for the value of a dollar. Claudia, the one who actually went to the store and bought milk, wasn't sure what to do. No matter what decision she made, she would end up disappointing or frustrating one of them.

Eventually Betsy gave in to James. Claudia had worked with Betsy long enough to know this wasn't what she wanted, so she came up with a plan to please her boss. If Claudia came to work and there was enough money on the counter, at least $5, then she bought organic. If there were only a couple of dollars, she bought regular. Either way, James and Betsy could blame Claudia.

Eventually the atmosphere returned to normal, and Claudia hoped she had made Betsy happy. She went through the motions with the kids, keeping her own worries to herself. Even the first morning back at work after she had made the discovery at the bank, when Claudia burst out crying on the walk from the subway to the Halls', she had managed to wipe her tears away just in time to face the children. As far as she knew, the Halls didn't have a clue how sad and desperate she was feeling. They didn't know that a woman so used to being broke had finally tipped over the edge. They didn't know that sometimes, on her way to work, she cried before she could stop the tears from falling.

"I didn't know you sent out a check for your rent," Cap had said when Claudia called him, screaming. "I'm sorry."

"You are not sorry!" she lashed out. "So don't come and say you're sorry because you're not sorry."

"I didn't know about the rent," Cap repeated.

"I could beat you!"

Claudia slammed down the phone. Then she did what she often did when things got tough. She went into denial.

Cap had walked into Claudia's life when she was a teenager, and through all of their ups and downs, he had been a magnet she could not shake. Twenty-four years after she first laid eyes on him, after she was sure he had cheated on her and stolen from her, it was impossible for Claudia to imagine a life without him.

On Cap's last visit home, before he cleaned out her bank account, Claudia heard more rumors about Cap cheating on her and having a baby with another woman. A letter had arrived addressed to him, and Claudia hid the letter away. She wasn't ready to read it yet. Cap found out about it and went to Tanisha for more information. He promised her he would take her into Manhattan for the day if she handed over the letter. She did, and then he went back on his promise, telling her he had been joking. When Claudia got home from work that night, Tanisha was upset.

"Daddy bribed me!" Tanisha told her.

After Tanisha had gone to bed, Claudia confronted Cap, telling him he had better lay his cards on the table before he went back to Dominica, but he refused to admit he'd done anything wrong. By the next morning, Claudia was feeling too many emotions to count. She was angry and sad and hurt and scared.

There was a time when Cap had made her feel safe in the world. Claudia was a sixteen-year-old girl the day she walked into a local dance club with a friend who introduced her to a handsome man seven years older than herself. Cap, who looked young for his age, was slim and tall and strong. He also played saxophone in a popular band. As soon as they started talking, Cap stole Claudia's heart. He bought her a malt that she could still taste years later whenever she ran the memory of their meeting through her mind. He was her first love, and all these years later, still the love of Claudia's life.

In the beginning it was all fun. But before long, Cap took on a controlling, older-man tone with Claudia. He didn't like her talking to her friends. If she wanted to go dancing, he had to be there. At the time, Claudia didn't understand what the fuss was about, but later she realized he had just been trying to protect her. Soon after meeting Cap, Claudia dropped out of high school and made the decision to move to the Virgin Islands, where she could live with her two brothers who had gone ahead of her. The one thing on Claudia's mind now, as much as she loved Cap, was helping her mother. The day she left, she knew Cap was outside working in his garden, but she just caught her plane and flew off without saying a word. It was too hard to say goodbye.

Claudia moved on to the next chapter of her life in Virgin Gorda. At first she missed Cap terribly, but then she met her brother's friend Elton, an electrician who wooed her and treated her like a queen. Claudia was supporting herself, sending money home to her mother, and dreaming of moving to the United States someday so she could build a better life for herself and her family.

Then Claudia found out she was pregnant. She considered having an abortion, but the pregnancy was too far along, so she had no choice. Claudia became a mother. Torn between caring for Dexter and sending money home to help her family, Claudia made a decision. She sent her newborn son back to Dominica to live with her mother and sisters. For the next few years, she saw Dexter sporadically, and by the time he was four years old, she had her visa for the United States ready. She flew to New York and did not see her son again for ten years.

Cap came back into Claudia's life when she left the apartment in the Bronx and moved to Brooklyn. She came home on one of her weekend breaks from the Manns' and there he was, now living in Brooklyn, too. Soon Cap began stopping by regularly. He was making a good living working in construction, and he was determined to get back together with her. At first, Claudia ignored Cap's efforts. But Cap was persistent, and because Claudia still loved him, she couldn't resist. They began talking again, and before long they became a couple.

"Why don't you leave your job?" Cap had asked when she complained about working for the Manns. "I'll take care of you. I can help you get your green card."

It was a tempting offer, yet Claudia declined. She may have been back together with Cap, but it was against her better judgment. She heard rumors, even back then, about him running around with other women. He denied the accusations, but as much as Claudia wanted to believe him, she couldn't completely trust him. On the other hand, Claudia wanted out of her job. She thought about everything that had happened over the years, particularly how Lisa had stolen money from her and flaunted her affair in front of Claudia. Finally, Cap's persistence paid off. Claudia decided not to go back to the Manns', freeing herself from that lonely suburban house for good.

Then Claudia found out she was pregnant again, this time with Cap's baby. She decided to have an abortion. Struggling financially and with her relationship still rocky, Claudia wasn't sure she could raise a child on her own. She made an appointment at a clinic, but in the end she couldn't go through with it. She kept the baby and considered sending Tanisha back home to her mother and sisters to live with Dexter.

Claudia's aunt insisted otherwise. "You can't do it. You can't let this one go. You have to keep her by your side."

That was all Claudia needed to hear. This time her baby wasn't going anywhere, and it was the best decision Claudia ever made. She and Cap had had their problems over the years, even breaking up while she was pregnant, but after Tanisha was born, the two grew into each other. The drama died down and Claudia and Cap had built a life together. They were a family.

"I almost sent her home, but I just couldn't do it," Claudia reflected. "I say, 'You know something? I can't have two leaving me.' So I just stick it out and stick it out and that's it. It got tough. But now I only have one void instead of two."

A decade later, Claudia's family had been blown apart. Her money worries and anger at Cap seeped into her dreams. Her old friend Ruth appeared in her sleep to tell her she had been right to warn Claudia away from Cap. Ruth had never liked Cap, and whenever Claudia went to see him, she purposely walked the long way around the village to avoid Ruth's house and another lecture about how he was no good for her.

Claudia dodged reality in other ways too. She dreamed of traveling the world, of seeing Paris and buying fancy pocketbooks and cologne. She watched QVC and fantasized about buying a set of four-hundred-thread-count sheets they advertised for just $50. She survived the monotony of her life as a nanny by imagining a better life somewhere in the future, where she had more money and earned a degree. Nowadays, though, these fantasies all seemed like a joke. She didn't have time for dreams. She owed two months' rent. Wishes couldn't pay the bills.

Weeks passed and Claudia did not tell Betsy and James or Royette or Grace about her money troubles; she certainly didn't tell Tanisha. She went to work as usual. Sometimes James was home and sometimes he wasn't. The more he was in the apartment, the more frustrated he grew with the lack of order. Things were always misplaced. Pen marks appeared on the walls and furniture. Scratches materialized on doorways and floors. The housekeeper the Halls had hired, a friend of Claudia's, mopped the floors without rinsing them, leaving a film behind that made James's shoes stick to the wood. Her incompetence made Claudia's life more difficult.

"You know," she told her friend sarcastically, "if you rinse the mop it works better."

There was a trickle-down effect. James complained to Betsy about the cleaning lady. Then Betsy alerted Claudia, who had a chat with her friend. The children ignored the hierarchy altogether, running around, pulling books and clothes off of shelves, playing games, knowing it would bother their working father but unable to contain their natural instincts to move, to shake things up, and to laugh all the way through it.

Fed up one weekend, James created and implemented a new system in the house. Monday morning, Claudia arrived to find that James had organized and labeled every food group in the pantry. Canned goods, cereal, pasta. Each one had a place on the shelf with a piece of masking tape under it, the name clearly written out in black marker. The linen closet was meticulously labeled as well. Twin sheets, queen sheets, washcloths, and towels.

"This is how everything should be put away now," Betsy told Claudia with a sigh, walking her through the apartment.

"Okay," Claudia said, eyeing her boss.

Betsy looked tired to Claudia, and Claudia worried that she was taking on too much. She had always admired Betsy's boundless energy, her ability to handle a high-pressure job and still come home with enough left in her to give to Lucy and Jackson. But Betsy was wilting now, dark circles under her eyes. Claudia wondered if James's working from home was taking its toll on Betsy, too. He took on a few big projects around the house but most of the household management fell to Betsy. Claudia couldn't imagine adding to Betsy's troubles by asking her for help with her rent.

"You can see Betsy trying and trying, but one day I think she just gonna lose it," Claudia said, describing everything Betsy did to keep the family going. "She's the one holding everything up."

It was a dark time for everyone, yet nobody said a word. Outside, the days had grown shorter and colder. Wind whipped down the streets, making it more difficult for Claudia to stay out of the house unless she had a play date or a class. Betsy was dragging under a lingering cold and a deep cough that worried Claudia. James was moodier than ever.

Meanwhile, Betsy noticed that Claudia, clearly distracted, was putting cans in the wrong section of the cabinet, placing towels where sheets should have been stacked in the linen closet. She sensed Claudia's depression, caught the distant look in her eyes and her lack of energy, but she chalked it up to marriage problems. She never guessed that Claudia, totally broke, was terrified she would be kicked out of her apartment and have no place to go.

Back at work after Christmas, Claudia stepped out the front door of the apartment, pushing Lucy in her stroller. Just as she was congratulating herself for getting out of the house smoothly and not interrupting James, the wheel of the stroller popped off. Claudia cursed it, and Lucy began to wail. The child sobbed and sputtered uncontrollably, reaching hysterical heights while Claudia, blocking out Lucy's tantrum, got down on her knees and tried to get the wheel back on. It was no use. Without saying a word, Claudia stood back up and looked calmly at Lucy's tear-streaked face. She did not try to hug Lucy or tell her it would be okay. She did not whisper in the child's ear or take her in her arms. Instead, she waited the fit out.

"Claudia, what's going on out here?" James asked, opening the apartment door and stepping out into the hall.

"The wheel come off the stroller."

James leaned down and took Lucy in his arms. He put his hand on her head, stroking her hair as he explained that the stroller had broken but that she would be okay. Lucy took in big gulps of air and calmed down. Wisps of blond stuck to her wet cheeks. After his daughter had stopped crying, James picked up the stroller and carried it back into the apartment.

"We'll have to get this fixed," he said as he closed the door behind him.

"Well, Lucy, I guess we'll have to walk," said Claudia.

The six-block walk to Lucy's dance class did not go well. Claudia was relieved that James had handled the situation back at the apartment, but on the street, a bitter wind hit Lucy in the face and she exploded. Claudia, who felt that Lucy was past the age of strollers, paid no attention to the child. She walked straight ahead, and when Lucy refused to take her hand, Claudia kept on going.

"I don't want to walk! I don't want to walk!" Lucy shrieked.

"Lucy. Your stroller is broken. You don't have a choice."

It turned out to be a slow, painful, cold journey. Claudia remained completely stone-faced while Lucy threw a vicious tantrum. Pedestrians stared at the pair, casting puzzled looks at Claudia — and sympathetic smiles at Lucy. To people on the street, Claudia seemed cruel, a woman ignoring the deep distress of a young child, but Claudia fixed her gaze straight ahead and kept her legs moving because she knew Lucy would follow. Lucy whined and sobbed and thrashed her hands, but as long as her nanny walked, she walked too.

"I don't want to walk! I don't want to walk! I'm too cold!"

Claudia picked up her pace to make the streetlight and Lucy followed, still sobbing. She waved her hands in the air, but Claudia did not respond. Instead, she glanced at the magazine covers displayed at a newsstand she passed near the subway stop. Celebrity gossip and advice on weight loss and speculation about the end of the housing bubble. She looked in a store window. Leftover summer shoes on sale and new boots at full price. Ever since she had arrived in this country, Claudia had fought the urge to return home. She had promised herself on her first lonely night in America that she would stick it out until things became easier, but as she faced eviction from her home, a devastated marriage, and a little girl sobbing on the street, Claudia was still waiting for that to happen.

The blasting steam heat and bright lights of the dance studio changed everything. Lucy stopped crying almost immediately. She kicked off her pink Converse sneakers, pulled down her aqua-colored pants, wiped away her tears, and jumped around with the other girls. A smile spread across Lucy's face as she looked at Claudia. Before she took off down the hall for class, she hugged her nanny.

Claudia breathed deep. Then the drama kicked up again: a nanny stood by the elevator in tears, surrounded by a circle of other nannies, a low murmur of voices rising as they talked with the woman and glanced warily at a mother who was within earshot, standing in the hallway. Claudia's friend Daisy stuck her head in the group, listened briefly, and then headed straight over to Claudia.

"She just got yelled at by a teacher in front of everyone," Daisy told Claudia. "She's stuck between a rock and a hard place."

Daisy explained that the nanny took care of two children who needed to be picked up at two different schools at the same time. She had collected one child, and then raced to the second school to meet the other child. It was an impossible task, and when she showed up five minutes late for class, a teacher had screamed at her. The nanny was humiliated and fed up.

"You can bet if she was a parent, that teacher wouldn't have said a word to her," Daisy remarked to Claudia, shaking her head.

"The teacher should have taken her aside to talk to her, not yelled at her in front of everyone," Claudia agreed. "I don't know what I do if that happen to me. The teacher would have to call Betsy or James, because I don't know what would fly out of my mouth if she talked to me that way."

Daisy and Claudia discussed the unreasonable demands put on nannies. Parents always expected more from their nannies than they expected from themselves. They didn't want their children watching television, but then they stuck them in front of shows all weekend long when their nanny was gone. They didn't want their children eating sweets, but then they gave in at the first sign of distress. They couldn't cook and clean and focus on the child's educational development and safety at the same time, but their nanny was expected to do all that and more.

What would happen if all the nannies and the housekeepers all over the city picked the same day to stay home from work? Complete chaos, Daisy and Claudia agreed. Manhattan would grind to a halt. Dishes would pile up in sinks. Kids would run around dirty. Refrigerators would sit empty and dry cleaners might as well close. By the time the sun set, the parents would beg for them to come back to work. And then, maybe then, the nannies would get the money they deserved for working so many hours and doing so much. Maybe then they'd get the respect they had earned after so many years of sacrifice and loyalty.

"Boy, did I have a crazy weekend," said a mother from across the room, unaware of Claudia and Daisy's conversation. "We were up in Connecticut, and I started having problems with my gallbladder."

"Oh yeah?" said Claudia. Claudia knew the mother from the neighborhood.

"It was awful. I had to go to the emergency room." The woman continued talking, her voice growing louder in the quiet room.

"Sounds painful," said Daisy.

With her mop of frizzy hair and disheveled clothes, the woman had the air of a frazzled stay-at-home mom. Claudia and Daisy both wore jeans and trendy shoes and newsboy caps on their heads. They were about the same age as the harried mother but looked ten years younger than she.

"Claudia, Sophia really likes Lucy. Maybe we can have a play date sometime," said the woman with the gallbladder problem, just as class was ending.

"Sure. Whenever," Claudia said politely. The woman was nice enough, but Claudia would try to avoid a play date. What would they have to talk about while the kids played?

The circles under Betsy's eyes were even darker when she came home that evening. Claudia's worry about her boss flooded back. Betsy acted peppy and friendly, but Claudia could see how tired she was and wondered whether she was hiding something. Betsy, meanwhile, was wondering about Claudia. Her nanny seemed defeated somehow. Sadness seeped out of her. When Betsy asked her about math class, Claudia changed the subject. She couldn't bring herself to cut it out completely, but Claudia was taking fewer classes and didn't think she'd be ready for the GED anytime soon.

"You seem kinda low," Claudia remarked to her boss when she walked in the door.

Betsy looked at Claudia in surprise. "Oh, I'm fine," she answered, dumping her heavy bag on the kitchen table with a sigh. She was wearing nude fishnet stockings, knee-high boots, and a fitted down jacket. "I was thinking the same thing about you."

"Who, me? I'm fine," Claudia responded, avoiding eye contact as she picked up her own bag to head home. "Nothing going on but the usual."

ELEVEN

PERCHED SIDE BY SIDE on Claudia's glass-topped coffee table were two snow globes: the Statue of Liberty and the Empire State Building. With their dark wood bases and thick round glass, they provided a comforting weight in the open palm. These were not the cheap plastic snow globes of Forty-second Street, last-minute souvenirs for tourists rushing out of town. These globes were little treasures, whimsical and strong, pieces of art worth keeping.

Claudia hadn't bought them for herself. James had come home from work with them and had handed them over to her because he did not want the clutter in his own apartment. Claudia loved them, the fantasy trapped under glass, the pristine New York City of her dreams. Shake them up, hold them upside down, flip them in the air, and catch them in your hand. The scene went white, but it did not change. Eventually the snow settled and left the green statue and majestic skyscraper standing in clear water, unscarred and perfect.

Claudia picked the globes up and dusted them off, then set

them back on the table. It was a chilly January morning. Outside, the cloudless sky was impossibly bright, the air sharp and cold. The sun hit the still-sleepy streets of Flatbush, glinting off of parked cars and pieces of broken glass. The pizza place, the cell phone store, the Chinese takeout on the corner were all closed. At ten o'clock in the morning, it was too cold to be out on the streets.

Inside, the steam heat mixed with the sunlight streaming through the windows, giving Claudia's apartment a drowsy, slightly out-of-focus feel, but she'd been cleaning nonstop. The scent of Pine-Sol drifted from the bathroom, a stew brewed on the stove. Banned from the phone because of her bad attitude at school, Tanisha lay in bed in front of the television, its soft hum floating through the rooms.

It was a slow Sunday, but Claudia kept moving. The eviction notice had arrived in the mail on Thursday, and Claudia had still not told a soul.

Claudia had known it was coming, but somehow it was still a shock to her when it appeared. The problems she had been ignoring were suddenly real. The envelope was just a thin, white piece of paper, yet it carried so much weight. Before Claudia had opened her mailbox, she had been a hardworking immigrant. After she read the letter, she felt like a criminal. The authorities were after her.

Claudia had received the Christmas bonus she was hoping for, $900, although she suspected Betsy had thrown in the last hundred behind James's back. Betsy also gave her a set of gorgeous silk pillows that Claudia refused to put on her black sofa. Her beaten and battered couch was not good enough for such rich fabric. She would save the pillows for the new couch she intended to buy someday.

The extra money was a relief, but it did not pull Claudia out of her hole. Instead, it had kept her floating through the holidays. Past due on both December and January's rent, she was now also facing February's. So she cooked and did dishes and dusted the pictures, a photo of Tanisha in a school uniform she now refused to wear, a print of Tanisha's older half sister, a child her father had during one of his breakups with Claudia. A few of the frames were hand-me-downs from Betsy and James. So was the unopened, dusty bottle of champagne.

Claudia had not gone to bed until after 1:00 A.M. the night before, and she was still tired this morning. She had babysat for Betsy and James to earn some extra cash. When they came back, glowing from a bottle of wine and a chance to be alone together, they were both smiling. Claudia was pleased to see them happy, and James was in a good mood when he rode down in the elevator with her to see Claudia off. He hailed the cab for her because he knew most drivers would not take a black woman to Brooklyn. Without James, Claudia might stand there all night getting passed by.

"I have to go back to the garage," the cab driver lied as soon as James stepped aside and Claudia slipped into the car. Without a word, Claudia climbed back out.

"If you don't take her, I'm going to report you," threatened James. Claudia liked this side of her boss. He had her back.

"Well, I don't know where I'm going," the cab driver claimed.

"She'll tell you," said James as he opened the door for Claudia.

Once again, Claudia settled into the back seat, smiling to herself, and the cab driver caught her eye in the mirror. Other nannies took cab fare from their bosses, pocketed it, and then rode the subway. That way they had more money and saved themselves the humiliation of being kicked out of a taxi or passed by as if they were invisible. But Claudia decided to enjoy the ride home, watching the city lights fade as the car made its way over the Brooklyn Bridge. There was a hole in the skyline where the World Trade Center used to stand, but the view was still impressive, all steel and lights and buildings climbing straight up to the moon.

Claudia remembered September 11 as if it were yesterday. When she emerged from the subway, the entire sky had turned black. "Is this the end of the world?" she'd wondered. "Is this what the end of the world looks like?" She had walked all the way home over this same bridge, instinctively inching her way back to Brooklyn along with the stunned crowds, dirt and debris falling down on her and everyone else like confetti, covering them in soot until they were ghosts. Later in the afternoon, she reached Betsy by phone and found out the Halls were all safe, too, but an acrid burning smell hung in the air around their apartment and lingered for months. She worried the air wasn't good for the kids.

By the time she reached home, Claudia felt sorry for the cab driver for getting dragged so deep into Brooklyn, where there was no way he'd catch a fare back to Manhattan. After all, he was just trying to make a living.

"Look, buy yourself a drink," Claudia said, handing the cab driver a nice tip when they pulled up in front of her apartment building. The man smiled at her in the mirror.

There were two reasons Claudia hadn't confessed to Betsy that she was being evicted. First, she didn't want to burden her boss with more problems. The vibe at the Halls' was still strained. There had been a few messages on the machine about Jackson, confirming mysterious doctors' appointments. Claudia had seen a change in Jackson this year. He was more withdrawn, more disorganized. When he did not get his way, he threw tantrums, unacceptable be-havior for an eight-year-old, in Claudia's opinion. Still, she did not worry about him the way his mother did. Betsy was so concerned about her son, she couldn't even talk about it. Claudia accepted the silence because she knew how fiercely protective Betsy was of her children and her family.

This did not mean that Claudia was blind to what was going on. She picked up on the clues. She found extra writing assignments Jackson was working on and schedules mapping out every hour of the day for him, detailing tasks like making the bed and collecting his papers for school. Claudia caught the look in Betsy's eye when she watched her son walk away. She took note of the questions Betsy began to ask, details she mined about her son that she never used to seek. "How did Jackson seem after school? Did he see any of his friends at the park? Did they let him play?"

Claudia watched Betsy worry and let her get it out of her system. She knew Betsy had a physical reaction when she watched her son, a longing in her chest, a force compelling her to fix everything for him.

Meanwhile, Claudia was completely confident that Jackson would find his own way in his own time. She did not feel his pain like his mother. She observed Jackson from a distance, assuming he was going through a necessary rite of passage. One day a friend of Jackson's would push him away and Betsy would panic. The next day, Claudia would answer the phone when one of his friends called wanting to hang out. Claudia saw both the ups and the downs over the days and hours she spent with the boy. Betsy didn't always get the entire story, because she was working.

Jackson could take his time completing tasks and he had trouble mastering things like swimming, but he was also smarter than most. Claudia was sure of that. He was good-looking, intelligent, and loved by his parents and his nanny. "Sometimes he act like a two-year-old, but I love him anyway," Claudia said, stating her affection as an irrefutable fact.

• • •

The second reason Claudia had not approached Betsy was pride. In the eight years Claudia had worked for the Halls, she had never gone to them for help. No matter how broke she was, Claudia did not ask for anything. Pride and reserve were Claudia's two biggest assets, her only access to power. There was power in keeping her struggles to herself, dressing modestly, and holding her head high even when all she wanted was to crawl under the sheets. If Claudia felt like giving up, she certainly wasn't going to let anyone know it.

Instead, she told white lies to cover things up. When her cell phone bill got so high her service was cut off, Claudia told Betsy that Tanisha had broken her phone. Sometimes she began to believe the lies herself. Claudia's money problems weren't all Cap's fault, although he had dealt the deathblow. It was also her fault. It was hard to live on what the Halls paid her, but Claudia also bought things she couldn't afford. She didn't always want to live the lifestyle she could realistically pay for. At the same time, she didn't want to leave the Halls for a higher-paying job or take side babysitting gigs on the weekend.

None of it mattered now, as Claudia cleaned and the soft thud of music came through her ceiling from the upstairs apartment. There was no point in blaming anyone. Claudia had to figure out a way to get the money. The theme song to *Barney & Friends* blared from the bedroom, and Claudia laughed to herself. Her twelve-year-old daughter was watching a show for preschoolers.

"What are you doing with *Barney*, a big child like you?" asked Claudia when Tanisha passed her on her way to grab something to eat in the kitchen. "Poor thing, you're not talking on the phone so you're bored."

"I like *Barney!*" Tanisha said as she stormed back into her room.

When Royette showed up later with Ava, Tanisha came out of her room again and Claudia shooed the girls to the bedroom.

Within seconds, Royette spotted the eviction notice Claudia had left lying in plain view. Her secret was out. "Claudia! What are you going to do?" Royette asked, holding the paper in her hand.

"I have to do something."

"You'll stay with me if you have to," Royette said.

Grace came over next, bringing Monique with her. The three girls jumped around the back room, laughing and joking and trying on clothes. The three mothers sat at Claudia's dining table, shoved in a tight spot just outside the kitchen, behind the front door.

"Maybe I should give you my student-loan check," Grace, who was in nursing school, said. "You and Tanisha can't end up on the streets."

"I can't take your student-loan check," Claudia answered, touched by Grace's offer. "I'll figure it out."

A few hours later, Royette and Grace collected their daughters and went home. It was dark outside now and Claudia's entire apartment was clean. The stew was in the refrigerator. Tanisha was asleep. Claudia thought about Grace's and Royette's offers. She knew they wanted to do what they could, but they were limited, too.

The eviction notice required that she appear at housing court that Friday. She would show up and ask for an extension. Still, she didn't know how she would come up with the money. She needed $1,438 for two months' rent, plus another $719 for February. Maybe if she had more time, she thought, she'd figure out a way to get the money. Eventually, the morning light shone in her living room again. Claudia stood up. She had to go to work.

Betsy was on her way out of the building just as Claudia made her way in. Lucy was still at preschool, and Claudia was planning on dropping off her bag before she went to pick the little girl up. She had already been to her math class that morning. Somehow, she couldn't bring herself to stop going, even though she couldn't afford the extra $20 or $40 a week it was costing her. Giving up her math class meant giving up her future.

Color had returned to Betsy's face; the circles under her eyes had faded. She seemed less burdened to Claudia, who still wasn't quite sure what her boss had been going through over the past few weeks.

"I need Friday off," Claudia told Betsy abruptly.

"Why?" Betsy asked. She was annoyed. Her Friday schedule was booked, one meeting after the other. She was also worried. Claudia's eyes were puffy, her expression drawn and sad.

"I need to take care of something."

"Well, what?" Betsy pressed Claudia.

"Betsy, I have to go to court."

Claudia braced herself. There was no way Betsy would let this one go.

"For what?"

"They send me a letter for eviction. It says I have to be at court on Friday."

The words poured out. Betsy didn't even have to push. Taking the notice out of her pocket, Claudia handed it to her boss. She did not feel the shame she had expected. She felt relief. She did not have to hide anymore.

"Why do you have to go to court? Let me just call your landlord. We'll work this out. How much do you owe them?"

"Two months." Claudia didn't mention that she didn't have the money for February's rent either.

"Let's go upstairs and deal with this," Betsy said, turning around to press the elevator button.

After weeks of agony and sleepless nights, Claudia's problem was solved in fifteen minutes. Betsy whipped out her checkbook. She didn't have time to think about how she felt or what the broader implications were. Claudia had never come to her for help, and now it was time to act. Claudia called Grace to get their landlord's number. Then Betsy took over, getting the landlord's office on the line. One of the owners, a man named Jonathan, took her call.

"If I write you a check for the last two months, can you just halt this process? She's a mom with a twelve-year-old kid," Betsy said.

"Is your check good?"

"Of course it's good!"

"Well, sorry to ask. It's just the people I deal with." Jonathan laughed.

Claudia knew all along that if she had asked, Betsy would have helped her, but Betsy's reaction had been so quick, so immediate, that it almost knocked Claudia off her feet. It wasn't that Claudia felt she didn't deserve the help after all these years — she just didn't expect it.

"You know I always pay my rent, even if it means I don't have any food," Claudia said before she could stop the words from coming out.

Betsy was silent. She was in a state of disbelief, totally blindsided. Claudia was no longer the person Betsy had hired eight years ago, although she hadn't seen that until now. When Claudia first took the job with the Halls, her husband had been working in construction, bringing in a good salary and taking care of Tanisha. But Claudia was alone now, and she had a daughter to support. Standing in the kitchen with her checkbook in hand, Betsy realized how complicated hiring a nanny really was. Claudia had no savings, no college education, and no property to her name. She lived check to check. Remove one piece of the precarious structure of Claudia's financial life and it all fell apart.

Betsy and James Hall were Claudia's only safety net now.

"It's a good thing my business is going so well," Betsy said as she headed out to her gallery, leaving Claudia behind in the kitchen.

"Then why don't you pay me more?" Claudia thought, but she kept her mouth shut.

A week later Claudia was evicted anyway. The housing marshal came while she was at work, changed the locks, and slapped a large orange sticker on her front door. Claudia had been branded, exposed to all her neighbors as someone who could not pay the rent. When Tanisha returned home from school, she found herself locked out. She ran to Royette's and called her mother.

Claudia had worked in big houses in the suburbs. She had worked in apartments uptown and downtown and even Queens, neighborhoods she couldn't afford to live in herself. But Claudia's real home had always been her one-bedroom apartment in Flatbush, where she nodded at the people she knew in her courtyard, borrowed eggs from Grace, and depended on Royette to watch her child. The moment she heard about the eviction, she lost her center, her core, her anchor, and her refuge. That night, with nowhere else to go, Claudia and her daughter slept at Royette's.

The next morning, Betsy sat at her kitchen counter, waiting for Claudia to call her again. When she heard about the eviction, she canceled her appointments for the entire day. Betsy was ready to focus on her nanny. She blamed herself for thinking she could solve Claudia's problems by waving a magic wand and "trusting a slumlord." For a few days after Betsy had written that first check, she had been totally relieved. Everything seemed back to normal: Claudia was her old self, cracking a few jokes, giving Betsy some of the local gossip. In the end, after Claudia had confessed that she was short on February's rent too, Betsy had written checks for all three months of rent. Betsy and James gave Claudia one-third as a gift and they all agreed on a $30 a week payment plan for the remaining two-thirds. It seemed like the perfect solution.

Now Betsy was right back where she started, still waiting for Claudia to get her life in order so Betsy could go to work, earn money, and pay for it all. As usual, Claudia was light on the details and didn't have her landlord's number. It was locked away in her apartment. She didn't have any luck tracking down her neighbors for the number, and when Betsy called information, the office wasn't listed. Claudia finally decided to walk over to the real estate office in person. She promised to call Betsy when she got there.

Stuck at home, waiting to hear from Claudia, Betsy felt powerless to resolve the situation herself. She tried calling Royette's house but got no answer. James kept quiet and stayed out of the conflict. Betsy knew he was horrified by the entire situation. He agreed wholeheartedly that they should bail Claudia out; he just had trouble understanding how she had fallen into the situation to begin with. James hated financial messes as much as he hated any other kind of mess. In fact, when it came to handling money, Betsy and James were both conservative. While Betsy might splurge on a beautiful suit, she'd wear it for years. James was even more frugal.

"James was basically appalled," said Betsy. "I mean, for the guy to buy a pair of sneakers, it takes six months of considering, does he really need a new pair of sneakers?"

Claudia finally called Betsy from the real estate office. She was fed up and furious. They had told her to wait without offering her a chair. Over an hour later, she was still standing awkwardly in the office, ignored by everyone.

"I am not moving," she told Betsy over the phone. "I think they just want me out. I've been hearing rumors they just want me out because Cap cursed them out a long time ago."

"Who are you talking to?" Betsy asked. She had been trying to gather information on the company that owned Claudia's building, but it was impossible because it was listed under so many different names.

"Jonathan."

"Let me talk to them," demanded Betsy. Claudia happily handed over the phone.

"Look, we don't want this lady out," Jonathan told Betsy. "We've done six possessions in this building. We've gotten rid of them. She's a nice lady. We're not trying to get rid of her."

"Why didn't you cash my check? Claudia did what you told her to do."

"Once we get the marshal involved, we don't cash checks. We just get them out. That's policy. She still has to go to housing court," said Jonathan. Thinking the matter had been resolved, Claudia did not show up at court to explain that she had paid the rent. When she didn't appear, the marshal automatically came to her apartment. Even now, with Betsy involved, Claudia would have to go to court.

After a bit more back and forth, Jonathan agreed to give Claudia a new set of keys if Betsy gave him a certified check. As soon as Claudia put Betsy on the phone, someone had offered her a chair. She was sitting now, listening to Jonathan's end of the conversation. The secretary then took the phone and tried to charge Claudia an additional $500 in legal fees, but Betsy challenged the additional amount, suggesting she would call her lawyer to look into the issue. The secretary and Jonathan suddenly dropped their fee request.

Working the phones, negotiating a deal, getting the information she needed, Betsy was in work mode. In her office in Chelsea every morning, she dropped her bags on the floor, picked up the phone, and threw her feet up on the desk. Photos of her two children and her husband sitting in front of her, a view of the gallery out her door, Betsy made deals, resolved conflicts, answered e-mails, and succeeded by using her guts and instinct. She had a long list of things to do that day, but right now she was involved in the moment, giving it as much of her time and energy as she would any project at work. She was going to fix this situation and worry about the rest later.

Knowing Betsy was on her side made Claudia relax. For the first time in a while, she wasn't facing the problem on her own. "I think if Betsy didn't come in, they would make me pay back the five hundred dollars. But they realize I wasn't alone. I had people on my side who aren't my color," she later said.

Betsy and the landlord came to an agreement. Claudia would pick up the certified check from Betsy's and then return to Brooklyn for her new keys. While Claudia traveled to Manhattan, Betsy went to the bank to get the check. She was angry at Claudia's landlord. But she was also irritated that Claudia hadn't come to her sooner, the minute she found out about the eviction notice. Why hadn't she just asked for the money instead of burying her head in the sand and hoping the problem would go away? This was her nanny's big flaw — passivity — which Betsy also came up against when Claudia watched her children. Claudia did not get involved enough with the kids when they were having problems and Betsy wasn't there to help them out. Claudia didn't play with them or referee their fights with friends. She fed them and made sure they were physically safe, but she did not intervene.

"When you hire someone like Claudia," Betsy thought, "you take on full responsibility for her." She talked to a friend of hers whose nanny owned a house in Queens and rented out a floor. Because this nanny's tenants sometimes didn't make their rent, she ended up in the same situation as Claudia. Betsy's friend had to help her nanny out when that happened so she didn't default on her mortgage.

Stories like these made Betsy want Claudia to go to school even more. Claudia deserved a better life, and Betsy worried about what would happen when Claudia grew old and had no savings. She and James had once given her a few thousand dollars to start an IRA, in the hopes that it would motivate Claudia to save. The money was probably gone by now, though, and Betsy knew better than to ask.

"Next time just come to me before it gets out of hand," Betsy told Claudia when she arrived to pick up the check. "Because it feels like the hydra. You know, you cut off one head and then there are two heads?"

Early on the morning of February 13, Claudia woke with a start. Anxiety raced through her. While the sky was still pitch-black, she got up and ran herself a bath. She combed her hair and brushed her teeth. She flipped the television on and got dressed in jeans, a white V-neck sweater, and a pair of red socks. She rubbed gloss on her lips. The entire time, her stomach was in knots. For the first time in her life, Claudia was going to court. It was housing court, but she felt like a thief.

She had been locked out for only one day, but it might as well have been a month or a year. Walking through her door for the first time after the eviction, she had seen her apartment from a distance, as though it wasn't her home but a close relative's. Everything was intact and in the right place. The black couch, the snow globes on the coffee table, the ceramic fruit placed perfectly in a bowl. Against the opposite wall stood her neatly made bed alongside Tanisha's.

It was all so familiar, but Claudia had stood there looking at her apartment as though she were seeing it for the first time. She had raised Tanisha here, fought with Cap here, and had friends over so many times. It had been her refuge at the end of the day and her hideout on the weekends when she could no longer face the world. Coming back after having that sticker slapped on her door, she'd felt robbed, stripped bare. She had lived here for ten years, but in the space of one night, it had been tainted with shame.

Claudia was going to court, but for her neighbors, this was just an ordinary day. They headed to work wrapped in jackets and scarves, coffee cups from local bodegas in hand. Stuffed book bags weighing them down, kids walked to school. Claudia passed the stores on her street, the combination hair salon and recording studio, the market selling African and West Indian food. On Flatbush Avenue, most of the storefronts still had their gates down, shut tight with thick padlocks. When the wind picked up, plastic bags, pieces of newspaper, and other bits of garbage flew through the air. Carrying a bunch of heart-shaped balloons, a lone girl wandered past Claudia. A group of younger girls shuffled up the block, giggling, clutching single roses in their hands. It was the day before Valentine's Day, and all the kids were celebrating in school.

Claudia made her way across the street without noticing a thing. She couldn't believe she was going to housing court. "It's a place I just don't appreciate. I don't want to go there. I just don't want to go there." This was one of the worst, most humiliating episodes of her life. She had had nightmares of people coming to lock her inside the apartment. When she woke up, she half expected to be kicked out onto the street again.

A white dollar van pulled up to the corner on Flatbush Avenue. It was crowded, but spotting a seat in the back, Claudia climbed in. Dollar vans, also called commuter vans, were a popular way for immigrants to get around in the boroughs, where buses and trains were less reliable. Claudia knew the van would get her to downtown Brooklyn faster than the local bus, and with its padded seats, it would be a more comfortable ride.

The other passengers sat quietly as the van rocked back and forth. Claudia took a dollar bill and a quarter out of her purse and handed them to the woman in front of her, who silently passed it to the driver. The scent of the van's pine deodorizer filled the air. Fragments of Brooklyn flew past the tinted windows: the jumbled storefronts of Flatbush, the bare trees of Prospect Park, the Brooklyn Botanic Garden, and the main branch of the library at Grand Army Plaza.

The driver had the radio tuned to a local West Indian station broadcasting a talk show that had an immigration lawyer on as a guest. The questions poured in about how to get papers. The van approached downtown Brooklyn, where the buildings stood tall and the sidewalks near Court Street and Fulton Mall overflowed with pedestrians. The talk show ended and news of Haiti came on the radio.

Claudia climbed out of the van at 114 Livingston Street, where she passed through a metal detector and headed up in the elevator. "What do all those people going to court feel like when they know they're going to jail?" she wondered. Jail must be the worst place in the world. The thought of it made her shudder.

The elevator opened onto a generic hallway lit by fluorescent lights. A few people stood waiting for the session to start. Everyone looked anxious and slightly confused. Claudia checked her letter to make sure she was in the right place. When a white man in a suit passed, a black woman who was waiting tapped him on the shoulder and asked if he was a lawyer. The man shook his head. The woman's lame attempt to get legal help amused Claudia, but she also understood the impulse. She wouldn't have minded having someone powerful by her side today.

A few more people appeared, including a skinny black man wearing a priest collar and a silk purple shirt, his hair in tight braids. Claudia took one look at him and thought of Snoop Dogg. For the first time that morning, she smiled to herself.

Finally, the group was called into the courtroom. It was small, with rows of wooden benches, just like every television-show courtroom Claudia had seen. Dispersing, everyone chose seats far apart from one another. One woman read a book; a man flipped through a tabloid newspaper; others stared off into space. Claudia pulled a copy of *Essence* with Mary J. Blige on the cover out of her bag.

"Does anyone need a Spanish interpreter?" a man called out from the other side of the room, and the rest of the room answered with a collective, muted no.

After the judge sat down, Claudia was called first. Quickly she explained that the rent had already been paid when her locks were changed on her.

"You've got your keys?" the judge asked. "You're all paid up?"

"Yeah," answered Claudia.

The judge dismissed the case and told Claudia that she had the right to sue for unfair eviction.

Outside the courtroom, Claudia smiled. Not only was the nightmare finally over, but the judge was on her side. She felt validated. Since she had been evicted, Claudia had been telling herself that it never should have happened, that her landlord was just after her, but deep down she worried that she'd been in the wrong. With just a few words, the judge made Claudia feel freer than she had since she found out Cap had taken her money. Her landlord had been wrong to kick her out and change her locks when Betsy had already given them a rent check. Claudia had no intention of suing, but it was satisfying to know she could. Right now all she wanted was to go home, unplug the phone, and hide out for the entire weekend. First, though, she had to get through the rest of the day at work.

Before she headed for the subway to Manhattan, Claudia grabbed a quick breakfast at a local deli. She thought about everything that had happened. She had been kicked out of her home, treated like dirt at the landlord's office, and slapped with $500 in fictitious legal fees. Yet once Betsy had picked up the phone, the landlord returned Claudia's keys and dropped the fees, too. Just like that.

It reminded Claudia of how naive she had been before she had moved to this country. She hadn't known a thing about slavery in the United States, and she had never even heard of Martin Luther King Jr. She knew racism existed, but it wasn't anything she had ever experienced; it wasn't something tangible. Even when she was in school in Dominica, a former colony with a slave trade, the history of slavery was never taught. Thinking back, she remembered a historical monument to slavery she had passed regularly in her hometown. She had never read the plaque or stopped to think about what it all meant. Now she felt racism regularly, and Tanisha had been hitting her with questions she didn't really want to answer, especially in the past couple of weeks.

It was February, Black History Month, and Tanisha was asking questions about the marches in Selma, Alabama; Malcolm X; and the civil rights movement. She wanted Claudia to rent the 1970s miniseries *Roots*.

When Tanisha was just a little girl, maybe five or six years old, Claudia came home from a nanny job and found her daughter covered with baby powder in the bathroom.

"Tanisha, what are you doing?" Claudia had asked, puzzled.

"I just want to get white," she answered.

"Tanisha, you know you're beautiful. Black is beautiful," Claudia had said, wiping the powder off her child. "We are all colored people, white, pink, blue. God made us all."

Later, Claudia thought about the white children she cared for and whether Tanisha was jealous. Did she think Claudia would spend more time with her if she were white? Did she think Claudia loved white children more than her own dark-skinned daughter?

Tanisha's tone had changed as she learned more about racism at school. "Why white people don't like black people?" she had asked Claudia recently after learning about segregation in the South.

"Oh, Tanisha, that's a long story," answered Claudia, not even sure where to begin.

"White people are mean."

"Not all white people are like that," Claudia explained. "Just a few. We all the same. I cut myself, I bleed. They cut theyself, they bleed."

When Claudia got back to work, James was in the apartment with the kids. Betsy was already at the gallery. There was nothing unusual about the day. The job was almost soothing after the drama of the past month. Claudia tried to relax, but she still felt slightly unsettled. She remembered how Lucy sometimes called her Miss Claudia. "I told her, 'Lucy, don't call me Miss Claudia. That sounds like a slave name!' But she's only three. She don't know what I'm talking about."

All the people in the courtroom that day had looked scared and nervous. Their homes were at stake. Claudia didn't know why they hadn't paid their rents, but she imagined they weren't much different than her.

"You know what you should be when you grow up?" Claudia told Tanisha when she got home that night. "A lawyer."

TWELVE

KIM SHOULD HAVE turned down the job with the Porters as soon as she read their contract. Ten single-spaced pages, it was the longest, most detailed employment contract she had ever seen. More than an outline of her responsibilities and a confirmation of her salary and schedule, it was a reflection of Brian's obsessive and controlling nature. When she first read it, Kim had laughed to herself and sighed, brushing it off as an over-the-top document created by two clueless but eager parents-to-be. Now, after working for the Porters for real, the contract didn't seem so funny anymore. She saw it as a misguided list of instructions on how a stranger should raise and love someone else's child. Kim had loved every child in her care instinctively, the feeling growing naturally. Putting that emotion down on paper, along with monetary compensation and other legal terminology, transformed her ability to nurture into a commodity to be bought, sold, and monitored.

By contract, Brian required "the nanny" to support Cooper's entire well-being, from ensuring that he hit his developmental milestones to giving him ample physical affection during the twelve hours a day that his parents worked. While Cooper was only an infant, his nanny was to be part intellectual coach, weaving reading, music, and math into every moment; part caregiver; and part iconic mother, the kind of woman who struck the perfect balance between love and discipline.

Kim was expected to prepare Cooper's birth announcement, arrange Cooper's birthday parties, pick out gifts for Cooper to take to other children's parties, write his thank-you notes, and purchase his clothes. Brian, creating the contract before Cooper was born, had also decided how his child would be disciplined, mandating that the word "no" would be banned from the house. Examples were given of the right and wrong way to instruct the as-yet-unborn child. Instead of, "No, you can't run into traffic," Brian suggested the alternative, "You may not run into traffic. But you can run on the sidewalk."

Brian took pains to anticipate his nanny's personal behavior. Even on her off hours, she was not allowed to have unapproved visitors, and she could not keep alcohol in her room. Making a scene was forbidden. She was asked to apply Purell to her hands every fifteen minutes while the child was still an infant.

Kim would be with Cooper for most of the baby's waking hours, while Brian and Holly remained in the background, directing how their son was taught, fed, and disciplined. By instructing their nanny to do things exactly as they would if they were home with Cooper, Brian and Holly would essentially be raising their child. They might not be there to implement the rules, but they could still dictate that Kim wash her hands after she took Cooper's shoes off.

On other jobs, Kim had done most of what Brian was asking for without needing to be told. She had always fallen in love with the children under her care. But she hated the way all these instructions were presented as though she didn't know how to do her job. From the moment she walked in the Porters' front door, Kim had felt micromanaged and disrespected. Now she saw that it had started before she even arrived.

Kim was unwilling to break her one-year commitment to the Porters just because Brian was difficult; instead, she forced herself to adapt. She kept a low profile, slipping upstairs and down, depending on where Brian had parked himself that day. If he was away, Kim spent most of her time with Cooper in her arms as she chatted with Paul in the living room or with the construction guys working on the first floor. On days when Brian was home, Kim retreated to the tiny nursery, snuggling with the baby in between trips downstairs to make bottles.

There was no turning back now, she regularly told herself. Kim had made the decision to stay on a twenty-four-hour-a-day job with a boss she could not stand the sight of. Her employer was like a bird, always on her shoulder, peck, peck, pecking at her every move. Even when she hid, Brian managed to find her.

"His diaper needs to be changed," Brian announced one day, catching Kim relaxing in the glider, a happy, sleepy Cooper in her arms.

"No, it doesn't need to be changed," Kim sighed, barely able to make eye contact as Brian marched toward her. If Brian had hired her for all her years of experience and her glowing references, why didn't he trust her to change a diaper? she wondered for the hundredth time.

"Yes, it does need to be changed!" Brian leaned down and plucked Cooper from Kim's arms just as she had seen him grab the baby from his wife on their first day home. Feeling the diaper with his hands, he glared at Kim. "See, it is wet. He does need to be changed."

"You know what?" Kim snapped. "A baby's diaper is wet all the time, but if you change it every time it's wet, you'll go crazy."

And so the daily, petty battles went on between nanny and employer in the Porter home. Brian and Kim argued over the way to put in a car seat, over Cooper's diapers, over the temperature of the air conditioner. When she lowered the air, Brian turned it up again. When she offered to fix the car seat, Brian shrugged her off, telling Kim he knew what he was doing. There were light moments that got Kim through the day — running jokes she had with Paul or friendly chats with the men on the construction crew or a tender exchange with Holly when she took breaks from her home office to coo with Kim over Cooper — but she never had the same ease with Brian.

Everything about Brian got under her skin, from the hacking sound he made when he brushed his teeth in her bathroom during the day to the thick layer of suntan lotion he slathered on his nose to protect himself from ultraviolet rays. She hated the expressions on his face when he gave orders and the way he wore his pants just a little too high on the waist and the way he swung his hands as he talked to emphasize that his way was the best way and no other way would work.

The tension took a physical toll on Kim. Her room was still a mess and it felt more like a crash pad than a home. In the evenings, she zoned out in front of the television in the dark room, falling asleep on the side of her bed that was clear of clutter. The other side was still covered with clothes she could not unpack until Brian okayed the use of the closet he was sure was ruined by water damage. Some evenings, when she had the energy, she charted her physical decline in her journal, noting her hair loss or a gain of two pounds. Other nights, she jotted notes about Sam and how much they had both lost when he shut her out and refused to make the marriage work.

At the end of the month, Kim realized she was falling apart. She wanted to stay on the job but Brian's constant monitoring was killing her. Talking it over with Paul, she decided to confront Brian about his behavior.

"You know," Kim began nervously, as the two stood in the living room at the end of yet another tension-filled day, "you hired me to do my job and you hired me because of my expertise and I just feel like I can't breathe without you being right here."

Kim watched in fear as Brian's entire face changed. His cheeks grew red. His eyes scrunched up. His hands curled into tight fists. It was, Kim later described to her friends, an angry, evil look. It was a look she would not forget.

"I don't know what you're talking about," Brian answered defensively. "I haven't done anything wrong."

Kim shot back with a prepared list of moments when she felt he had crossed the line. Then, just as quickly as the anger had appeared, it slipped away. The evil expression dissolved as Brian's eyes filled with tears. Shocked, Kim didn't know what was worse, facing Brian's anger or watching him cry.

"Please don't leave," he pleaded with her, promising to improve.

"Okay," Kim agreed. "I've said what I had to say and I'll give it another week."

This was not the first time Kim stayed on a job against her better judgment. Her loyalty to others over herself often got her into trouble. Before she and Sam were married, Kim went to work for a lovely family in Lakeway who had three children. Alison and Andrew Morrison were well off, but they didn't have any of the negative traits Kim found in other families of privilege: unhappiness mixed with an infuriating sense of entitlement. This family had money and a huge house, but it was a home, a place with a soul. In the mornings, Kim opened her eyes in the guesthouse where she lived, taking in the view of the backyard strewn with children's toys, and the main house, an imposing structure that managed to retain an air of charm and intimacy.

The first year and a half with the Morrisons was uneventful. But then Kim started to notice a change. Andrew, who had always been polite and respectful to Kim and loving to his family, was increasingly rude to everyone around him. In April, Andrew told his four-year-old daughter to take a bath with Kim and left his three-year-old son unsupervised while he walked out of the house to work on his motorcycle. Kim watched this once devoted father forget all of the children's events that month. She stood by as his behavior grew more and more unpredictable and he frequently lost his temper with the children and with Kim.

That July, Alison and Andrew went to a marriage counselor. When he came home from their first appointment, a paranoid Andrew ranted that his wife was going crazy. He told Kim to take the children out to dinner. He grew increasingly agitated, making no sense. Kim did what she always did in a crisis: she remained very calm and went numb.

Knowing Andrew kept guns in the house, Kim secretly packed the children's bags and loaded up the car. Then she collected all three children, promising them a fun adventure as she got them out of the house. She had never been so scared in her life as she pulled out of the driveway, but she knew she was doing what she had to do to keep the kids safe. She called Alison at her office and told her boss to meet her at a local restaurant. After Kim had told her about Andrew's bizarre behavior, Alison agreed that she couldn't take the kids back to the house. When Alison was unable to find a hotel room in the area, Kim called a friend in San Antonio who said that she could put them up for a few nights. Kim was sure this would be the wake-up call everyone needed to get Andrew help.

Andrew was hospitalized and diagnosed with bipolar disorder. He was prescribed medication, but his behavior didn't improve upon his release. Kim desperately wanted out of the situation before it got worse, but her sense of obligation to Alison and the kids was too strong. If she wasn't there to help, wouldn't they all fall apart? Who would protect the children from Andrew? All three children were suffering. The oldest boy went from being happy and well-adjusted to angry and unreachable almost overnight. Kim watched as Andrew ridiculed his daughter, going so far as to call her a "nightmare." The younger boy regularly asked Kim if his daddy still loved him.

The next couple of months were terrifying. Kim came across two handguns Andrew now kept in the house and even caught him trying to make ecstasy in the kitchen. Andrew was soon fired from his job but turned around and bought a new house behind his wife's back. He also shaved his head and bought yet another gun. Every morning, Kim felt a jolt of fear that Andrew had killed Alison and the kids while she was sleeping. Alison was a mess, the kids were a mess, and Kim lived in constant terror. She began sending e-mails to her family and friends, detailing the dramatic events of her daily life. "Get out," they all told her. But she stayed. "I have every reason to quit and it wouldn't come as a surprise to anyone," she admitted in one of her e-mails. "But right now the last thing Alison needs is to interview new nannies. Even if she could, I don't know if she could get one to stay."

Andrew turned his study into a shrine decorated with candles, incense, and bowls of vitamins and herbal supplements that Kim worried the children would get their hands on. Kim used all her strength to stay and Alison lavished her with praise and gratitude. "You have deftly maintained some sense of normalcy in the kids' lives and provided among the best advice and counseling I've received from professionals," Alison wrote in a note to Kim that came along with a bonus. Whenever Kim thought of leaving, she remembered how much Alison and the children needed and appreciated her, how this had once been her dream nanny job. Even Alison's parents sent Kim a note of thanks.

Finally, Kim's fear overtook her guilt and she gave Alison her notice. Andrew wasn't getting any better and continued to be obsessed with guns, even asking Kim to buy him one at Wal-Mart. The day she left, she sent a quick e-mail to her friends and family. "I feel like a kid," she confessed. "I'm so scared I just want someone to pick me up and hold me."

A year and one month later, Kim heard the news that Andrew had killed himself. Alison moved away with the kids. Driving by the family's old house sometimes, Kim liked to remember the warmth the home once held and how fond she was of Alison. Then she remembered the chaos that erupted when Andrew's mental health deteriorated. Staring at the house through her car window, she pushed the memory of Andrew falling apart out of her mind and thought again of the view she woke up to every day in the guesthouse. She could still see the early morning light hitting the children's toys scattered across the green grass.

The more time Kim spent at the Porters, the more often she found herself thinking of Andrew. Brian's behavior, his paranoia and his obsessive nature, reminded Kim of the first signs of Andrew's breakdown. On the one hand, Kim knew she was quick to jump to conclusions after watching one boss fall apart, and Brian was obviously functioning in his daily life. On the other, she couldn't help finding parallels. Nothing had changed after her confrontation with Brian; it was as if his tearful apology had never happened. A few days later, he marched up to her in typical fashion and delivered yet another ridiculous order.

"The front door is broken, so you have to stand guard until it's fixed," he announced.

"How long will it take?" she asked, shocked that he was being so paranoid.

"All day," he answered, as though it was the most normal thing in the world to ask his nanny to stand by the door for hours.

Up on this hill, hidden from the road by a gate and trees, the house, Kim knew, would be safe from burglars. But Brian wasn't worried about robbers. He was worried about the construction workers.

Kim did as she was told, bringing Cooper downstairs for the day as she kept her eye on the door. Inside she was furious. The construction crew was the nicest group of men she had come across in years. If the house was on fire, she knew they would be the first to run inside to save her and the baby. They helped Kim with bags after a shopping trip, chatting about the baby, smiling behind Brian's back when he snapped at her in front of them.

"We don't know how you do this job," they joked with her when Brian was out of earshot, and she was grateful for the validation.

Once again, Kim thought about quitting. But instead of walking out the door, she did what she was told and just watched it. Holly, working upstairs for the day, called Kim on her cell phone when she couldn't find the baby.

"What's going on?" she asked. "Where are you?"

"I can't come upstairs," Kim explained. "Brian wants me to guard the front door."

"Why?" Holly asked.

"It's broken and Brian doesn't want anyone walking in." Kim kept the explanation short. She had never dragged Holly into her dynamic with Brian and she didn't want to start now.

"You're kidding me," Holly said with a sigh.

"If you need anything, call me," Kim said. "And I'll send it up with one of the guys."

Almost immediately after arriving home from the hospital, Holly, though technically still on maternity leave, began working. She spent her days on the telephone and typing on her laptop. Holly reached out to her nanny for parenting support, which came as a huge relief to Kim after Brian's micromanaging. Kim encouraged Holly to take more breaks, to rest and get her milk supply up for breastfeeding. She tried to think of things she could do to make life easier for Holly, and she did her best to instruct and support her without sounding condescending.

Brian might question her every move with Cooper, but Holly was totally open. If not a natural mother, she was a natural learner. Egoless and willing, she peppered Kim with questions and took every answer in. Kim, in turn, felt useful and knowledgeable, at the top of her nanny game.

It was in the moments with Holly that Kim finally felt like a nanny, and especially the nanny of a newborn. She simultaneously cared for Cooper and helped his mother navigate a whole new world. Doing her best to keep her tone neutral, Kim let Holly make minor mistakes as she guided her through Parenting 101. Giving Cooper his first bath one night, Holly had a hard time cleaning him while also keeping him steady. She moved her hand away from Cooper's head to wash his feet, and Kim watched the baby sinking under the water. Without missing a beat, Kim plunged her own hand into the water, propping Cooper up again before his face was submerged.

"Okay, this is where you really want to make sure you keep one hand under the neck at all times," Kim had said calmly, silently relieved that the baby was in her hands now.

As far as Kim was concerned, where Brian had no business being a parent, Holly was fabulous. She wished the woman didn't have to work so many hours and had a more understanding husband. When Kim did fantasize about quitting, she always considered Holly. "I'm supposed to be relieving her stress," she would think, "and I'm just going to triple it."

On short trips out or just hanging out in Cooper's tiny nursery, the sound of hammering or drilling ever in the background, Holly and Kim didn't necessarily grow close or become the best of friends, but they had a relaxed interaction, a calm and rewarding working relationship. Kim cooed at Cooper, loving his baby smell and his little eyes, the soft touch of his head.

"I think he's going to be a peacemaker," Kim had told Holly, who listened intently to Kim's every word about her son. "He won't be a class clown, but he's always going to be smiling and happy, and when he walks into a room, he is always going to brighten it, and if people are down, he is going to cheer them up. He won't take life too seriously, but he won't be a joker either."

"Tell me more!" Holly had exclaimed eagerly, and Kim laughed, amused that this boss, too, believed in her ability to read children.

Just a few weeks after giving birth, Holly was asked to interrupt her maternity leave to return to her office for an entire day of meetings. She brought Kim and Cooper with her, placing them in an empty, windowless office that the company used as a lactation room while she headed to a conference room on another floor. Holly wanted to keep Cooper on his feeding schedule, but hours passed and still she hadn't returned to breastfeed the infant. Kim began to worry, wondering where Holly was and how long she would be gone. Pulling her cell phone out of her bag, Kim saw that she had no signal. Now she realized Holly would be just as worried as she was. They had no way to reach each other.

Kim pictured Holly standing in front of her colleagues, exhausted from being a new mother, pulling it all together to focus on the task at hand. Holly was a workaholic, respected in her field. But at home, Kim was surprised by how meek Holly was around her husband, how she put up with his overbearing behavior. Here was a woman who loved her newborn, who was the only one in the marriage with a full-time job, whose husband insisted she do all of her night feedings in another room so he could get his rest while she wasn't getting enough sleep of her own to produce enough breast milk. Kim felt it was her job to ease some of the pressure.

Cooper began to fuss, and then he fussed some more. Kim looked around the empty office, calculating the hours she had been sitting there. It was way past Cooper's feeding time. She hadn't eaten lunch or had a bathroom break. She had formula as an emergency backup and she knew she would have to use it. Sticking her head out of the office, she asked a woman passing in the hallway if she could bring her a bottle of water. After all the work his mother had put in to keep him exclusively on breast milk, Kim would have to give Cooper his first bottle of formula.

When, a few minutes later, Holly finally appeared at the door, Kim said immediately, "I had to give him formula."

"Why did you do that?" Holly began, but then she stopped herself. A newborn who normally eats every two to three hours could not go this long without milk. Kim watched Holly's face fall, knowing she was angry at herself, at Kim, and at the situation.

"I tried calling you but I didn't have a signal," Kim said, feeling terrible for Holly.

Holly sat down. Kim watched her pick her baby up and start to cry.

A few days after their trip to Holly's office, Kim sensed a new dynamic between her and Holly. She got the feeling that Holly was torn about her nanny's close bond with her child. This was not the first time Kim had watched a mother struggle between gratitude and jealousy.

"Cooper just seems very attached to her," Kim heard Holly telling a friend over the phone, a note of pain in her voice. "I know I should be glad about it but at the same time it's hard."

That night Kim decided to take her loving down a notch to make more room for Holly. She would make an effort not to kiss Cooper and to hold him less often if Holly was around. It was a delicate situation, but Kim knew she could navigate it. It was part of her job and much easier to handle than Brian's behavior.

Turning on her computer, Kim put Holly out of her mind as she read through her e-mail. When she was done, without giving it much thought, she logged on to Sam's e-mail account using his password. They hadn't exchanged a single word since she moved out, but she thought about him every day. She heard the soundtrack of their relationship whenever she turned the radio on in the Accord — Shania Twain or Celine Dion. She ached to see Jessica and Amber, furious that Sam had turned them against her, convincing his children that their stepmother simply gave up and walked out the door, when he was the one who had shut her out.

Scanning his e-mails, she read several messages from two different Internet dating services. She was shocked. Dating was a world Kim hadn't even considered entering. If the kids only knew how quickly their father was replacing her, they might see her side of the story. Instead of dating online like Sam, Kim had been researching the possibility of freezing her eggs in case she ever did meet someone new.

Lying in bed alone, she couldn't help picturing Sam getting ready for one of his dates. He got to live in their house while she was stuck in someone else's. He was moving on with other women while she couldn't even imagine flirting. Curling up on the empty half of her bed, Kim went to sleep, marking off one more day in her yearlong commitment to the Porters.

THIRTEEN

VIVIAN COULD DO MANY things better than a mother. While mothers stressed about starting solids, weaning babies from the breast, and potty training, Vivian was bursting with confidence and know-how. As a nanny, she dove into the messy domestic lives of first-time parents, putting everything in its place. She categorized every area of a child's life until it made as much sense as a perfectly formulated math equation. Childhood, in Vivian's hands, was a methodical process in which every problem was anticipated, dealt with, and consistently managed.

She could do all of this because she did not have the same "umbilical cord emotions" as a mother, she said. The sound of a child crying did not shake her to the core. The sight of a child refusing to eat did not send her into a panic that he might starve. Fear didn't rule her thinking. She saw things clearly, knowing the long-term benefits of ignoring a tantrum or a milk strike or an angry little face. She did not make the same mistakes that many parents made; parents, Vivian knew, could be so desperate to make their kids happy, they sacrificed life lessons by giving in to the moment.

"That's something I can do that a parent can't," she explained. "I can separate what's for me and what's for the child. When you want to give the child a bottle after a year, that's not because the child needs nutritional development from the bottle, that's because you still want a baby."

Vivian had recently counseled a mother whose baby had become accustomed to sleeping with her at night. In order to transition her child out of the habit, the woman set up an air mattress on the floor of the nursery. She'd lie down with the baby on the mattress, eventually moving the child to the crib and then returning to the air mattress before finally leaving the baby on his own once he was asleep.

"Why don't you just put the baby in the crib and let him cry it out?" Vivian asked.

"Oh, no," the sleep-deprived mother answered. "That's too traumatic."

"No, it's more traumatic to have this thirty-day weaning out," Vivian insisted. "That's for you, that's not for the child."

There was no quick resolution after Vivian's frustrated declaration that the job was no longer working. There was no grand discussion that solved everything. Catherine had ignored Vivian's threat to quit, and Vivian hadn't brought the matter up again. After their blowup, Catherine had come home from work, and slowly things went back to normal — with a few changes. Vivian's love for Devan and David remained fierce and protective, but a small shift occurred that spring that she may not even have noticed herself. She began to truly understand that they were not hers. She began to accept that if she was going to stay with the boys a little longer, she would have to start letting go.

"The whole Trevor thing could have been avoided if there had been communication beforehand, so that's the lesson in that story," Vivian said matter-of-factly, looking back on the events of the previous weeks.

Over the years, she and Catherine had been many things to each other. They'd been employer and employee, big sister and little sister, mother and daughter, and also friends.

Slowly, the reality of the situation sank in. Vivian could not go back to the way things were, no matter how much she hated change. It was no longer her and Catherine making decisions about the boys, it was her and Trevor and Catherine. Sometimes it was just Trevor and Catherine. The dynamics had shifted, but Vivian was still hanging on.

"You have to remember, we already had five years of having little blowups and big blowups," Vivian said, explaining why she'd stayed on the job after threatening to leave. "It was already established that we were invested in each other. We were family. There was too much to let go."

Trying to keep things in perspective, Vivian had turned her attention and energy back to her personal career goals. She worked on getting her Nanny of the Year materials together. The conference she had organized in the fall had been a huge success, and she truly felt that she, more than anyone, deserved to win the honor, but she didn't know what politics might come into play within INA. Vivian vowed to make her packet so outstanding that nothing could get in the way of her election. She proofread her resumé, gathered her written recommendations, laid out her articles, and selected before-and-after shots showing her weight loss. In the first photo, she stood in all black, eyes shining in her chubby face, arms around a decorated Christmas tree. A year later, her expression a bit more subdued, her hands clasped together, she stood beside David and Devan as the boys sat on Santa's lap. She was 133 pounds lighter, half her old self.

Along with a loving nomination letter from her proud mother and high praise from Catherine, Vivian was thrilled to include another letter from one of Boston's premier nanny agencies, highlighting her major achievement of the past year. "The Boston conference attendance was the largest ever recorded for any nanny meeting," wrote the agency owner. "In an industry that has local agencies sometimes at odds with each other, she successfully enlisted and motivated the heads of Boston-area nanny agencies to work elbow to elbow." That was Vivian, pulling everyone together by sheer will.

She handed in all her materials in March. In April she got the phone call she was hoping for.

"It's ninety-nine percent that you'll get it," INA president Pat Cascio told her. "We called Catherine for a reference."

The INA's only concern was Vivian's ability to be an effective spokesperson for the industry. Vivian had earned a reputation for her emotional outbursts at INA meetings, and a few board members were worried that she wasn't savvy enough to deal with the press. Vivian admitted she could sometimes go overboard in arguing her case, and that her confrontational style was an ingrained part of her personality, but she also knew that when it came to the media, she could generate interest in the profession and handle questions like a pro. After being a nanny, PR was what she did best.

Vivian hung up the phone and immediately began to cry. She wanted this more than anything in the world, and there it was right in front of her. What if she didn't get it now? Everyone she knew — colleagues and friends — told her she was a lock for Nanny of the Year. But what if it didn't go her way? Suddenly Vivian was scared. If she didn't win this, if someone else was named Nanny of the Year at the first INA conference held in Vivian's hometown, she would be utterly humiliated.

This wasn't the first time questions about Vivian's personality had come up, and Vivian tried to take Pat Cascio's comments in stride, accepting the fact that she was often misunderstood. She described herself as a goal setter, orderly, organized, passionate, emotional, truthful, and a straight shooter. She also knew that there were those who saw her as an overbearing control freak who was sometimes emotionally unstable. Vivian knew that there were women in the industry who steered clear of her.

"They don't like me," she said with an impish smile. "They're intimidated by me. I'm a warrior. I don't back down. I'm an advocate and I'm passionate. I'm not going to go with the flow just to make peace. They're jealous. Women get jealous."

It was this contrast, the way others saw her versus the way she saw herself, that had Vivian worried. She may have done more than anyone else to benefit the nanny industry over the past year, but she may also have offended people along the way. It was possible that Vivian wouldn't win Nanny of the Year because some members had a personal dislike for her.

"If I don't get this," she reasoned, "I'll know it's just political, because I really deserve it."

While she waited for INA's final word, Vivian kept busy at work, grateful for the distraction the boys offered her.

She'd been keeping a close eye on David, who'd had a cough for several days, and one afternoon he seemed particularly uncomfortable. With Catherine in back-to-back meetings and Trevor out of town, Vivian decided to call the doctor.

"I'm calling for David Pritchard. Date of birth: six, three, ninety-nine," Vivian said, speaking quickly as she often did, anticipating the questions the nurse would ask. "He's had a persistent cough and it hasn't subsided. He has no other symptoms. I'm afraid it may be allergies or his asthma acting up. Normally I wouldn't be concerned, but he has had it for three days and it's beginning to irritate him. I've given him cough medicine but nothing has helped."

"Who are you?" the nurse asked.

Vivian sighed. "I'm Vivian McCormick, David's nanny."

"I can't talk to you," the nurse said. "You need to have the mom call."

"Look, I've been his nanny since he was born," Vivian said, irritated. She had little patience for people like this, people with no clue how vital a nanny was in a family. "If you look in his medical file, you'll see that."

"Well, I'll try to look for it and I'll call you back."

For the next hour and a half, waiting for the nurse to get back to her, Vivian fumed. How could that nurse dismiss her like a stranger on the street? How come Vivian ruled the boys' lives inside the house but to the outside world she was just a babysitter? This was exactly the reason she had gotten so active in the nanny industry. She picked up the phone again.

"Dr. Putter knows me," Vivian said when the nurse answered. Then she went in for the kill. "I'm the same nanny whose eight-month-old you gave a Band-Aid to after I told you not to and he swallowed it and ended up having a fluoroscopy. Yeah, that's right, I'm *that* nanny. Remember me now?"

"Yes. I do remember you now. You need to fax over a medical release form."

Vivian slammed down the phone, pulled out the binder where she kept all of the important papers related to the boys' care, and then faxed a copy of the release, granting her complete medical authority in the event that Catherine and Trevor were unavailable. She wanted to scream at the nurse over the phone, to march into the office and make this woman understand just how important she was in David and Devan's lives.

Thinking back on all the times she'd taken the kids to the doctor's office in the past four years, Vivian shook her head in frustration. "Trevor's only been there once," she explained. "I've been there a million times. Catherine usually meets me. She's been alone with Devan once. I've been alone with David *three times.*"

When she was on the defensive, Vivian was the type to keep score. She wanted credit for a role that was not fully understood by the world. Sometimes, when she didn't get the respect she wanted from others, she relied on small victories at work to keep up her morale. A few days after her showdown with the nurse, she and Catherine had a disagreement that Vivian perceived as yet another challenge to her authority.

Yu-Gi-Oh! and Pokemon trading cards had recently become popular with the boys and their friends, and Vivian objected to what she saw as their negative influence. She went to Catherine with her concerns about the games: a Baptist, Vivian felt the Pokemon characters were "demonological" and should be banned from the house.

"From a Christian perspective, I get worried that they're a culty thing," she said to Catherine, who didn't listen. A few minutes later, the women were together in the family room with the twins when the play turned rough and Devan pulled David's arm aggressively.

"Stop! Stop! You're going to pop his arm!" Vivian yelled and turned to her boss. "See, Catherine. This is Pokemon."

"How do you know that?" Catherine asked skeptically, her arms folded across her chest as she leaned on the kitchen counter.

"I'm their nanny. I know new behavior. " Vivian looked Catherine straight in the eye. "Ask the boys where they learned that," she dared her boss.

"Where did you learn that?" Catherine questioned her sons.

"Well, what were you doing?" Vivian prodded them. "It looked kind of neat."

"I was taking Devan the bad guy into the pool like they do in Pokemon," David explained.

"See, I told you!" Vivian exclaimed. "I'm their nanny. I get a gut feeling and I know it."

It was like she knew the boys better than they knew themselves. She didn't have to think or analyze behavior, because she knew immediately, instinctually what was going through their heads. She had a bond with them that would not break. And it was this knowledge that allowed Vivian to finally accept that she would have to step back and let them continue to grow on their own. The awful, unimaginable thought of leaving that had first entered into her head in September now became a part of Vivian's reality.

"My bonding with the kids isn't going away," Vivian said without a trace of distress. "But the job is coming to an end. Slowly. It's winding down. It's the next stage of the game. I'm getting better about that stuff."

Catherine came home from work early one April evening in a particularly buoyant mood. It was still light outside, but the boys had already finished dinner, and they and Vivian were sitting on the couch in the family room, chatting and giggling. In her beige Talbots slacks and blue button-down shirt, Catherine looked modest and reserved, but her face was open and bright.

"Boys, I have a secret to tell you," she said as she leaned down to whisper in their ears.

Vivian watched as broad grins spread across the boys' faces and their eyes grew wide. "Congratulations, Nanny of the Year!" they shouted, jumping into Vivian's arms.

Vivian whooped as Catherine gave her a hug and the boys began to dance around the room. Vivian buzzed inside, thrilled that her own boys had broken the news. This was going to be a big thing, she thought to herself. Her job now was to be the best role model possible, to represent to the public all that a nanny could be. This was the moment she had been dreaming about for so long, the pinnacle of her entire career, and instead of happiness filling her up, Vivian felt a bit out of place, a little off kilter and downright surreal.

In the car on her way home, Vivian spread the news by phone, hoping it would sink in if she repeated it enough times. Her mother wasn't home but she did get a few of her close nanny friends on the phone: Laura, who had helped her with the Halloween party, and another INA nanny named Claire.

"I'm proud of myself," Vivian said.

"You really deserve this," her friends agreed.

"I know. I really do," she answered, soaking up the feeling of accomplishment.

Having reached the goal she had set almost twelve months earlier, Vivian now gave herself another: her acceptance speech had to be perfect, hitting all the right notes, outshining every Nanny of the Year speech that had come before. Last year, she had watched Amy Lynn at the podium, imagining how differently she would handle the opportunity to stand before one hundred of her peers. This had to be a speech that would resonate throughout the entire nanny industry. The biggest flaw in past speeches was an excess of personal emotion. Vivian's would be different; she would use her personal experiences only as a bridge to define her broader views. This speech would be a call to arms, encouraging all nannies to join in the fight to gain respect. Above all, Vivian vowed, she would not turn into a sappy, sobbing wimp. She would stand strong before her friends and colleagues. She would use the opportunity of being awarded the highest honor in her field to instruct and inspire. She would be the consummate professional.

"The speech should be more like you get elected for president than you win Miss America," she said.

Lost in her thoughts, Vivian made a wrong turn on the streets she usually navigated so well, heading toward oncoming traffic. She made a quick turn and headed back in the right direction, making a to-do list in her head the entire way.

The worst thing about being fat had always been the clothes. Now Vivian could fit into a regular size 14. A slew of stores opened up to her and she headed straight in, giddy with excitement. Using the extra money she made from a weekend nanny job, Vivian hit all the places she had once been forced to admire from a distance. She marched into Bloomingdale's, requested a personal shopper, told her she wanted to see all things "young and flirty," then spent $900 in a single afternoon. Her eyes shining, she inspected skirts, admired shoes, and found herself in a world she had never been allowed to enter: the world of trendy clothes. It wasn't that Vivian hadn't cared about or wasn't aware of what other women her age were wearing; up until now, she just hadn't had access.

She added bursts of color to her dark-hued wardrobe, skirts that showed leg, and sexy strappy sandals. Running the conference itinerary through her mind, she tallied up the events and made sure she had a new outfit for every occasion — the opening cocktail party, the Nanny of the Year luncheon, the closing festivities. Her outfits ranged from cute and conservative to sexy but elegant.

"Last year I looked like a lesbo at conference," she joked, remembering her boxy suits.

When the new wardrobe was complete, Vivian continued the makeover with a new haircut, going for a short, sassy, layered bob that concealed her recent hair loss. She had her nails done and sat in a tanning bed. A year ago, Vivian had packed her suitcase with her outdated suits and awful flats, telling herself she would at least look professional. But on this late April weekend, the new Vivian left the old Vivian behind. She was tan and smooth, her outfits impeccable, her hair fashionably styled. This was no longer just the INA conference; this was Vivian McCormick's coming-out party.

She made her debut at the opening cocktail party on Friday night. Stepping into the main ballroom at the Hilton Hotel near Logan Airport, Vivian felt strong and confident. In a pair of high-heeled sandals, a knee-length black cocktail dress, and a sheer black shawl thrown over her shoulders, Vivian looked better than any other nanny in the room and she knew it. She took note of everyone's double takes as she passed.

"I didn't even recognize you!" several women said as she walked across the room.

"I had no idea Vivian was so pretty," one nanny whispered to another.

By Monday morning, Vivian was in a horrible mood. Just a few hours before the Nanny of the Year luncheon, all of the pressure she had put on herself to craft the best speech in the history of INA was finally taking its toll. She was unable to bear the thought that anything would go awry, that something would happen off the script she had so perfectly formulated in her head. She stood smack in the middle of her own fairy tale, terrified it wouldn't have a happy ending.

Standing in the sunny hotel lobby, in a crisp white sweater set, Vivian was uncharacteristically quiet and subdued. Outside, a soft spring breeze ruffled women's skirts and the backs of men's suit jackets. Airplanes flew low, heading for runways just a shuttle ride away. Inside, elevator music played softly in the background. In the lobby, with its high ceiling and glass atrium, Vivian looked a little lost, a smaller version of herself, as her mother, Susan, and grandmother, Bea, made innocent chatter. In a blue and tan suit with a matching silk shirt, earrings, and necklace, Bea was an elegant grandmother. Susan wore a red and white sweater with a pair of tan pants and red clogs, a simple gold cross around her neck. She looked excited and proud.

Vivian was the first to spot her father, making his way into the hotel through the lobby's revolving door. A tall man with wide shoulders, dusty blond hair, and ruddy cheeks, Billy McCormick looked like a much steadier presence that morning than he had been over the course of Vivian's life. Taking in his suit and tie and the amused, proud grin on his face, Vivian was momentarily relieved. Her father had cleaned himself up for her big day; he'd made an effort. She had invited him against her mother's and grandmother's wishes, and she hoped he wouldn't make her regret it.

As they waited for the rest of the group to assemble, Vivian's mother fussed over her daughter, adjusting her corsage until Vivian snapped at her to leave her alone. "When I'm stressed, I get bitchy," she said by way of apology.

Catherine arrived at the hotel next, with David and Devan in tow. The boys were decked out in their party shirts, matching short-sleeved button-downs in green and blue. Vivian's face lit up as they ran to her, and in their frenetic, happy presence, she relaxed. She and Catherine hugged, and then groups formed as pictures were taken. Vivian smiled wide for all of them.

"Their mother is young-looking," Billy said to no one in particular, eyeing Catherine. Vivian made a mental note to keep her father away from her boss. Catherine was a pretty woman and Vivian knew without a doubt that if given the opportunity, her father would hit on her. Freshly scrubbed, Billy was a well-dressed time bomb.

"The boys are getting big!" Susan sang out, presenting Devan and David with a gift of coloring books and crayons. Vivian also had a present for the boys, T-shirts she had bought at the conference. Over the years, Vivian had given the boys several such shirts, with sayings like, "She's not my mother, she's my nanny" and "I love my nanny this much," with a picture of two arms outstretched.

"You boys should put those on," Susan said.

"No. They're wearing their party shirts, specially picked for today," Vivian remarked sharply.

As the small group headed up the escalator, Vivian chatted with the boys while keeping an eye on her father, who was inching closer to Catherine.

"I'm taking a cruise to Alaska," Susan declared to Catherine, who smiled kindly as Billy cut in.

"I just took a trip," he said. "To Troy, New York. I found a pub there and felt right at home."

"You know, I didn't even recognize you!" Bea said, quickly changing the topic of conversation to Vivian's dramatic transformation.

Vivian led her group into the International Ballroom, heading straight for the table she had on reserve. Placing the boys on either side of her, and Catherine next to Devan, Vivian seated her father several seats from her boss. A waiter appeared at Vivian's side, putting kids' meals in front of Devan and David. Vivian, of course, had thought ahead and had them special ordered. Just when she was getting comfortable, her father spoke.

"Let me ask you a question," Billy said, leaning over to address Catherine. "Have you and Vivian ever been at odds?"

"Once or twice," Catherine answered with a smile. "But we really get along. We're opposite personalities but we mesh."

"You know," Billy continued, putting his finger down on the table for emphasis, "Vivian was always strong-willed. I did a lot for her over the years."

Vivian knew where her father was headed — down a path of lies. Susan intervened, bringing up her Alaska trip again. Devan and David tore into their new crayons. Catherine leaned in to Devan, helping him open the container.

"I sent these to the cleaners." Billy held his suit jacket out by the lapels. "These are mine. They aren't rented."

Vivian knew her grandmother suspected he was drunk, but she decided to give him the benefit of the doubt, writing his awkward behavior off as a case of nerves. She believed he was proud of her, but she knew he wasn't comfortable at formal events. Vivian pulled David onto her lap. The boys sat quietly, drawing and eating, chatting politely, behaving just as they had always been taught. From a distance, the table looked perfect, just as Vivian had pictured it a year ago. She felt the glances of other nannies in the room, their whispers to each other about how cute the twins were, how nice it was to see Vivian there with both of her families.

Finally Vivian was called to the stage to join the four other nannies who had been nominated for Nanny of the Year. She stood up from the table, smoothing down the front of her black pants. For just a moment she hesitated; then she smiled at David and Devan and went up to take her place among the others. When Vivian was announced as the winner of the award, the room broke into applause. Amy Lynn, the previous year's winner, placed a tiara on Vivian's head, slipped a Nanny of the Year banner over her shoulders, and handed her a bouquet of roses. Vivian cringed at the moment's resemblance to a Miss America pageant. Then, she was speechless. Looking out at the faces of her peers, at her mother and grandmother, at her father, at Catherine, and, most of all, at Devan and David, Vivian paused, took a deep breath, and started to cry.

"This is overwhelming . . ." she said as she struggled to get her emotions under control. Wiping her eyes, she focused once again on David and Devan. She began her speech by talking directly to the boys. "I love you and I love being your nanny. Thank you for sharing your days with me, and I would like to thank your mom, Catherine. Thank you for unselfishly sharing your wonderful sons with me. I value the friendship and relationship we have built."

"It's very emotional," Susan said to Catherine, whose eyes were filled with tears.

"Vivian was a brat when she was a child," Billy announced.

Vivian's speech was a success. Once she had cleared her throat, she launched into all she had done for the industry and all she hoped it would become. At the end she called Devan and David up on-stage with her to sing a song they had chosen. It was the theme song to *Teenage Mutant Ninja Turtles,* but by the time they were through, almost every nanny in the room was crying.

"I'd especially like to thank my employer Catherine," Vivian said on closing, tears once again welling in her eyes. "For letting me truly love these boys."

Later, when the banquet room was empty and Catherine and the boys were gone, Vivian slowly gathered up her things. Her father had left without saying goodbye. Tired and relieved that the big event was over, Vivian walked back to her room with her mother and grandmother.

Vivian's hotel room was like the backstage of a fashion show. Clothes were strewn here and there, a bouquet of flowers sat on the dresser, the Nanny of the Year gift basket took up space on the bed. As she changed into casual clothes, the hotel room mirror reflected the loose folds hanging from her arms and legs. Though Vivian had lost 133 pounds, her skin hadn't adjusted to her new, smaller self. A year later, she would undergo a twelve-hour body-lift surgery, but on this day, she moved around the room, aware that she had a problem but not really caring. She was done putting on a show.

"Can I borrow this for my cruise?" Susan asked her daughter, pointing to the black cocktail dress Vivian had worn the first night of conference.

"You have to have it dry-cleaned. There's deodorant under the arms. And you have to dry-clean it after," Vivian instructed, holding the dress out to Susan. "You should bring a black jacket to go with it so you don't get cold."

"You've lost too much weight," Susan said, looking her daughter over.

Vivian looked at her mother blankly. Over the past two days people had been stopping to offer congratulations and tell her she looked great, but Vivian's perception of herself still hadn't caught up to the reality. She could buy a new wardrobe, twirl around in front of a mirror, and bask in the glow of envious stares, but she could not shake the feeling that she was still, as she had been her whole life, the obese girl. But as she handed her new dress to her mother, it suddenly struck Vivian that if her mother could wear her clothes, and her mother wasn't fat, then she must not be fat, either.

Vivian left her room a mess, guiding her mother and grandmother back downstairs. She still had workshops to attend, along with the final party, an All-American Feast with apple pie and hot dogs. In the hotel lobby, Vivian hugged her mother and grandmother and said goodbye. Seeing the pride on their faces, she felt a deep sense of satisfaction.

"You know, Vivian," Bea said before leaving, recalling Vivian's speech, "you were right. Catherine really does let you love those boys."

FOURTEEN

Betsy and james's living room looked out on another living room in the building across the street. The two buildings had been built before World War II, and as they rose upward cheek to cheek, they blocked the sunlight one floor at a time. They stood as reminders that even if you made a decent living and had a large apartment in New York City, you still lived in claustrophobic conditions where a view of the sky came in tiny patches.

During the daytime hours, no one appeared in this other living room. With its bright white couches, neatly lined bookshelves, and one perfectly arched orchid placed in the center of the coffee table, the apartment was as quiet and staged as a museum exhibit. It was a reminder of everything the Halls' apartment was not and everything James wanted it to be.

The Halls' living room had the bones of a showplace — meticulously chosen furniture, stretched canvases on the walls, and perfectly placed family photos — covered in the clutter of family life. Signs of the children were everywhere: books, toys, papers, single shoes, random plastic game pieces left behind when boxes were put away. At the end of her long days, Claudia stacked. She turned the clutter into strategically placed piles: books on the coffee table, toys in the corner, papers in a neat mountain on the dining room table.

Lucy and Jackson's room was always a particular challenge because Lucy spent her days pulling her clothes out of her drawers, throwing them in the air, watching them fall on the floor. She jumped on the pile of clothes, draped her body over them, closed her eyes for a few seconds before bouncing up again. She pulled dresses over jeans, shirts over sweaters, mismatched her colors and patterns, and sauntered out to the living room in her wild outfits, looking for Claudia's approval.

With James home regularly, it was impossible for Claudia to keep up with the kids' messes. When she knew the schedule, she rushed around and put the place in shape for their parents' return at the end of the day, a habit that bothered Betsy. James and Betsy had made it a house rule that the children clean up after themselves. It took work, directing them to be responsible for their things, but as parents they felt it was important to develop the routine in them over the long run. Claudia, Betsy knew, picked up after the kids even though the Halls asked her not to, because it was faster for Claudia to do it herself and allowed her to avoid conflict with James.

By now all the nannies in the building knew about James. When Claudia's friends asked for a play date, she would decline, saying, "I got Mr. Grumpy back at the house," or "Mr. Grumpy home today." First she said it with affection. Then for comic effect.

After James had been working at home for several months, Claudia sighed with irritation. "It's like he's just grumpy from being grumpy. I don't know what's wrong with him. Maybe it's something inside of him, because you can't be fine one minute and then a fly pass by and suddenly everything changes."

There was speculation among her nanny friends about the source of James's moodiness. "Maybe he's gay," they ventured, and Claudia laughed, knowing it was a ridiculous thought.

Whatever it was that was causing James's mood swings, Claudia was ready for it to be over. She wanted the apartment to herself again. She worried that Betsy's cheerfulness would fall apart and she would finally let her husband have it. Most of all, she wanted James to be nicer to the kids. Lately, they either fought with him or stood frozen in anger as he yelled. A week earlier, while Claudia was getting Lucy dressed in the living room and James was working at his desk, the little girl paused and looked straight into Claudia's eyes.

"You know what, Claudia? My daddy does really want me," Lucy said. Claudia felt a surge in her heart.

"Of course he does, Lucy!" Claudia said, raising her voice so James could hear. "Of course your daddy wants you. He loves you."

Some days, if James was in a bad mood, Claudia simply went numb. To her it was as if he was there yet not there at all. Although she didn't think anyone had noticed, she had changed after the eviction. While she had always struggled with boredom on the job, Claudia had also had moments of lighthearted banter with her friends and Betsy. Her soft giggle came easily when she hung out with the kids. Recently, though, Claudia had lost that sparkle, and now she dragged herself through the entire day. Claudia's signature calm had become full-blown passivity. When Lucy dressed up, she watched and gave a half smile. When Tanisha gave her grief and demanded attention, Claudia didn't return her daughter's attitude with her normal wit. She ignored her.

Claudia had become a lesser version of herself. She was muted, her movements a little slower and her sighs a little longer. She began avoiding eye contact more often. When she'd been evicted, Claudia had made a vow to herself: she would never get that close to the edge again. She would cut out the extras and start saving money. She'd join another susu, and when her hand came up, she'd put all the money into an emergency savings account.

The first luxury to go was math class. But life without math was like a long winter with no sun. Nothing could grow under those conditions. Claudia stopped talking about the GED. If someone brought it up, she'd say casually, "I'm still going to take the test. I just have to go to the library and get a list of the dates." But she never went to the library, and eventually everyone stopped asking.

Betsy did notice the changes in Claudia. She noticed because Claudia's depression was making her life more difficult. Betsy didn't blame Claudia for being depressed. What bothered her was the domino effect Claudia's problems had on her life. As a part of her long-running campaign to put things in order, Betsy had recently spent an entire day organizing the kids' drawers. Previously, James had labeled all of the cabinets and the linen closet. Now she was doing something similar.

Yet soon Betsy and James were finding clothes in all the wrong drawers. And the Friday before she left for a business trip to London, Betsy got a call from James at her gallery: he was furious because he had found Lucy's socks in Jackson's pajama drawer. Sitting at her desk, with a long list of calls to make and e-mails to write before she left for her trip, Betsy suggested James write Claudia a note and leave it on the counter. She didn't want to get in the middle. Betsy didn't have time to run interference between her nanny and her husband. She had already given up countless hours helping Claudia get back into her apartment during the eviction.

"She could return the favor," Betsy said to James, wishing her nanny was more proactive, especially after they had helped her financially. Then she shifted her tone. "It might not be her fault. Lucy does put her clothes everywhere."

"But Lucy only has two matching pairs of socks left, and it should be Claudia's job to tell us things like that," James argued.

"That's true," Betsy agreed before hanging up the phone. She tried to focus on work. The last thing she needed was an angry phone call from her husband over some minor domestic details. When Claudia added to the disorder in the house, it drove James up the wall, and then it all came back to Betsy, whose job it was to manage Claudia.

Although the Halls' apartment was relatively spacious, Betsy and James still felt it needed to be run like a tight ship, with everything in its place. Only, Betsy didn't have the inclination to keep up with it. She just didn't care that much. It wasn't that she liked having Legos and books and board games scattered all over the house; she just didn't let it affect her the way it did James. On the one hand, Betsy felt bad about Claudia. She'd be depressed herself if she were in the same situation. Then again, she was paying Claudia to do a job, and she didn't have the time to pick up the slack. "It's just so busy at work right now," Betsy said. "I don't want to have to deal with these domestic issues. That's why you pay someone."

When she came into work on the first Monday in March, Claudia spotted the note from James on the kitchen counter. It was going to be a long week. Betsy was in London for five days of meetings. With their mother gone, Jackson and Lucy would need more attention, and Claudia prepared herself for the challenge of working alone with James. She picked the note up, read it over, and then put it back down, her face remaining expressionless. It didn't bother her one way or the other. Nothing did these days.

The apartment was quiet, the counters clear, and the top of the dining room table was bare. With Betsy away, the house was un-characteristically neat. Passing Lucy and Jackson's room, Claudia was surprised to see pictures on the walls and new comforters on the beds. Claudia was pleased to see James had done things for the kids over the weekend. An entire wall was lined, top to bottom, with books, and James had built a bunk bed so Jackson could have his own space. A mobile of racecars swayed from the ceiling.

Claudia left the apartment and walked down the street toward Lucy's school. The air was warm, but the sky was a heavy steel-gray. The clouds cast a shadow on the neighborhood, and the streets looked colorless: the buildings, the sidewalks, even the newspaper stand and cluttered storefronts seemed flat and lifeless.

She opened the door to Lucy's school and the gloomy day burst into Technicolor. Bright orange strollers stuck out in hallways, and children's paintings covered the walls, making a bold collage of reds and yellows and blues. Mothers and nannies clustered together as children in pinks and purples and greens and blues ran around them, demanding snacks and play dates and undivided attention as they told breathless stories about their school day. A few nannies said hello and nodded at Claudia. She parked herself next to Cynthia, and they talked about getting together the following week with the kids. Five minutes later, when Lucy's class was over, Claudia stepped inside to get the little girl. A smile spread across Lucy's face and she ran over to Claudia. After the daily goodbye song, the pair headed out.

The two strolled down the street together as they did every day of the school week. Lucy held tightly to Claudia's hand, her head bowed in a rare moment of contemplation. Claudia was puzzled by the child's concentration, and then she realized Lucy was gazing intently at her own feet. She had on a pair of bright white, slightly oversized, brand-spanking-new sneakers.

"Did your daddy buy you new sneakers this weekend?" Claudia asked.

"Yes!" Lucy shouted with pride. Claudia felt a wave of affection and happiness for the child.

"Claudia, can I watch TV when we get home?" Lucy asked.

"You know what? It's nice outside. Let's go to the park after lunch."

"Just one little show!" Lucy demanded. Claudia ignored the child, ducking into the drugstore with Lucy and grabbing a discounts circular to read. Then they walked the rest of the way to the Halls' building and rode the elevator up to the sixth-floor apartment.

Lucy requested a nonnutritious lunch of buttered toast and a cup filled with one-half lemonade, one-half Coke to drink. Cringing as she poured out the lemonade and Coke, Claudia obliged, wondering if this was what James had served them to drink over the weekend.

"I said just a little bit of TV!" Lucy howled again in the apartment. Claudia was unmoved as she placed a plate and cup on Lucy's table and called the girl over to eat. Already upset, Lucy picked up the toast and scraped all the butter off until it hung from the tips of her fingernails. Then she stood up and began to cry, circling around the kitchen with her hands held stiffly in the air.

"Screaming doesn't help," said Claudia calmly. "You need to eat your lunch."

"Mommy! Mommy!" Lucy cried. "I want Mommy!" Then she begged for television again and asked for a chocolate chip cookie.

"Cookies is not lunch, Lucinda. You know that," said Claudia with a smile. She was amused by the child's persistence.

"It's not funny!" yelled a furious Lucy.

Claudia sighed, put down the magazine she was reading, and wiped off Lucy's hands. Finally, she coaxed Lucy into taking a few bites of toast before she handed her a cookie. Then she went back to her reading, flipping through the pages. She picked up the family calendar and saw that after Betsy returned from London, they were having a ninth birthday party for Jackson at Lazer Park. Two weeks after that, the family was going to Aspen to ski.

If Cap came to town again while the Halls were away, Claudia would have to figure out some way to spend her time off. She could not stand the thought of watching him sitting on the couch all day like he was king of the castle. Even after he'd taken the money from her account, Claudia still felt she had to let him stay in the apartment when he visited, for Tanisha's sake, but Claudia refused to spend time with him herself. If she had the money, Claudia would fly to Miami and stay with a friend who lived there. She could go see her brother in New Haven, but Cap would probably insist on joining her.

After a while, Lucy calmed down and began to play with her Angelina Ballerina board game in the living room. Then Daisy called to invite Claudia to the playground later in the day. Claudia agreed, hung up the phone, and tried to reach Royette to invite her along too. Royette had finally landed a job. As it turned out, she was working in the same neighborhood as Claudia, in a building along the West Side Highway with views of the Hudson River. She had held out as long as she could for a $600-a-week salary, but in the end she had to take what she could get. Now she was putting in fifty-five hours a week caring for a five-month-old baby and making $450 off the books. Royette lived in fear of losing this family too and made Claudia promise to keep the job a secret from their friends until she was sure it was going to last. So far it was a good job and the people she worked for were decent, but Royette complained that the apartment was so stuffy, she was sure she and the baby were coming down with colds.

"Claudia?" Lucy asked quietly as her nanny got her dressed for dance class and the playground.

"Yes?" replied Claudia, pulling the girl into her arms.

"I miss Mommy."

"Well, where is she?"

"In London."

"Oh. Well, then, she went to visit the queen?" Claudia giggled.

"No!" Lucy laughed. "She went for work, but I really miss her."

"Before you know it, Lucinda, she'll be right back here with us," said Claudia, hugging the child. "She'll be right back here with us."

"Good," said Lucy, and the two headed out the door.

Although the winter freeze had lifted, Claudia was still dressed as though snow could fall at any minute. Her puffy down jacket zipped all the way up, newsboy cap on her head, her practical brown boots on her feet — the ones Tanisha called her "white girl boots" — she huddled next to Daisy on a playground bench. All the other nannies loosened their scarves and took off their hats, but Claudia shivered, clutched her collar with her hand, and breathed out through her mouth, half expecting to see her own breath in the chill. Then the sun broke through the clouds, shining directly on the bench.

"It's warm out here," said Daisy. "Why don't you take your jacket off?"

"I'm cold. I'm always cold," said Claudia.

"This summer I'm going to take the kids to Battery Park and go to the playground there." Daisy quickly looked around the park and located Violet, playing underneath a jungle gym. "This playground gets too crowded."

"I'm not going over there," said Claudia, standing up to look for Lucy. "It's too, too far."

She walked to the other side of the playground, scanning for a blond head. Lucy was playing with a pack of girls her age. Turning around, Claudia headed back toward Daisy but caught the eye of a man wearing a pair of shorts, the same crazy father from Lucy's fall ballet class. Claudia nodded her head at him and hoped to avoid a conversation.

"Claudia!" he called out, walking over to her with his hands in his pockets. "Just the one I wanted to see."

"Oh yeah?"

"My wife and I are having a party, and we're looking for a babysitter for the night. I thought you might know someone who wanted to make some extra cash."

"I might."

"There's no cleaning involved. But the woman can't be big because she has to climb the stairs."

"Okay," Claudia said and looked around. She had no intention of recommending a friend to work for this man. There was an awkward moment of silence and then the man turned away.

Back at the bench, Daisy was settled next to a nanny with dreadlocks and a kind, deeply lined face. Claudia liked the woman, knew she worked part-time while she went to school, but could never remember her name — Lolita — until at least ten minutes after she saw her. Lolita wanted to be a schoolteacher. Over the next couple of hours, the three women chatted, fell into silence, kept their eyes on their own children and anyone else's they recognized. They commented on the weather, on their children's schedules and personalities.

Lucy surfaced to have her shoelace tied and gave Claudia a quick hug. Violet came by next and giggled with Daisy, who affectionately called her "V." Lolita took her baby out of the stroller to give her a bottle.

"How are things going with Mr. Grumpy?" Daisy asked when Lucy and Violet had run off again to play.

"Oh, they the same. He always in a bad mood."

"I don't know how you deal with that," said Daisy sympathetically.

"I'm going crazy in my own way," said Claudia. She raised her eyebrow, gave a little smile, and finally unbuttoned her jacket. Even she had to admit it wasn't that cold out.

Claudia took Lucy straight to ballet class in order to avoid running into James back at the apartment. Daisy kept her company the entire way. They moved at the slow, meandering pace of a family, stopping to tie a shoe, to point out a single red balloon flying overhead, to wait for the light to change even when there was no traffic coming. Other pedestrians rushed by the foursome, pocketbooks thrown over shoulders, faces set in serious, unwavering expressions. It was a fast-paced weekday and everyone had important things to do, important places to be, but Daisy and Claudia took it slow, oblivious to the world moving so quickly around them. They were on kid time.

Ballet class was about to begin, and all the little girls were antsy. They bounced, laughed, waved their hands in the air. As soon as the teacher called them, they took off down the hall, blurs of pink and black. One child stayed behind as her babysitter finished pinning her hair and then gave her hug after hug after hug before sending her off. Preferring her Bible to conversations with nannies, she was the quietest caregiver of the bunch.

Classical music played softly on the other side of the loft, making its way over a makeshift divider of white bookshelves. They held an eclectic mix of books: a Webster's dictionary, *War and Peace, Love Medicine* by Louise Erdrich, a novel Claudia had heard about but never read. Recently she'd devoured *The Lovely Bones*. She'd found it in the basement at work while she was doing laundry, and loved it.

There were five nannies in the room and no mothers or fathers. When the dance instructor walked in, they sat up a little taller, a little straighter, and fell silent.

"Can you bring this to Mom?" the instructor asked in a loud voice to a woman who spoke perfect English. The nanny took the note without saying a word.

Thigh to thigh on the couch, Daisy and Claudia leaned back and began to chat about manicures and weight loss. Claudia took off her coat and laughed with her friend. She was cheering up.

"I used to be so skinny! Even skinnier than her," Daisy said, pointing to a petite Asian nanny reading a *New York Post* someone else had left behind. "I tried that Atkins diet for two weeks but it made me sick. It wasn't healthy."

The nanny with the Bible put it down and slowly made her way to the bookcases to spy on her child dancing. Daisy and Claudia watched the woman come back smiling.

"You know, they're too young for all these classes. They're just back there running around," Daisy said to Claudia. "If a child shows promise or talent at something, then I understand putting them in a class to encourage them. But otherwise it's just a waste of money. There are people starving in the world."

"Well, if one child in the neighborhood goes, they all go," answered Claudia.

"I just took Violet to her private-school interviews," Daisy told Claudia. "I have to be the one to do it because if she goes with her mother, she clings to her."

"Why doesn't she go to the public school around here?"

"I don't know why they want to waste their money. Everyone

knows the school here is really good. I didn't like the private schools anyway. They interviewed Violet, but they didn't take the time to really see her. Except for Brooklyn Friends. They took the time, and I'm glad she's going there. At least it's not the Little Red School House. That place is too, too elite."

Class ended, the girls returned, and the nannies snapped into action. Claudia and many of her nanny friends had opinions about their kids and their schedule of classes, but they generally kept those opinions to themselves. They observed the families they worked for and made their own assessments, but they did not share their thoughts with the parents unless they were asked. It was a line they did not cross.

"Where is my child?" Claudia called out affectionately, pulling Lucy into her arms. On the way out the door, Daisy and Claudia paused and looked at a piece of paper taped to the wall. It was a Xeroxed photo of President George W. Bush smiling, his face crossed out and the words "Bush is scary, we want Kerry" scrawled underneath. Repeating the rhyme like a song, they laughed as they headed down the stairs.

Claudia decided to spend the rest of the afternoon back at the park, avoiding James altogether. She had one more hour to kill before she had to pick Jackson up at soccer. Daisy sat with her. Claudia unzipped her jacket and relaxed as they continued chatting. She smiled, made jokes, laughed for the first time in weeks. Lucy and Violet stayed out of trouble and for now, the job seemed easy.

As the afternoon turned into early evening, one by one the nannies gathered their children and snapped them into strollers. Some toddlers cried and arched their backs, desperate for a few more minutes in the playground. Others fell back with a sigh and let themselves be pushed home. The screams of children dimmed and the park grew calm. Empty Baggies and paper plates from the nearby pizza place lay under benches. One lone sippy cup sat on the ground near the playground gate. Finally, Claudia stood up, stretched, and said her goodbyes to Daisy. She called out to Lucy, who came willingly.

"Will Daddy be home?" the little girl asked as she walked with Claudia to pick up her brother.

"I don't know. Probably," answered Claudia, checking for on-coming cars before leading Lucy across the street.

Claudia looked down at Lucy, caught the white flash of her new sneakers, and thought of the new comforters on the kids' beds at home. She remembered the mobile on the ceiling. She imagined James at home alone over the weekend, running around taking care of the kids, pouring them Coke and lemonade to make them happy. She pictured him organizing their room and how happy his children must have been watching him make the changes.

James was difficult and moody and angry, but Claudia felt she could see deeper, past the bluster and the huffing and puffing, to his heart. Inside, James was a good person. She was certain of that. For eight years, she had seen him love his wife and kids. The problem, as far as Claudia could see, was that James was not at peace. He wasn't happy at his job so he'd quit. Now he worked for himself, but he had not found the satisfaction he'd been looking for. James was frustrated, and sometimes his frustration blew right out of him.

Now that Claudia thought about it, she and James were not all that different. No matter how hard she tried, Claudia never felt she'd done enough with her life. She'd moved to a strange country, sent money home, raised a daughter, and here she was, still long-ing for more. James had finished college, was successful and well paid, had a great wife and two beautiful children. As far as she could see, he'd achieved the American dream. Yet when Claudia looked at him, she saw the frustration etched into his forehead, the clenching of his jaw. She recognized that longing.

"James wants to get someplace too," Claudia said, sympathizing with her boss. "But like me, he just don't know how to get there."

FIFTEEN

OPENING HER EYES early on a Saturday morning in September, Kim looked around at her third home in three months. This was a hotel room Brian had insisted she move into so he could tear out her closet and attack the water damage he was sure had taken over. Kim had resisted the move because it made absolutely no sense to her. Why tear out and replace the closet now only to send her to live in a hotel again when they did more renovation a few months later? Why not do all the work at once? Brian ignored her resistance, made the hotel reservation, and promised Kim she would love it, claiming it would be just like having her own apartment for six weeks, only better.

The hotel was nothing like Brian described and Kim knew he would never stay in a place like this with his own family. A small room on the ground floor, her "apartment" came with a half kitchen equipped with exactly one fork, knife, spoon, plate, and cup. At night, after a twelve-hour day at work, Kim came back to this room and listened to people passing by her door. Then came the clomp, clomp, clomp as they walked up the stairs. Even with the curtains tightly drawn across the window that faced the parking lot, Kim still felt exposed listening to car doors close and people chatting just outside. She was relieved to be away from Brian in the evenings and to finally have her own space, but she resented the commute to work and having to once again pack her things up and move.

When the Porters gave her a spa certificate to thank her for her trouble, Kim held it in her hand and doubted their motives. In the past, she had always been touched when employers bought her gifts or wrote her notes of thanks, but this certificate felt like an empty bribe. Money came easily to Brian — he threw it at all kinds of problems. It was a true feeling of gratitude that eluded him.

These days, Kim resented everything about her job, and on this Saturday morning, the morning of Cooper's baby dedication ceremony, she found herself dreading an event she would normally have looked forward to. Kim loved birthdays and celebrations, but her other families had always invited her as a guest. The Porters had acted like they were inviting her as a guest on her weekend day off, but she knew that they would quickly put her to work. Kim would go because she loved Cooper, not because she felt like part of the family.

After several confrontations with Brian, nothing had changed for Kim in the Porter house. But instead of leaving, she had fallen into an old trap. She turned herself into a martyr. "It's a pattern with everything in my life," she explained. "It's not what I want, it's what's best for everyone else. And it's gotten me in a lot of bad situations, this putting everyone else's wants and needs in front of my own."

This was not a trait Kim felt was exclusive to her. It was a classic personality flaw in many of the nannies she knew, women like her who chose nannying as a career. They were natural people pleasers who had trouble speaking up for themselves, who found confrontation almost painful. "Anybody who puts themselves last tends to be in a service position, which is what we are," she said. "In our world, your complaints are about the way someone keeps a house or the way someone is a parent. It's a very difficult world to complain in."

Picking up the phone, Kim called Diane to get her dose of support for the day. The deeper in she got with the Porters, the more Kim had begun to rely on her old boss for validation that she wasn't crazy. Diane was always on her side, always the first to point out that Brian didn't know how valuable a great nanny was and showed Kim no respect.

"You could get there late," Diane suggested when Kim said she didn't want to be put to work on her day off. "Just say your alarm didn't go off and then when you arrive, everything will be set up already."

Kim toyed with the idea but climbed out of bed and headed to the shower instead. By the time she was dressed, in a long skirt and blouse, her hair blown out straight and her makeup on, there was already a message on her cell phone from Holly, asking Kim to stop off on her way to the house and pick up all the food for the guests. Grabbing her keys, her purse, and her gift for Cooper, Kim headed out to begin what she knew would be a day of errands and following orders.

Kim drove to Central Market, a gourmet supermarket with catering services. At Brian's request, Kim had done most of the planning for this fifty-person event. She had even, as instructed a month earlier, noted where the sun would hit at the exact time of day the dedication would take place so the rented chairs could be strategically placed in the shade. Kim had laughed at Brian. He prided himself on this kind of attention to detail but he didn't listen to her when she pointed out that without her room available, the Porters would have only one working bathroom for a large number of guests. It was bound to flood.

Kim parked the Accord in the lot outside the shop and rushed inside. Makeup on and hair blown out, Kim was a more sophisticated, elegant version of her workday self.

The woman behind the counter met her with a blank stare when Kim requested the Porters' order. Asking a few other employees, the woman then informed Kim that the order was never placed. Back in the car, after doing some quick thinking, Kim called the other Central Market in the area and found that the Porters' food was on order there. It was a twenty-minute drive away. Why hadn't they bothered to give her the right store location, Kim fumed, worried that she would miss Cooper's big moment. Already on the phone with Diane to vent again, Kim began driving.

"Now how hard is it to tell you the right Central Market?" sniped Diane, feeding into Kim's growing irritation.

"If they start the ceremony without me, I'm going to be furious," Kim told Diane, and then she hung up to take a call from Brian on the other line.

"The toilet is backed up," Brian said quickly. "I need you to get a plunger."

Kim sighed to herself, and then she had to laugh. Just as she had predicted, the single toilet couldn't handle the number of guests. It did feel good to be right.

"Mr. 'Things Have Got to Be Done My Way' is screwed, and now he doesn't have a bathroom for all these people!" Kim said to Diane, calling her with another update.

Pulling up in front of the house, Kim's mood shifted once again that day. It was quarter past eleven and she was sure she had missed the ceremony, a major milestone in Cooper's life. Parking the car, she noticed the florist still running around with flowers, more than two hours late.

"Is it over?" she asked Paul when she walked in the door.

"It hasn't started," he answered.

"Oh my God!" she said. She hurried back to the car and began unloading the platters of food.

Slowly, one platter at a time, Kim walked across the muddy lawn and up a flight of stairs, putting the food on a table set up in the back. The guests sat on chairs on the shady patch of lawn. Brian spotted Kim and waved, but he didn't get up to help her with the food. Paul, who had begun shooting with the video camera, didn't come to help either. As her skirt dragged through the mud, and sweat dripped down her forehead, Kim realized that nobody was helping her because she was the help. Trip after trip, not a single person offered her a hand. The ceremony began. Paul looked at her, shrugged his shoulders, and kept filming. After climbing what Kim thought must have been four hundred stairs, she made her last trip to the car and double-checked to make sure it was empty. Instead of returning to the house, she got in the driver's seat, started the engine, and drove away without saying goodbye.

Kim spent the rest of the day holed up in her hotel room, watching movies. The next morning, she woke up and returned the gift she had bought for Cooper. She had already given him *The Giving Tree,* and she'd reconsidered spending the money on an expensive outfit too. Holly had left several messages by now, but Kim did not return a single call. "This is it," she told herself, the black-and-white reason she needed to quit. Over the past months, she had already called her nanny placement agency several times for advice. When she described the situation, they assured her repeatedly that she could leave and it wouldn't be a mark on her otherwise stellar record. But Kim had been waiting for a single event that would allow her to quit guilt-free, and now she had it.

Kim had become, in the short time since she had moved into the Porters' house, a disgruntled employee, the type of person who kept count of everything and complained all the time, the type of person she herself avoided being around. When Brian left his dishes in the sink, she simply washed hers and left his right where they were. Because she did not feel like part of the family, Kim viewed this job differently than all the others. There was no incentive to go the extra mile.

Her journal, which she'd started in an attempt to deal with her divorce, was instead littered with complaints about Brian. Along with those complaints was a running list of physical ailments and a daily tally of her weight. She had regular bloating and stomachaches, and often counted the number of laxatives she took when she gained just a few pounds. After hitting 112, she vowed to eat only salads for two days. Under so much stress, her old food issues had resurfaced.

This was not the healthy, caring person she wanted to be. Paul came to work every day with a smile on his face and a consistently upbeat personality. She was the negative force. She had a hard time getting through a single day without complaining about her job. And, even worse, she was uncharacteristically smart-mouthed.

One evening when Holly and Brian were planning to head out with the baby to see friends, Kim witnessed a fairly minor scene unfold that managed to rile her up. Holly clearly didn't want to go out, and Cooper was asleep, but Brian insisted on waking the baby up so that they could leave the house on schedule.

"He needs to be fed before we go," Holly had said to Brian. Kim stood in front of the sink washing bottles, listening to the exchange. As she predicted, Brian shut her down: "We don't have time," he said. Kim felt a pang of sympathy for Holly. She knew Holly would prefer to breastfeed in the privacy of her own home, and that Cooper hadn't eaten for four hours.

"You know," Kim had remarked to him in passing as Brian ushered Holly and Cooper out the door, "at some point you've got to learn to put your child first."

"Bye," he had said dryly as he closed the door behind them.

On the Sunday after the dedication ceremony, Kim finally returned Holly's many calls.

"Brian was up all night," Holly said. "He was just so upset. It was his son's big day. He just didn't understand how you could do this to his son."

Kim was caught off-guard. Holly was distraught. She was sure that something awful must have happened to make Kim walk out in the middle of the event, after leaving all that food in the sun.

"First of all, when I left it out there, it wasn't in the sun," Kim told Holly. "I just felt so disrespected that I had been running all over the place and no one helped me."

"I'm so, so sorry," Holly said. "We really didn't realize what was going on."

She apologized for herself and for Brian, who'd had no idea so much food had been ordered. He had thought there were only one or two platters for Kim to set out. On the one hand, Kim was sure it was just an excuse Brian had made up. On the other hand, it was a plausible one. What if it was true? The entire day had been a disaster. She wasn't so sure about quitting now. What if it was all just one big miscommunication?

The next morning, Kim went to work.

Kim's first day back had been calm and uneventful, but Holly was finally clueing in to the fact that things weren't working out between her nanny and her husband. She called a meeting with Kim and Brian and tried to mediate the situation before it got completely out of control. Kim was relieved Holly was intervening. She hoped it would make things better.

They sat on the sectional, piles of toys and books and half-empty boxes cluttering up the room just as they had the day Kim arrived. As soon as Kim began to express her concerns, stressing Brian's controlling behavior, his lack of respect for her as a professional, career nanny, Brian's face went red and he sputtered in anger, denying her charges.

"When I was working for my last company, we had a team-building weekend and the theme was being a compassionate person," he spat, glaring at Kim. "You don't even know what that means."

"Yes, I do know what it means," Kim said evenly.

"Well, if you know what it means then you would be compassionate, because you are not compassionate and a compassionate person is someone who does good, who puts other people first, who doesn't always think of themselves first."

Kim sat silently staring at Brian. "You have no idea who I am," she thought. She was the one who did her best to put Cooper's nursery together just right. She was the one with constant stomachaches and hair falling out just because she didn't want to abandon Holly and the baby. She was the one who remembered everyone's birthdays and anniversaries, buying gifts and always, always sending cards, even buying special, fun stamps if they were going to children. She was the one, at seventeen years old, who bought her father his own set of dishes and silverware when he moved out of her mother's house for good.

Kim sat as still as possible. Using all her willpower, she did not bounce a leg or move a finger. She could not remember even blinking. If she moved just one inch, Kim knew she would not be able to stop moving. She would fly out the door for good. All she wanted in this moment, when she could not breathe because the air was so tight, was to get out of there.

"I know this is a difficult living situation," Holly said, agreeing that they were all in tight quarters and pointing out that Kim still didn't have her own space. "I've discussed this problem with my parents and they both said, 'You know, she's used to being in a home, by herself, full charge. She's not used to being around all these construction guys and Paul.'"

"I have no problem with that," Kim interrupted. "I love Paul being around. I love the construction guys being around. I have no problem with that. But I cannot have so many changes in my life. Moving out of Sam's house, then moving into a bedroom-bathroom situation until I get my space, then moving to a hotel, then I'm moving back here to more construction and not knowing when I am going to finally get my own space."

"Well, we need to talk about that too," Holly said.

"The construction won't be done on the house," Brian added. "You won't have the apartment we promised by January. It's going to be at least another six months. There have been so many delays." He was calmer now, hands clasped together on his lap.

"Maybe we can give you more room," Holly offered. "You can have our office and the bathroom and we'll just make the upstairs the living room. But if we have a guest, then your area has to be used for guests. Of course, we also understand if you want to leave. This isn't the living situation we promised you."

Kim agreed to stay but declined Holly's offer to change rooms. She told herself once again that if she could just ignore Brian, this job would work out. Cooper was such a loving baby and Holly really needed her help and she always looked forward to hanging out with Paul, talking about his girlfriend and laughing about Brian's quirks.

On Friday evening, Paul left the house for the weekend after saying goodbye to Kim. A few seconds later, Kim's phone rang. She expected it to be Brian but Paul's name came up instead.

"Hey," Paul said softly into the phone.

"Hey," answered Kim with a smile.

"Turn around," he said, and she turned to face the window. Paul stood outside, a big smile on his face. "Have a nice weekend."

Kim smiled back. It was a sweet moment and it made her happy. It was just the kind of thing that kept her from quitting her job.

For the first time since starting with the Porters, Kim woke up looking forward to her day. Brian had meetings out of the house, which meant she could pass the hours with her two favorite people: Paul and Cooper. The sky still dark, Kim turned on a light and climbed out of bed. She ate her breakfast in front of the morning news. Kim now made a habit of eating her meals in private — if she ate in public, Brian inevitably managed to find her and put her to work.

Since the dedication ceremony blowup a few weeks before and the end of Kim's stay in the depressing hotel room, Holly had returned to work full-time, leaving Kim alone with Brian for twelve hours a day. Kim stayed in touch with Holly at the office, sending her text messages and e-mails with pictures of Cooper taken all over the house in different poses so Holly could still feel connected. Paul often came up with ideas for the photos, from spiking Cooper's hair to silly outfits he could wear. Brian glanced at the pictures without even a hint of a smile. He was still impossible to work for.

A few days after she moved back in from the hotel, Brian stopped the microwave while it was still going, pulled Kim's dinner out and put his own in to warm up, leaving hers on the counter. Instead of calling Brian on his behavior, Kim took a deep breath and tried to ignore it. Over the next few days, she let her frustration out by talking to friends and family, telling and retelling the microwave story over the phone. Once again, they all urged her to quit.

Putting her bowl in the sink, Kim headed upstairs to see Cooper. She loved the mornings, when the baby greeted her with a smile as she pulled him out of the crib, pressing his tiny body against her chest as he nuzzled his face in her neck. Downstairs, in the blissful quiet, Kim gave Cooper a bottle. A couple of hours later, Paul arrived, bringing his work into the living room so he could hang out with Kim for the day on the Porters' sectional. Brian's mail was spread out before Paul on the glass coffee table.

At around noon, they ordered lunch and continued to camp out in the living room, taking bites of food as they chatted and worked. Kim held up a book, reading to Cooper as he sat in his bouncy seat. Paul spoke to Kim about the latest drama with his girlfriend. Almost ten years younger than Kim, Paul often came to her for advice about his love life, while she relied on him to listen to her complaints about Brian.

"Oh! This is interesting," Paul said with a smile, pulling a Victoria's Secret catalog out of the pile of mail. It was addressed to Brian.

"Oh my God!" Kim laughed as she looked at the half-dressed model on the cover.

"We should do a photo shoot of this to send to Holly today," Paul suggested. "We'll prop the magazine in front of Cooper like he's reading it."

"That would be hysterical," Kim agreed.

The photo was meant to be a joke, a silly shot of a three-month-old boy sneaking peeks at sexy ladies in lingerie. Months later, remembering the exact moment she decided to go along with Paul's idea, Kim would shake her head, wondering what she was thinking. Embarrassed, cheeks growing slightly red, she would insist it wasn't in line with her personality. Just as they were about to set up the shot in the bouncy seat, Brian walked into the house. Spotting the catalog on the table, he immediately grabbed it.

"No, no! You can't take that!" Kim said with a smile, reaching out to grab it back. "That's going to be a photo-op for Cooper. Paul is going to take a picture of it in front of Cooper and underneath we're going to write, 'Uncle-Paul-Approved Reading Material,' and then we're going to send it to Holly at work."

"I don't know if that's such a good idea. Are you sure that meets with nanny's approval?" Brian said, eyeing Kim.

"Yes," she answered.

"Well, if it's approved by nanny then it's okay with me," Brian said as he walked out of the room, heading to his office.

Kim and Paul laughed together as they propped Cooper up in front of the catalog. Typically modest by nature, Kim covered the side of the catalog in Cooper's line of sight with a copy of the book she was reading him, *Goodnight Gorilla*. It was a silly idea and a silly photograph but Kim hoped Holly would enjoy it. The day Holly had gone back to work, she had cried and held on to Cooper. She had worked through most of her maternity leave and now she would be gone even more. Kim felt awful for Holly. It wasn't the first time she had seen a mother torn between work and staying with her baby.

When the photos were taken, Paul and Kim decided on the best shot and e-mailed it to Holly at her office.

"Ha. Ha. Very funny," Holly wrote back.

Their fun time over, Paul and Kim got back to work. Paul sorted through the rest of Brian's mail while Kim washed bottles in the tiny kitchen. The bottles drying on the rack, Kim picked Cooper up and headed upstairs to feed the baby and put him down for his nap.

• • •

An hour later, just as Kim was about to put Cooper in the crib, Brian flung open the nursery door. It was still bright outside, and late afternoon sun filled the room. The banging and drilling of the construction crew had come to a stop for the day. Brian stood silent for a moment, breathing heavily. Kim immediately recognized the look of anger on his face from their past fights. His face was bright red, and sweat shone across his forehead. Brian's eyes narrowed as they focused on Kim, who was standing with Cooper in her arms. Kim's heart beat fast. She was scared and intimidated. The first thought that entered her head was the time. It was 4:00 P.M., the exact time the construction crew usually went home. She didn't want to be alone with Brian and she hoped Paul hadn't left for the day as well.

"You took the picture!" Brian screamed at Kim. "After all of that, you took the picture anyway."

Before Kim could speak, Brian turned around, stalked out, and slammed the door behind him. She heard his footsteps as he stomped downstairs. Kim stood for a moment, confused and startled. Then she began pacing across the room, holding tight to Cooper. Five minutes later, Brian reappeared. Now Kim was terrified. If she screamed and the construction crew was there, she knew they would come running to her rescue. But she was alone, except for the baby in her arms, as Brian exploded into rage. He had checked his e-mail between visits to the nursery and received a note from his wife about the picture.

"Don't you ever do this fucking shit again!" he screamed, his entire body shaking.

Kim thought she would fall down on the floor right there if she wasn't holding Cooper. She held the baby even tighter. He kept her upright.

"You are such a bitch! I don't know who you think you are!

You're trying to cause problems between me and my wife! You're opening my mail. You're planting things to destroy my marriage. How dare you? Who the hell do you think you are?"

"Brian, calm down," Kim said softly. Her entire body shook. Nobody, nobody in her entire life, had ever spoken to her like this before, not her brothers or her father or either of her ex-husbands. Everyone who knew Kim knew not to even swear around her because she hated it so much. Now here was her boss, a sweating, angry man who was twice as strong as her, cursing away.

Then, as quickly as he had come into the room, Brian turned around and stormed out again. Kim stood in shock this time. She didn't move. She could barely think. Brian sounded paranoid, making wild accusations. She thought again of Andrew Morrison. She was still clutching Cooper when her cell phone rang. It was Paul.

"Are you all right?" he asked.

"No," she answered, relieved that he was still in the house.

Paul came upstairs to check on Kim. She took one look at him, put the baby back in his crib, and began to shake uncontrollably. Paul helped her to the glider.

"Breathe," he said.

"Did you not hear when we explained to him exactly what we were doing and he said, 'If it's nanny-approved, it's fine'?" Kim asked when she was calm enough to speak.

"Yes. And I will absolutely back you up on that," Paul answered.

After Holly came home from work that evening, Kim listened anxiously to the soft murmur of husband and wife talking upstairs.

When the house was quiet outside her door, Kim finally typed the resignation letter she had wanted to write since her first night in the Porter house. If the dedication ceremony and Brian's daily criticisms hadn't been enough of a reason to quit, this latest episode definitely was.

No matter how much she loved Cooper or felt for Holly, the price of working with Brian was too high for Kim. Her letter was short and to the point and she gave Brian and Holly one month's notice. When she was done, Kim opened her bedroom door and walked to Brian's office, placing the letter on his desk. Then she left a telephone message updating her nanny placement agency.

Exhausted, Kim spent the next few hours lying in bed. She heard Brian and Holly busying themselves in the office, and knew that they had found her letter. Her room was as cold as it had been her first night at the Porters' and she shivered under her blanket, remembering that this day was also the two-year anniversary of Andrew Morrison's death. Once again, she thought of Sam and the life she had lost. All night long, Kim thought about her door and how it didn't have a lock on it and how at any time, Brian could fly right through it.

The next morning, nobody said a word about the letter. Brian walked in and out of his office without looking at Kim, and Holly rushed out the door for an early meeting. Confused by their reaction, Kim simply went to work, getting Cooper dressed for the day and giving him his morning bottle. When she went into the tiny kitchen to wash her dishes, Brian stepped out of his office and walked toward her. As they stood side by side in front of the sink, Kim wrung out the sponge without making eye contact. She hated it when he stood this close.

"Well, we got your resignation," Brian said flatly. "I'll get in contact with the agency and have you replaced."

Kim stayed silent.

"The best thing to do in terms of replacing you and talking to new nannies and you getting another job is to say that it didn't work out because your private apartment wasn't ready. And that you're going through a divorce, so your private space is important to you."

"That's fine," Kim agreed. "But I don't want you to say anything about the divorce, because that has nothing to do with what happened here."

"Okay," Brian said.

Then he walked out the door with Paul. Kim was finally alone. As bad as the night before had been, this was a good day. Kim had the house to herself and she was free. The episode with Brian was just the sort of thing she had been waiting for. It was her guilt-free ticket to quit a job she had made a one-year commitment to. This was it. Kim found herself surprised and even a little thrilled that her resignation had been accepted so calmly.

"Well, I heard," Paul said glumly when he returned from lunch with Brian.

"Oh, yeah? What did he say?" Kim asked.

"He said that you had given your notice and that you had given him five or six weeks and that there was just a lot of tension and cramped quarters and that now your space in the new house was going to be delayed."

Looking at Paul, Kim realized how much she would miss him. Then she began to think of Cooper. She had started with Cooper the second he was born and she had hoped to be with him for years. Now she had to let go early, before he turned from baby to toddler to boy.

"I will never see you roll over," she thought, looking down at Cooper. "I will never see you walk. I'm not going to hear what your voice sounds like. I'm not going to see what color your hair turns into." Kim repeated these sentences in her head for the rest of the day as she held Cooper or looked down at him in his crib. Gazing at the sleeping child, she began to feel awful for him.

"I hope you get a really good nanny," she said as much to herself as to him. "Because you're going to need all the help you can get."

Even though she knew it was arrogant, her guard went up just thinking about another nanny taking over for her. Nobody could take as good care of Cooper as she did. No matter how bad the job had been over the past three months, Kim's commitment to her work as a nanny had never wavered. She had fallen in love with this long, skinny child, with his funny smile and upbeat personality.

Over the years, Kim had let go of many children she loved, including her own stepchildren. The first time she left a child was the hardest. After two years with that little girl, Kim cried openly when she said goodbye. Within blocks of the house, she had to pull her car over to the side of the road because she was sobbing so hard. For the entire week afterward, Kim could still feel the girl in her arms. Leaving Cooper would be difficult, but it was a process Kim was used to by now.

"As the years go by it gets easier," Kim said. "I don't know if that's an age thing, if when I was younger, I didn't protect my heart as much. It's not that I love them less now, because you can't help yourself. You say you're going to protect yourself, but you just can't. You definitely go through withdrawal afterward."

"I'm just surprised that the first big thing that happens like this, you would quit," Holly said over the phone to Kim later that day. Kim explained that the incident with the picture had been only the latest of many.

"Holly, it's been happening," she said gently.

"Is there anything we can do to change your mind?" Holly asked, agreeing that Brian had overreacted. "I know that Brian has a problem with the way he deals with people; he even has a workshop coming up to deal with his issues. Maybe that would help?"

"I'll think about it," Kim said, but in her heart she knew she was leaving.

• • •

It was not the easy goodbye Kim had expected. Holly begged Kim to stay while Brian wooed her with his money. First came little presents. Spa certificates, gift baskets, scented candles. Then came wild promises of her own rent-free apartment and a car in her name. None of Brian's gestures changed Kim's mind.

"I apologize," Brian said one afternoon, catching Kim alone with Cooper in the nursery. "The way I spoke to you was wrong. I've never spoken to anyone like that. And it won't happen ever again."

"I accept your apology," Kim answered, and then she took a deep breath before she continued. It was getting late and Kim was nervous. The construction crew was gone, Paul was gone, and Holly wasn't due home for at least an hour. She was alone in the house with Brian. Holding Cooper close to her, she continued. "But I have a really hard time accepting that at thirty-five years old, somebody acts like that for the first time in his life. It's just my experience with people. I can't fully believe you."

"I was just very upset that you were going through my mail."

"Brian, I have never, ever done that. I didn't even open my husband's mail. You asked Paul to go through two boxes of mail that day and he found the catalog."

"I know you're right. It was Paul. I'm sorry I yelled at you about it."

But the conversation did not stop there, where it should have, with a mutual acceptance that they simply weren't the right fit. Instead, Kim was suddenly faced with an intimacy she did not want or ask for. It was a classic live-in nanny situation: an abrupt, awkward closeness based more on proximity than authentic connection.

"It's just that Holly's very insecure about her weight, her body," Brian began, trying to explain why he was so upset about his wife seeing the catalog addressed to him, propped up in front of his son in the photo. He began to cry. "Holly is just really reserved about the whole subject of sex. I thought the e-mail would just really upset her."

Kim stared at her boss from her chair. Her ears buzzed. She wasn't even aware of breathing. She did not stand up. She did not stop him from talking. Somehow her body lifted outside of itself, as though she were above it all and in her mind she simply repeated: "This is not happening. I am not hearing this." She wanted to run but she kept silent instead, willing the conversation to be over.

"If you stay," he said, "we *will* buy you an apartment."

"I'm shocked," she finally answered after a long pause. "Given the way we've been butting heads, I'm shocked that you would want me here. You know you need someone a little bit younger, someone you can control more."

Pain ripped through Kim's stomach. She didn't know if it was something she ate or the tension or an ulcer suddenly erupting, but she knew she had finally, after over an hour of talking, had enough. She stood up, put Cooper in his crib, and turned to Brian.

"I'm sorry, I have to go."

"Okay, we'll continue talking about this," he answered.

The next evening was a repeat of the first. Brian cried and begged Kim to stay as she sat in the glider with Cooper in her arms. He asked her to seriously consider staying on the job while he was away for the next few days on a business trip. Kim knew it would be the best thing for her to do financially, but she just couldn't see doing it.

She had never been in the job for the money, and while she had been drawn to the perks of this job, she was willing to take a pay cut, to do whatever she had to in order to find a better job. If working for Holly and Brian had taught her anything, it was that money could buy a lot of things but it couldn't buy her. When their house was finally finished and magazine perfect, she knew it would be the same exact place it was now: claustrophobic, isolating, and miserable.

Downstairs with the baby, she stood in the doorway watching Brian pick up his bags for his trip. Paul stood nearby, finishing up some last-minute work. Brian walked over to Kim, gave her a hug, and then paused with tears in his eyes before kissing her forehead. Once again, she was stunned. Pulling back, she looked up at his tear-stained face as he turned to walk away.

"What was that?" Kim asked Paul after Brian was finally gone.

"I have no idea!" he said, throwing up his arms.

The next day a huge floral arrangement arrived. The day after that came a basket of bath products.

"You need to stop this. It's too much," Kim told Holly, assuming they were from her.

"I'm not doing it, Brian is."

Kim began making her final plans to leave.

For the first time since she'd left the house she'd shared with Sam, everything fell into place. While Brian and Holly kept their hopes up that Kim might change her mind, she moved forward. Diane had suggested Kim come back to work for her, and then Diane's husband, Jeff, suggested that Kim look into buying a townhouse of her own. Diane followed up their conversation with a long e-mail.

"If you don't leave this job, I'll slap you silly," joked Diane. "But if you decide to stay, I'll support you. Even when Brian chops you up into little pieces. I'll be the one to put them all together and bury them in a coffin."

When she had a good day at work, joking with Paul, cooing over Cooper, who was becoming increasingly interactive and cheerful, she felt pangs of regret.

"Brian should leave instead of me," she said to Paul.

"Let's vote him off this island!" Paul said, laughing.

But they both knew it was already over. On her next day off, Kim drove back to Georgetown, passing Sam's house. He had cut down the tree in their front yard and finally put up the white picket fence she had always wanted. Staring at the house, she missed him desperately. She wanted to feel her husband holding her again. She wanted to grow old with him, like they had promised. She had left phone messages, sent e-mails and text messages about seeing him and the kids, but nothing was returned. Staring at the house now, she thought, "I can't believe that we will never have forever." But eventually, she drove away.

Kim found her new townhouse much more quickly than she expected, a modest place tucked in a complex in Northwest Hills. The complex was built in the 1970s and showed some signs of age, but it was also comforting. At the beginning of October, all her plans in order, Kim finally called Holly at work and told her that her resignation from a month earlier still stood.

"Why are you leaving?" Holly asked yet again, and Kim found herself sighing. How many times could she explain herself? How many ways could she diplomatically tell this kind woman that she had married a jerk who was impossible to work for?

"I don't know how you can stand him!" she wanted to scream, but instead Kim told Holly it just wasn't the right fit.

When Brian heard the news was final, he approached Kim one last time with tears in his eyes. She stood, unmoved.

She was, she realized, tired of the struggle of her life. She was worn out from her breakup with Sam, from the pain of still not having her own children. She was exhausted from her long conversations with Brian.

She did not cry when she left, because it had already been a long, drawn-out goodbye. She had been quietly, slowly letting

Cooper go during her final days. She would miss Cooper terribly, from the way he smelled to his bright morning smile. She wished she could take him with her to her new life and protect him forever. She wished she could make sure he did not grow up to be like his father. But she also accepted that she was just a nanny who had stepped into Cooper's life for a brief period of time. Hugging Cooper for the last time, Kim handed him over to his parents, who stood together in the doorway.

"You'll see him again soon," Holly said as she took Cooper in her arms.

"Yes, I'll come over and we'll all take a walk," said Kim.

"That's a good idea," Brian said with a smile.

Kim got into her own car, a beat-up Mazda stick shift she had bought used from a fellow nanny. Driving back down the hill, Kim told herself she would visit Cooper soon and always stay in touch with Paul. But deep down she knew, even though they had all promised to make an effort, that she would never see the Porters again.

SIXTEEN

VIVIAN WAS BACK in Wellesley the day after her Nanny of the Year speech, running on almost no sleep. Hair wild, face drawn and pale, she was dressed in a pair of loose jeans that hung low on her hips and an oversize white T-shirt with a picture of a Mary Poppins carpetbag on the front. White sneakers on her feet, arms tucked inside an old blue fleece, Vivian was once again transformed. Midnight had struck, she had turned back into a pumpkin, the fairy tale was over. She might have won Nanny of the Year, but right now she had a job to do.

Charging around town, Vivian marched into various stores, searching the aisles for Pokemon party favors. Catherine had assured Vivian she would take care of the boys' birthday party, only to throw the planning back on Vivian at the last minute. She was irritated that Catherine hadn't given her a specific budget, not to mention any guidelines. Vivian had pressed her on how much she wanted to spend and what her expectations were for the party, but Catherine had simply shrugged and told her to get whatever she needed.

Devan and David had requested a Pokemon party, and though Vivian wasn't happy with their choice, she'd cleared the shelves in Wellesley of all things Pokemon — plates and napkins, tablecloths and hats. She'd picked up the piñata. At around eleven, she ducked into another store, hoping to find even more Pokemon paraphernalia. Rolling her eyes at an incompetent salesperson, Vivian flipped open her cell phone, called information, and grilled another salesperson at a store across town about its Pokemon stock. She had one hour left to shop before the boys got out of school. She had to be quick. On her way out of the store, she grabbed a stack of blue folders to use in the membership kits for her local nanny group. Over the weekend, at the INA conference, she had signed up several new nannies from the Boston area. Heading up to the counter to pay, she looked tired even from behind. Head slightly bowed, shoulders hunched, swaying side to side, she was beaten down and close to tears. The tension of the last few months, working nonstop, waiting to hear if she had won and then preparing for the big day, had taken a lot out of her. She was overly sensitive, stretched to the limit, and a little bit paranoid.

Back in the car, Vivian sighed. At moments like this, she hated adults. They were idiots. Nobody moved fast enough, nobody knew how to take care of business. Nobody could handle things like she could.

"I have more patience for children than adults," she huffed, her eyes growing wet. Adults were fools who got in the way of her goals, including Catherine, who was being way too laid-back about the party. Kids were just kids. They could be trained and molded.

Vivian had taken on the biggest goal in the industry and achieved it, just as she had planned. She had stood before her colleagues, impressing them with her speech and bringing tears to their eyes. She had conveyed to everyone in that room, with Devan and David at her side, just how important this job was. Now it was all over. She had a party to plan, but what was the bigger, driving purpose? Vivian promised herself she wouldn't lose sight of her professional objectives. Back on the job, she was just an average person running errands. But Vivian would never settle for average. By the time her term as Nanny of the Year was over, she vowed with renewed energy, she would be a media star.

At noon, Vivian walked through the gate at Chipmunks. Children scrambled across the gravel-covered yard as usual as she pulled out a newspaper article that had run over the weekend about her Nanny of the Year win. It was an impressive spread. In a perfect picture taken in the Pritchards' family room, Vivian sat on the Thomas the Tank Engine rug, Devan and David leaning in on either side to kiss her cheek. Now surrounded by the boys' teachers, back in the spotlight for a moment, Vivian passed around the article, taking in all of their congratulations. When she spotted David and Devan running toward her, her expression changed immediately.

"What happened?" she asked sternly, investigating a trickle of blood coming from David's nose. She stuffed the newspaper back in her bag and kneeled down to address the boys at eye level. "You were playing Pokemon, weren't you?" she asked as she wiped David's nose with a Kleenex.

The boys kept their eyes to the ground, their mouths drawn in deep frowns. They looked sad and vulnerable but Vivian didn't buy it. She kept coming at them from every angle, interrogating them until they finally confessed that they had been practicing their karate moves on each other. Vivian reminded them that they had been told specifically by their coach never to use karate on each other outside of class. Parents milling about, teachers standing nearby, Vivian didn't hold back. She lit into the boys, telling them that they would not be going to karate class that day, threatening to take away other privileges, and expressing her deep disappointment in their behavior.

In the car, Vivian called Catherine and left a rambling message about the karate episode. Pulling into the driveway, she told the boys to go play in the backyard while she got their lunch ready. That morning a crew had arrived to add a climbing wall to their cedar swing set, and she knew the boys were eager to explore it. She didn't like rewarding their bad behavior, but she took the opportunity to sneak all their birthday gear into the front room of the house.

After the car was unpacked, Vivian started a pot of water to boil for lunch and checked the Weight Watchers points on a Frappuccino she had had that morning. Glancing out the glass doors, she watched the boys fly by.

"You climb up the rock wall and then you slide down the pole!" she yelled through the open door. "Once you get up there, and whenever you're up there, I want that trapdoor closed. If you hit someone, you're done."

Devan, of course, immediately climbed straight to the top, teetering over the edge.

"Whoa, Devan! Hold on tight," she called, joining them outside. The wind had kicked up and there was a chill in the air. "Are you cold? Do you need your jackets?" she asked.

The karate incident behind them for now, the boys played happily. Vivian watched them for a while, then turned to go back inside.

"I'm going inside to make your lunch," she called out. "Do you guys want to play inside or outside?"

"Outside!" they sang.

"Okay. But do not leave the yard." She paused as Devan began climbing up the wall again. "Careful, Devan! Two hands!" she yelled from the door.

Inside, Vivian went about her business. Her mood had improved being around the boys, even if they were in trouble. When the phone rang, she guessed that it was Catherine.

"So," Vivian began. "Devan and David did karate on each other and David got a bloody nose. And that's not okay so I figured I should mention it. And I should call you and scare the crap out of them. That's why I left you that long message. Devan knew he was in trouble." She spoke with her boss about the birthday party, and after they'd agreed on a course of action to address the boys' behavior, Vivian hung up the phone and got the boys' lunch together.

By the time she'd called them inside, their cheeks were flushed, the karate incident long since forgotten. Given the green light from Catherine, Vivian brought it up again after they ate.

"You will tell Coach about the karate incident and that you gave David a bloody nose." Vivian lifted Devan's chin and looked him in the eye. "You're telling him, not me."

"Me?" Devan's green eyes grew larger, his cheeks burning red. He couldn't have looked sweeter in that moment but Vivian was unmoved.

"Yes, you," she said sternly. "And he might not let you do karate anymore. He might make you a white belt again. Or Coach might take a stripe away. That's my feeling."

"The yellow stripe?"

"The character stripe? Yes, maybe. The yellow stripe is the one that says you did good behavior and good listening. Or maybe the pin. He might take away the pin. I don't know. You'll have to talk to him on Thursday, since you're not going today."

Devan and David stood in silence. Vivian peered at their faces, calculating whether they had listened, understood the gravity of the situation, and knew to never repeat the behavior. Satisfied her words had sunk in, she sent them back outside to play.

Vivian smiled to herself. She had told the boys they couldn't go to karate class, but the truth was they didn't have class anyway. They were both scheduled for a doctor's appointment, something Vivian had been looking forward to for a while so she could look the nurse who had been rude to her right in the eye, so that nurse could watch her in action with the boys and see how integral she was to their lives. She walked toward the glass doors and watched the twins play. The day was only half over, but all her earlier frustration was gone. She had taught the boys another valuable lesson.

When her contract with the Pritchards expired in May, Vivian didn't push for a renegotiation immediately. By June, though, she knew she had to resolve the matter with Catherine. In the past, Vivian had felt guilty asking for a raise, because she loved the boys so much. Now she pushed all the guilt out of her head. Vivian asked Catherine for a salary increase of a dollar an hour. With the boys quietly settled in front of a movie and Catherine just home from work, the two women had a tense discussion in the kitchen.

"I can't afford that," Catherine said, shaking her head. "My whole salary will go to you."

"But you have a retirement package. You have all this stuff coming out of your salary," Vivian answered quickly. "You have a combined salary with Trevor. So that's only a percent of your whole household salary going to me."

It was the classic nanny-parent conflict: A nanny wants more money from a parent who already feels strapped. The parent worries about saving for the kids' college education or getting a better place to live or taking a summer vacation. With little or no savings, and often living from paycheck to paycheck, nannies view those expenses as luxuries, shaking their heads as they tell their friends that their employers claim they can't pay more. They point to Bugaboos in playgrounds, BMWs in driveways, upgraded apartments or houses, and ask each other, "If they can afford these things, why can't they pay me more?"

The boys were happily engrossed in the movie, blissfully unaware that their own future was being negotiated. Outside, the swing set, with its new climbing wall, stood empty. The bushes in the yard were perfectly manicured. A fresh green lawn was slowly growing over the patchy brown of winter. A shadow passed over the yard as the sun set.

"I've got the bling bling here!" Trevor sang out happily, entering the house through the side door, carrying a large box. He set the package down on the countertop, and Vivian saw that it was a new cappuccino maker. She shot Catherine an "I told you so" look, the edges of her mouth turned into a mocking half-smile. If they could afford another overpriced toy, they could afford a dollar-an-hour raise for their nanny. Trevor quickly made himself scarce, sensing the mood in the room.

"You're working less hours now. The boys are in school," Catherine argued. Another classic nanny-parent conflict: the parent questions paying a nanny the same salary when her children are in school, but still expects the nanny to be on call, to pick the kids up from school and get them to their various afterschool activities.

"I didn't get a raise last year at all," Vivian pointed out.

As the women stood in silence for a few moments, at an impasse, Vivian looked around the room. It was such a sunny, cheerful place to spend her days. Her love and dedication were everywhere, in the carefully labeled toy bins and the intricate scrapbooks she had put together. No matter what Catherine said, no matter how hard she tried to argue, Vivian knew she wouldn't back down.

"Have you been unhappy with my work in any way?" she asked.

"I think you went on a witch hunt against David's teacher," Catherine said, referring to Vivian's dislike of Sylvia. With her hair pulled back in a black headband and a plain cotton shirt on, Catherine looked almost like a child herself. "You think David can do no wrong."

"Please!" Vivian sputtered. Catherine knew Vivian came down hard when the boys misbehaved. "Anyone who has seen me around those kids knows I think they can do wrong."

"But you're too protective of the kids," Catherine said, and Vivian didn't argue. She knew it was true and she didn't care. In Vivian's eyes her protectiveness was perfectly natural, what should be expected of any nanny.

The back-and-forth continued, touching again on what was going to be expected of Vivian when the boys started kindergarten.

In the end, Vivian was successful. She walked out of the house that evening with the best contract of her life. With health insurance and other benefits, Vivian would earn about $50,000. She would also have her INA conference and membership fees covered.

Vivian was pleased with herself that night and she was pleased with herself the next morning. In years past, she would have woken up worried, feeling bad about asking to be paid to love. But now she knew her worth. She was the INA Nanny of the Year and that kind of nanny could make twice as much money as the Pritchards paid Vivian, even with her new raise.

Winning Nanny of the Year had given Vivian a new perspective; she felt more relaxed about where she stood in the Pritchard family, less compelled to control the boys' upbringing or be an equal player in the family's decision making. While still staunchly committed to Devan and David, she was taking her new title seriously, seeking out as much media attention as possible.

"The last Nanny of the Year didn't really do anything," she explained with a half smile. "The standard has just been raised."

Along with the feature article in the *Boston Globe,* Vivian appeared in the *Daily News Tribune,* the *Boston Parents' Paper,* and *Twins* magazine. She also went live on local television as a nanny expert. Continuing her activist work, she wrote a letter to the *New York Times* blasting the efforts of New York City–based Domestic Workers United to establish a minimum hourly wage of $14 for nannies. She argued that salaries should instead be awarded on merit. She contacted the United States Office of Exchange Coordination and Designation to highlight problems she saw with the agency's au pair program. In her opinion, too many inexperienced women who participated in the program to work part-time and see America were being hired as full-time childcare providers.

Vivian was growing up, right along with Devan and David, who had left toddlerhood behind for full-fledged boyhood. With every accomplishment, every pound she lost and every accolade she received, Vivian's confidence grew. At twenty-eight, she had swung wildly from overconfidence to deep insecurity. After she won Nanny of the Year, she cut Reed off for good, made her peace with Trevor, loosened her grip on the boys, became active in her church again, and promised to join her congregation on a missionary trip to Kenya.

Shortly after her salary renegotiation, Vivian got her first big opportunity. A literary agent who had read her feature story in the *Boston Globe* contacted her, asking if she'd be interested in writing a book. Vivian went straight to work, putting her best pieces of parenting advice down on paper.

"I'm going to be bigger than Oprah," Vivian joked. "I'm going to be the Dr. Phil of nannies."

She knew, without saying it aloud because she still loved the boys, that she was itching for something new. Her only hope was that, when the time came, the job ended well and they were all ready.

In the end, Vivian's break with the Pritchard family came just days before Christmas. There was no blowup between her and Trevor, no tortured showdown with Catherine — no one quit and no one was fired. Trevor was simply offered a job in Los Angeles that he agreed to take. Catherine broke the news to Vivian, who did not fall apart. Instead, this very attached, very protective, very controlling nanny remained unusually calm. She knew Devan and David were ready to live without her daily guidance. She had given them an internal moral compass, taught them how to regulate their own behavior, and instilled in them a deep sense of love.

"When I think about it, it's crazy," Vivian said with a sigh, remembering how young she was when she first took the job with the Pritchards. "The kind of responsibility I had. I raised those boys."

Even with her own book on childcare about to be published and lots of ideas for what she would do next, Vivian had kept her focus on the job as the boys entered kindergarten.

"We had a fight on the first day of school," Vivian said, laughing. "Catherine didn't think the boys needed new school clothes. I'm like, 'This job is almost over anyway. I'm not sending my kids to school looking like a grub.' So I bought them new school outfits. I paid for it myself and Catherine was pissed that I went over her, but I didn't care. I thought it was my job to be an advocate and make sure they weren't teased and didn't look like retards."

Watching the boys adjust to a full-time school schedule, Vivian knew instinctively she wasn't the only one ready to let go. David and Devan had absorbed the lessons she had taught them. On a trip to the Museum of Science in Boston to see a laser show, David suddenly refused to enter the theater, planting his feet on the ground.

"I'm scared," he said, looking up at Vivian.

"You're not scared!" Vivian answered, pushing him forward. "You've never been scared, until the last time when you went with your mother. We're going in."

"I'm not going in!" David shouted as people pushed past him to enter the theater.

"You're walking or I'm carrying you in, because I know you're not scared."

Vivian finally reached down, pulled David up like a toddler, and carried him into the theater, where he was absorbed by the show within minutes. In the past, this disagreement would have carried over all the way home, Vivian explaining at length why she did what she did, while he sulked in the back seat. But that night, David was the one who did the explaining.

"I'm fine. I knew you weren't being mean," he told Vivian as they walked hand in hand through the museum. "You just knew I wasn't scared from last time."

And later, after another incident of bad behavior, David told Vivian, "I know you were never mad. You were just trying to teach me something. I know you weren't mad. You just wanted me to learn. You wanted me to make a good choice."

"How did you know I was being fake mean?" Vivian asked, smiling to herself.

"Because I know you love me."

Vivian couldn't have asked for a better indication that the parting was coming at the right time. She was proud of Devan and David, and of herself. Vivian vowed never to get so close to a set of twins again, determined to do a good job but to protect her emotions and focus on her personal life the next time around. The boys, meanwhile, knew that she disciplined them because she loved them; it was her voice they heard in their heads, helping them make the right choices.

"It's just like Mary Poppins said: We come to do a job and when the wind changes, it's time to move on," Vivian said.

She made sure each boy packed a box for himself to send on to Los Angeles. She advised Catherine to have their room set up for them in the new house before they arrived. Together, she and David and Devan picked out their goodbye outfits. Then she helped them say goodbye to their friends, assuring them they would all stay in contact.

The week before the Pritchards moved, Vivian had the boys to herself while Catherine and Trevor traveled. They woke up in the morning, chatting as they got ready for school. At the end of the day, she picked them up, and they spent the afternoons talking and hanging out, curling up together on the couch. One night, while all three lay in bed watching a movie, Vivian let a few tears stream down her face. They were the only tears she would shed.

On her last day as the Pritchards' nanny, Vivian drove David and Devan and Catherine to the airport. The boys were spending Christmas with their grandparents before leaving Wellesley for good. Trevor had gone ahead.

Inside the airport terminal, with people rushing everywhere, fluorescent lights overhead, and a loudspeaker going off every few minutes, Vivian said goodbye to Catherine, then leaned down to hug her boys goodbye one last time. Finally, she stood and watched them slowly disappear, two little black-haired boys, the loves of her life, heading to the other side of the country. When she could no longer see them, Vivian turned and left.

• • •

Vivian dropped the keys to the Chevy Tahoe on the counter, looking around the Pritchards' family room for the last time. The room was empty, the walls bare. The smell of fresh paint was in the air. Closing her eyes, Vivian could put the entire room back together in her mind, piece by piece. But this was not her job anymore, and it was not her home.

She had made phone calls to Catherine and to the boys' doctors and coaches and teachers and other parents from this room. Standing at the counter, she had felt Trevor slip past without saying a word. She had fed the boys and read to them and dozed on the couch with them countless times. This was the room where David and Devan were raised, Vivian taking on the day shift, Catherine taking weekends and evenings. Vivian did not hold the title of mother, but she knew with utter confidence that she was in a category all her own.

"Don't worry," Catherine had said to Vivian before they left. "You'll always be part of the family. You will always be a part of Devan and David."

There wasn't a single doubt in Vivian's mind that she would remain a part of the boys' lives. Someday, she knew, she would watch David and Devan get married, she would stand beside them as they took that step into adulthood.

Vivian left the house by the side door, just as she always had, and walked down the driveway to her own car parked on the street. She turned on the engine, buckling her seat belt and glancing in the rearview mirror at the empty seats behind her as she pulled into the street. Making a right turn, Vivian drove away from the Pritchards' house for the last time, heading back home to the Bentley.

SEVENTEEN

TWO MOTHERS STOOD on opposite sides of a playground, a wooden hanging bridge, a slide, a shiny silver pole, and a set of stairs between them, worrying about their children. They were both well dressed and looking their best. Betsy was in a short black summer skirt, mules with delicate heels on her feet, an antique necklace wrapped three times around her neck. Claudia was wearing orange and white right down to her manicure and her new pocketbook. She looked new and fresh, like the beginning of spring, even though New York City was deep into a humid summer. When winter had gone for good, Claudia had taken the tight twists out of her hair, replacing them with soft, purple-tinted waves.

The first month of summer had passed better than she'd expected. Jackson and Lucy had been more fun than trouble, and James hadn't been around as much. Now she was gearing up for vacation. The Halls were going to the Berkshires for the month of August. Tanisha was scheduled to fly to Miami to stay with her aunt. For the first time in years, Claudia would be free of children.

No Jackson. No Lucy. No Tanisha. She could get up when she wanted, go back to sleep if she felt like it, and eat at any time of the day. It was a luxury she could hardly even imagine as she sat in the park, eyeing her boss and keeping track of the kids.

"Betsy looks good today," Claudia remarked to Royette as the two sat together on a bench. "I told her this morning she looked sexy."

"She does look nice."

"But she shouldn't ride the subway with that necklace on. It isn't safe," Claudia said, forehead wrinkling.

Royette pulled her baby out of her stroller. Her pale arms jerking as she began to whine, the child twisted in Royette's arms. Royette popped a bottle into the baby's mouth, rested her foot on the red stroller, and sighed. "This is a child who cannot sit still."

Claudia wasn't listening to her friend. She was watching her boss standing underneath Lucy on the jungle gym, grabbing the child's legs as she scanned the park looking for Jackson. Betsy had come to the playground after a lunch meeting to catch a half hour with her children before she headed back to the gallery. In fact, an hour had already passed since she'd joined them, and as Claudia watched Lucy cry when her mother tried to leave, she knew it would be a very long goodbye. She estimated it would take Betsy another forty minutes to pull herself away from the kids.

Betsy, who had never felt guilty about having a nanny care for her children, had suddenly been hit this summer with the feeling that her children needed her more than ever. They weren't just babies with basic needs to fill: a new diaper, a warm embrace, a bottle. Now her kids had complicated lives of their own, social landscapes to navigate and academic challenges to overcome.

She didn't stress about Lucy, who, bursting with confidence, threw herself into any situation. Jackson, though, was more sensitive. Over the past year, he had been having trouble with friends, who were mostly into sports like baseball, basketball, or football, none of which interested her son much. His response was to push hard for them to play video games or freeze tag, to plead for their attention. Betsy watched him chase after the other boys. She wished she could shake him and tell him to be cool, play hard to get.

Betsy was sure of Claudia's love for Jackson and Lucy and told herself that was the most important quality for a nanny to have. But she wanted Claudia to help Jackson manage some of his problems instead of brushing his behavior off or leaving him to wrestle with his feelings on his own.

Claudia didn't offer her thoughts or advice about Jackson's problems. She had taken note of his behavior since he was small, before he'd even started school. He could read through ten books, but whenever Claudia asked, he refused to write. Rather than go to Betsy or James with her concerns, she kept her observations to herself, stayed out of the situation, and figured it would all get resolved in good time.

"Some girls go in and take over and the parents don't like that, but they don't say it," said Claudia, outlining her laid-back strategy. "So I'm not the type to go in and take over. I do what I have to do. It's your family. You go in and do what you have to do. I didn't go right in there and say, 'Betsy, you should give Lucy Carnation instead of Similac.' Some girls do that. If she asked my opinion, I would say, 'Let's try it this way.' But she don't ask."

Last week, Jackson had had a complete meltdown, and Betsy hadn't been there to soften the blow. Sitting in the playground with Lucy and Claudia, Jackson had grown bored, as usual. He wasn't a little kid anymore. He didn't want to go down slides or run through sprinklers. He wanted to go home and hang out with a friend or play with his Game Boy. He'd begged Claudia to take him home and asked a friend to come with them. On the way out of the playground, the friend's mother declined the invitation, saying her son had other plans. Jackson threw an all-out tantrum on the street. The mother walked ahead without a word, leaving Claudia to pick up the pieces.

"I don't like one bone in that woman," Claudia had told Betsy when she got home. "She didn't do one thing to help. She could have suggested another play date, but she just walked away, and Jackson was hysterical."

"Next time something like that happens, call me so I can get on the phone and talk him through it," Betsy said, wishing she had been there to manage the situation.

While Betsy fretted about Jackson, Claudia was busy worrying about her own child. Tanisha had disobeyed a direct order and had had her ears pierced for a second time. Now her ear was infected and Claudia had to make a decision. Should she let her daughter keep the piercing or should she remove the earring and let the hole close up? It wasn't the piercing itself that concerned Claudia; she was worried that Tanisha's defiance was a sign of things to come.

Sitting in the park with Royette, she went over the conflict. "She told me, 'But Mommy, I didn't know you wouldn't want me to do it!'" Royette was settling the baby down in her stroller. "Now I don't know what to believe."

"Oh please! She know what she's doing!" said Royette.

Claudia was sure that Tanisha was on the right track, but she didn't want her daughter to go astray when she wasn't around to monitor her behavior. A few weeks ago, Claudia had returned home earlier than expected, and the apartment had been empty. Tanisha was somewhere out on the streets.

When her daughter came home with a friend, Claudia hid in the bedroom, put her ear to the door, and spied on her daughter. Tanisha's talk was all innocence, banter about clothes and cute boys, nothing to worry about. Later that night, she grilled her daughter about her whereabouts that afternoon.

"You want to protect me from everything, Mommy," Tanisha told her mother. "I'm a big girl. I'm getting older. I need to get out. My friends call and they say, 'Tanisha, what are you doing? Are you in the house? When are you ever going to get out of the house?'"

Claudia felt for her daughter and knew she had to start letting go. It had been a tough year for them both. Tanisha had been evicted along with Claudia, and then she'd witnessed the final breakup of her parents. On Cap's last visit, in the spring, Claudia had confronted him on the rumors she'd heard, that he'd had a baby with another woman, but he denied it. After yet another fight, Claudia had had enough. She no longer believed a word her husband said to her. It was time to cut Cap loose for good.

Bracing herself for a confrontation, Claudia told Tanisha, "Your father can't stay here anymore."

"You go, Mommy!" Tanisha said, surprising her. "But can Daddy visit at all?"

"He can come visit if he want. I don't own America. But he can't stay in this house."

Since her father had left, Tanisha had become needy and clingy. She had ended up in summer school. If Claudia had been home more, she thought, she could have made Tanisha focus. If she'd been home, she could have kept her off the streets. As often as Tanisha called her mother at work, Claudia still worried.

Twice in the previous two months, Claudia's apartment had been robbed, which only worried her more. Every day she reminded Tanisha to double-lock the door, keep the phone near her, and look behind her when she came into the building. There was no damage to the door, no lock picked, no signs of forced entry. But Claudia's purse and DVD player had been taken. She had asked her daughter if it was any of her friends, and Tanisha swore she hadn't let anyone into the apartment. Claudia changed the locks, but she never told Betsy and James about the theft. They had helped her out with the eviction; they didn't need to do more.

Claudia continued watching Betsy as she thought about Tanisha. Still unable to leave the playground, Betsy took the kids to the ice-cream truck. In a pink bathing suit with a skirted bottom, a big smile on her face, Lucy raced over to Claudia with a bar in the shape of a face with a bubblegum nose. Her blond hair sticking to her cheeks, her legs streaked with dirt, she was in heaven.

"Do you want a lick?" she asked her nanny.

"You promised me the bubblegum."

Lucy dug her fingers into the center of the face and pried off the nose. Claudia popped the gum into her mouth with a smile. Lucy raced back to her mother, who was now sitting against a wall with Jackson. When Lucy was done with her bar, Betsy rubbed more suntan lotion on her daughter. Lucy grabbed it and rubbed it on Betsy, who laughed and then picked up her bag to leave.

"Just stay a little longer!" Lucy pleaded with her.

"Can you get dinner started later?" Betsy asked as she walked over to Claudia, hoping to steal away. "Lucy, I have to get to work."

"Just a little longer!"

Betsy didn't promise to stay, but she didn't leave either. Jackson asked if he could have a friend play at home, and Betsy tried to talk him out of it. She knew his friends would turn him down, preferring to stay at the park, and she hated the thought of him being rejected again.

"Everyone is happy in the park now, Jackson. No one wants to go inside," Claudia said, sensing Betsy's worry growing. Betsy would never get to work if Jackson's frustration escalated. Claudia wanted to tell Betsy that everything would be fine. Boys would be boys. It was true that Jackson had his awkward social moments and needed extra help organizing, but Claudia had also been there when Jackson's friends came running to him, begging him to play.

"I want to leave the park!" Jackson whined. Betsy glanced at her watch, shook her head, and dropped her bag. She leaned in to whisper in Jackson's ear. Claudia went back to her conversation with Royette. This was a mother-son moment, none of her business.

Betsy put her hand on Jackson's head, telling him to breathe deep. His body relaxed. Soon he settled down on the bench next to Claudia, and Betsy handed him a book. Within a few minutes, he was lost in its pages. Betsy flipped her hair, pulled her bag back up over her shoulder, and kissed Lucy on the top of her head.

"Keep an eye on Jackson," Betsy mouthed to Claudia.

"Betsy, I've been doing that since a long time ago," Claudia answered with a smile.

"Now for the easy part of my day," Betsy said as she turned and made her way through the playground gates.

Claudia watched Betsy as her boss walked past a child screaming in his stroller, stepping under the shade of a tree and then out into the bright sun near the gate. She reached the cement path that led to the sidewalk, weaving through strollers and kids and nannies and mothers. As she picked up speed on the other side of the gate, she did not look back. Claudia caught one last glimpse of Betsy, the sun glinting off of her antique necklace. Claudia shook her head when she noticed the necklace, wishing she had remembered to tell Betsy to take it off before she got on the subway. She hoped Betsy would be safe.

Three weeks later, Claudia was on summer vacation in Brooklyn, surprised by how much she missed the children. Her last day of work before vacation had been endless, and the kids whined through every hour of it. James was out of the house running errands; Betsy was busy tying up loose ends at work. Claudia had invited Cynthia and Kai over to make the day go faster, but all three children acted aimless, on edge.

Cynthia blamed it on the rain and humidity. Even with the air conditioners blasting, the air in the apartment was close and heavy. The children parked themselves in front of the television, which blared with cartoons. Claudia stood at the kitchen island leafing through a magazine. A catalog on her lap, Cynthia dozed off and on. Tanisha had called almost every twenty minutes, her low voice, amplified by the answering machine, filling the house until Claudia picked up. It was Tanisha's birthday, and she was mad that her mother had gone to work.

"I don't have my daddy here. I don't have you here. I don't have anyone," Tanisha had complained that morning as her mother walked out the door.

"That's not true. You've had me every day for the last thirteen years," Claudia had shot back, and finally Tanisha had smiled.

Alone now in her apartment, it was easy for Claudia to forget how she felt on that endless last day of work before vacation. Jackson, Lucy, and Kai had tested her patience, Lucy throwing a huge tantrum when all three children tried to set up a store in the hallway of the building, selling their own belongings to neighbors. Claudia had dragged them back inside, and Lucy had erupted into tears.

Her hands raised in tiny fists, Lucy had screamed at Claudia: "You're the meanest babysitter ever! I don't want to see you!"

Slamming the door to her room, she'd left Claudia a little amused and a little bit hurt.

Jackson had ignored Claudia altogether and quietly continued to set up the store behind Claudia's back until she caught him, marched him to the couch, and told him to stay there.

"I'm going to have to talk to your parents about the way you are both acting," Claudia threatened, and Jackson crossed his arms.

"I'm really going to sell this stuff to people in the building and make money," he insisted, having stacked the family's books out in the hallway.

"You're going to be putting those books back."

Then Cynthia's cell phone rang and she went into the corner of the room to talk to her husband. Recovered from her fit, Lucy finally made her way back out of her room and walked over to Kai. Claudia pulled out an arts and crafts box to keep the two younger kids busy.

"Claudia!" Cynthia called out, laughing. "My husband says you should go back to Dominica in August and get your oil changed."

"Oh, no!" Claudia said with a smile. "Tell him it's too late for that. I'm rusty. My bones are creaking. I'm done with all of that."

Claudia still wasn't ready to date. One of Cap's friends, a man from back home, had made moves on her, but she'd brushed him aside. Still, he called every weekend like clockwork. Whenever the phone rang yet again, Tanisha answered it with her gruff, dismissive tone. "Mommy! It's your Sunday stalker!" she always called out, laughing while Claudia took the phone and made small talk one more time.

The day had ended with all three kids climbing in and out of a large cardboard box, pretending they were packages. Claudia suggested they go outside, but nobody listened.

"My husband said it's so hot out there Mayor Bloomberg should make it a law that women don't wear underwear," joked Cynthia. "I bet he would like that!" Claudia had answered coolly.

At first, Claudia's vacation had been bliss. She had a list of things to do, and she'd accomplished every task with plenty of time to spare for just sitting around. The first thing Claudia tackled was her $11,000 in credit card debt. She'd answered an ad for bankruptcy in the local newspaper, *Caribbean Life,* and made an appointment with a lawyer in downtown Brooklyn, two blocks from housing court.

A day later she found herself sitting across from a very nice woman who explained the entire process. For $760 — or two installments of $380 — Claudia could hire a lawyer who would handle the bankruptcy for her. Together, they weighed how it might affect her hope of going back to school to become a nurse. Would her bad credit make her ineligible for student loans?

"Nursing is a great idea," the woman said. "You could go to New York University. They have a good program."

Claudia laughed at the suggestion that she attend a school that cost thousands a year in tuition when she was just about to declare bankruptcy.

The second thing Claudia did was build a wall across her living room to surprise Tanisha with her own bedroom when she returned home from Miami. Royette's boyfriend did the job for her at cost. Claudia smiled just thinking about how shocked her daughter would be when she walked through the door. Claudia left a small space between the top of the wall and the ceiling so she would still have natural light in the rest of the living room, and so she could still listen to Tanisha's phone conversations.

Finally, she made her way to the library and picked up the list of GED dates. Sitting at her kitchen table, leaning on the white tablecloth, her head bowed above her bowl of ceramic fruit, Claudia looked through the GED dates for a time and place that best suited her needs. She would take the test even if her math was still shaky.

Now there was nothing left to do. Her apartment was neat, quiet, organized. She had thrown out all signs of Cap and added new touches around the apartment to help her forget him, replacing her pink bath accessories with a softer green, taking down old pictures, stacking the silk pillows Betsy had given her on her bed. Life was peaceful and under control.

Claudia was surprisingly uncomfortable with the feeling. For three weeks her life had been as perfect as the apartment across the street from the Halls', that childless oasis, the home where nothing was ever out of place. But Claudia felt empty and lonely. She missed Lucy and the way she threw her arms on her hips like a little woman when she made demands. She missed Jackson. She missed watching him read a book and spotting, just for an instant, the baby he'd once been beneath the boy he had become. Most of all, she missed Tanisha, her constant worry, her constant source of stress. She hadn't rolled her eyes once since Tanisha had left; she hadn't sighed or felt overcome with exhaustion. But she missed her little sidekick, the one who made her laugh, poked fun at her, and gave her what she thought she was still searching for: a secure sense of her purpose in this world.

All of Claudia's children made life harder, but they also made it richer and brighter. They had her heart. They were under her skin, whether she liked it or not, whether they were hers or the Halls'. "I feel like they're mine sometimes. Of course, it's almost been nine years. From baby, I grow up Jackson and Lucy. So sometimes you feel like they're yours. If you're lucky. If you're not just in it for the money. Sometimes I forget it's payday. It's like, I'm there for so long it's just part of my life. I forget I have to get paid until I see Betsy writing a check. Day to day, you forget," Claudia said in a rare moment of reflection. She dug up the Halls' number in the Berkshires and called, just to hear their voices.

"Lucy, it's me, Claudia. How's vacation going?"

"I miss you, Claudia," Lucy said, sounding distracted. "But I'm watching television."

By September, a week into the new school year, Claudia's mood had shifted again. She didn't miss the kids anymore; she missed her vacation. Things had changed over the summer. Betsy had announced that she was pregnant with her third child. Lucy had moved on from preschool to the pre-K program at the local public school. It was the same school Jackson had been going to for years, and Claudia stood inside once again, nodding hellos to the familiar faces while she waited for Lucy. She scanned the shelves at a book sale the parents were running in the lobby.

Lucy had a short day at school, and Claudia wanted to take the child home with her to Brooklyn to see where she lived. She had mentioned her plan to Betsy that morning.

"Is it safe there?" Betsy asked after she agreed to the trip.

"Where does she think I live?" Claudia thought to herself. "Does she think gunfire flies through the air all day?"

Then Betsy showed up at school, taking Claudia by surprise, saying she'd decided to spend time with Lucy that afternoon. Betsy's arrival meant there would be no trip to Brooklyn, but Claudia hid her disappointment. "I wouldn't bring her child to a place that's not safe. I see people walking with their kids in Brooklyn. A girl that lives just across the street from me brings the kids to her house. Cynthia bring Kai to her house to sleep, and all the girls bring the kids to their house to sleep," Claudia said, explaining her thinking.

Betsy was glowing and happy and content. Pregnancy suited her. Her black dress clung to her bulging belly and showed off her thin legs. A line of wooden bracelets slid up and down her arm as she moved. One of the parents from the book fair walked up to Betsy and Claudia, asking if one of them could run across the street to the diner and get change for their cash register. Claudia just stared at the woman. If she walked into a diner, a black woman, and asked for change, they'd look at her like she was crazy or a thief. Luckily, another parent stepped in and volunteered for the job.

Smiling at her mother and her nanny, Lucy emerged from her classroom. Her teacher, a young woman with great style, followed. Claudia always looked forward to seeing how the woman was dressed. Lucy hugged her mother, who led her out the door, telling Claudia to meet her at the playground in an hour.

A mother Claudia knew from Betsy's building stopped her in the hallway. "I heard Betsy's pregnant!"

"She is," Claudia answered.

"You've got a job for life now!" the woman remarked with a smile, but Claudia only saw a smirk.

"I guess I do," Claudia answered, and walked away.

Claudia could not get out of the building fast enough. She pushed through the doors and the sun hit her face. It still felt like summer, but Claudia knew cold was coming soon. Cars rushed up Greenwich Avenue, children yelled in the schoolyard, people raced past her on the sidewalk, but Claudia didn't see a thing. She headed to the playground a few blocks away, her home away from home, her office, her place to go to keep herself from going crazy. Anger filled her up, but she didn't know why.

The feeling was so intense, it took her by surprise. And then it hit her. This mother assumed Claudia wanted the job. She thought it was good news that the Halls still needed her. "She figured I wasn't good for anything in this life but being a nanny," Claudia said, her voice full of pain.

Despite the fact that she should have known better after everything she had been through that year, Claudia still told herself there could be more to her life than taking care of other people's children. With no savings, no education, and no experience outside of homes, Claudia sometimes wondered what would happen to her when she was too old to work. If the Halls, who were almost the exact same age as Claudia, retired someday, would she be retired too?

"When they have all their wealth and they're sitting on the beach retired, will they think of me?" she wondered. "Will they have something for me when I retire from them?"

All the nannies she knew worried about getting older with no savings, but they rarely talked about it. They were too distracted by the rent and their monthly bills to think about what might happen down the road. When Claudia thought about the future, she began daydreaming all over again. There was still time for her to get her GED, still time for her to apply to nursing school.

This mother at the school had assumed Claudia had no other plans for her future, that taking care of the Hall family was all she wanted. The woman had probably been trying to be nice, to be friendly, but a nanny would never have said those words to Claudia. "A nanny would say, 'Claudia, how you gonna cope with three, how you going to do it with three?'" explained Claudia. "Nannies would say, 'How you manage?' and then they would look to help me, saying 'I could watch Jackson while you run and take Lucy to dance class, and I could watch Lucy while you take Jackson to this or that.' That's how nannies operate."

Claudia crossed the street and walked into the playground.

Children were running. Nannies were pressed together in small clusters. Mothers were following their toddlers. Scattered around were bags of Pirate's Booty, pieces of fruit, and sippy cups. Claudia spotted an empty bench in the shade. She took a seat, dropped her bag next to her, looked around the playground, and leaned back. She didn't recognize anyone in the park, so she sat alone and tried to calm herself down. This was not the life Claudia was supposed to be living. Sighing, she crossed her arms, stared ahead, and waited for Betsy and Lucy to appear.

EPILOGUE

T HE LAST TIME I saw Claudia it was early in the morning. I was moving across the country to California, and I wanted to say goodbye. We met, as we often did, over eggs in a diner before she went to work. She liked white toast, her eggs fried. I spotted her from up the block as I approached the Q train stop near Seventh Avenue. On weekdays, we used to meet near her job in Manhattan, but time was tight that morning and she had agreed to meet me in Park Slope, Brooklyn, where I lived and she now worked. She threw me an amused grin as she watched me walk toward her with my newborn daughter, Georgia, strapped in a Baby-Björn.

In the past when we had met in Brooklyn on weekends, I always went to Claudia's apartment in Flatbush, and we would then make our way out into the neighborhood, stopping for a bite at McDonald's or to browse in a store. Once, we wandered into Prospect Park, where she was surprised to see the lake and the skating rink so close to her building. She immediately remarked that it would be a nice, peaceful place to read. I knew she would never actually go there on her own again.

Claudia was like that. She was wistful and longing, but life kept her to a fairly strict path of work and home, Lucy and Jackson and Tanisha. Long since broken up with Cap, she seemed a bit raw to me that morning in the diner, done with that specific man but still not ready to trust men in general. As we ate, I spoke nostalgically about Brooklyn and how much I would miss New York. She wondered what California was like. When I asked her about Betsy's new baby, the third baby, the child that had kept her on the job, I was surprised by her reaction.

"Oh, we are all in love with him," she said with a smile. "He lights up the house."

Nate had brought many changes. The entire family had moved from Manhattan to Brooklyn in search of more space. It was a shorter commute for Claudia but she had lost touch with all her Manhattan friends. After nine years in one spot, she didn't have the energy to start socializing all over again. Tanisha was keeping her busy, as usual. Most recently, Tanisha's high school, with a graduation rate of 36 percent, was labeled a failing school by the Board of Education and had closed. Once again, Betsy did a bit of hustling and got Tanisha an interview at a much better school in Manhattan. Tanisha was accepted and Claudia was hopeful that with a new crowd and more attention from teachers, Tanisha would graduate on time.

As we spoke, Claudia kept peeking over at my daughter, each time flashing Georgia a silent smile. She wasn't used to seeing me in this role. When I began working on this book, I was not a mother. Now that it was almost finished, I had two girls, Georgia and her older sister, Annabel. Motherhood had changed everything, of course. I now understood firsthand how vulnerable parents feel when they leave their children in someone else's care. Childcare became the central issue of my life. We couldn't afford a full-time nanny, and I quickly realized I'd be terrible at navigating the relationship anyway. I was the type of mother who would want the nanny to be her friend, who would worry about what the nanny thought of her and be uncomfortable in the role of boss.

I had managed to cobble together childcare through part-time babysitters, including my sister, and daycare. Often I didn't have enough hours of care to get my work done, and I fantasized about having a nanny like Claudia or Vivian or Kim, who could swoop in and free me from domestic life. As it was, my husband accused me of stealing my best parenting techniques from the women I met reporting this book, from wrapping our babies tight to soothe them, to sleep training, to time-outs.

Only toward the end of our visit did Claudia reveal her most intimate news. Taking a sip of her coffee, she put the cup down and looked me right in the eye.

"I saw my son, you know," she said. "We spent two weeks together. I traveled just to see him."

It was the first time Claudia had ever mentioned Dexter voluntarily, without me gingerly approaching the subject. Tanisha had flown with Claudia to the Virgin Islands, where Dexter now lived. At times the visit was awkward. She and her son didn't talk openly about her leaving him as a baby or how little they had seen each other over the years that followed, but she felt calmer about him now. A few times on the trip Dexter came up to her and whispered, "I want to tell you a secret." Then he softly kissed her cheek.

"I am not haunted anymore," Claudia said as she finished her coffee.

Vivian reaches out to me by every possible form of communication: cell phone, landline, e-mail, regular mail, instant messaging. After her job with the Pritchards ended, Vivian worked with two other families for about a year each. She also became a consultant, wrote four parenting books, and shifted her attention to her church, taking missionary trips to Kenya and Italy. She met her husband, Matthew, through a Christian dating website. They were engaged within three months, eloped shortly after, and she became pregnant.

She approached the birth of her own child with all the unbridled enthusiasm and focus she had brought to David and Devan. By the beginning of her second trimester, her baby already had a fully decorated nursery and a closet bursting with clothes and baby gear. I know; she sent me pictures of the actual closet and links to her registry and baby clothes. We batted around baby names.

Vivian had also interviewed and chosen her child's pediatrician, and she went to two obstetricians just to make sure she had covered all her bases. One was in the town where she lives with her husband, and the other, a highly regarded doctor in Boston, worked at the same practice as the doctor who delivered Devan and David. She worried, a lot, about the baby and her pregnancy. She already had the ultimate mother's dilemma: unable to live on one income, Vivian knew she would have to work. In her third trimester, she had been laid off of her most recent nanny job. At first, she called me in a panic. Then she quickly recovered and began planning to work exclusively from home as a freelance consultant and writer so she could be with her child. I told her she would be floored by motherhood. Laughing at herself, she agreed.

Yet, even with all this time and distance away from David and Devan, Vivian felt like she had already raised two babies. "I know I've had a taste of motherhood," she wrote to me. Since her years with the boys, Vivian had remained passionate about her work as a nanny but she also wasn't as consumed by the other families.

She admitted her relationship with the Pritchards wasn't always healthy.

"It's like when you have your first kid you are like that," Vivian said, thinking back on her time with the boys. "Then with each one you get less like that. You know, the first kid you never let have the pacifier off the ground. The second, you lick it clean. And the third, you just give it back immediately."

Devan and David were excited about the new baby and Vivian had taken their suggestions for names under advisement. "Viv, you're gonna be a great mom," David had said on a recent phone call. She did not regret anything about her time with the boys, but she realized that in her relationship with them, and with their parents, particularly Trevor, she had been too emotional, too invested. She was so young when she started, after all.

"I really grew up on that job," she explained. "That was my time where I really matured from a kid to an adult — and back again a few times — but eventually got there."

I took a couple of trips to see Kim. She had met a man named Robert and was married again. She was also a stepmother again and talked about Robert's son often. They lived in a bigger townhouse than the one Kim had bought on her own. Driving down the interstate on my most recent visit, I was nervous I would be late. I pictured her straightening up her house, thinking about what to serve me for lunch, maybe a little nervous I would make her relive — yet again — that terrible time she had with the Porters. It was not a period of her life that she liked to think about anymore.

Kim hadn't seen the Porters again. She hadn't spoken to her ex-husband again. But when she talked about them all, her speech slowed down, and she nodded her head slightly as though the memories were so vivid, they passed in front of her eyes. She felt each detail all over again. After one of our meetings, she reread her journal, which she had shared with me. She was surprised by how often she talked back to Brian and was embarrassed that she had stayed so long in a job that was clearly wrong from the start.

I knew which townhouse was Kim's even though they all looked alike. Hers was the only one with a wind chime hung up, a welcome mat at the door, and a bird feeder hanging from a tree. Inside, I met Robert, who was working from home that day. We shook hands. He was friendly and casual. At lunchtime, we wandered into her kitchen and she served me pasta Robert had made the night before. Before long, Robert joined us in the kitchen and Kim handed him a bowl of pasta too. He leaned on the counter while he ate with us.

Life had stabilized for Kim. She looked healthier. While she didn't work for Diane anymore, she still had one of the part-time nanny jobs she took when she left the Porters. According to Kim, that family was a dream to work for. When her bosses got a raise, so did Kim. They never came home late; they always appreciated her efforts. She now lived in the same townhouse complex they did. They were friends who respected each other, but the friendship was relaxed, low-key. It lacked the intense connection she had with Diane and the forced intimacy she had had with Holly and Brian.

"How do you deal with the isolation of being a nanny?" I asked, pointing out that she spent all her working time with children. She didn't have any nanny friends. "How do you deal with the fact that there is no ladder to climb on your job, no way to get a promotion?"

"Some women just aspire to be a mother and that was always my aspiration," she answered. "My aspiration wasn't to have any titles or have the world know what I was doing."

Now into her forties, Kim told me she was finally accepting the fact that she would not have a child of her own. It hadn't happened naturally with Robert and, getting older, she didn't want to adopt or go into debt paying for fertility treatments. I couldn't help feeling sad. It was such a simple wish, such a small thing to ask out of life. I wanted her to have it.

ACKNOWLEDGMENTS

I HAVE KNOWN Sally Wofford-Girand for more than half my life. Over the years, she has been a mentor, a big sister, a super-agent, and, most importantly, a good friend. This book would not exist without her tireless effort and steadfast vision.

I was incredibly lucky to end up in Andrea Schulz's hands. She gave me all the space I needed to get these stories onto the page and all the guidance I needed to get them right. She has made the book infinitely richer, and without her edits it would not be whole. Thanks also to Lindsey Smith, whose changes made this a smoother, sharper read.

To my family: Jesse Snyder, for being a best friend. Taisy Conk slept on my couch when I needed her most. Christina Washington was on call so many nights. Cree Snyder was a second mother. George Conk and Marilyn Armbruster gave me some of my best memories at Stone's Point. Rose Mackiewicz was a fearlessly opinionated and very funny role model.

My mother, Susan Maye, never judged me or pushed me to do anything in life but what I love.

My father, Michael Blaine, laid the foundation for who I am today. He taught me to read and write and gave me my first journal to record all my dreams.

To the Rothfelds, Evelyn, Stuart, Eric, and Jodi, for their support.

To Jon Cherins and David Coun for never asking if I would ever be finished with this book or placing bets on whether it would end up in a bookstore. Randi Coun traveled across the country in her third trimester and weathered a horrible storm without complaint. Ally Cherins, friend for life, has been with me through every step of this book and every step of becoming a mother. Special thanks also to Cindy Cordes for getting me through the most intense periods of reporting. Heather Paoloni gave me the blue room in Clinton. Wendy Doucette, a faraway friend, will always feel close. Stephanie Staal has been my partner in angst and long phone conversations. Jenny Lee's energy always got me back on track. Ruth Gallogly, the busiest person I know, took the time to read an early draft with an insightful and kind eye. Elisa Zuritsky, also an early reader, never stopped believing I could do this. And Jenny Offill was my bright spot on days of drudgery. I couldn't have managed the first years of parenting without her wit and fondness for a late-afternoon drink.

I would also like to thank Scott Adkins at the Brooklyn Writers Space for giving me what I always dreamed of: a quiet place to write that felt like home. Susan Gregory Thomas kept me entertained during many lunch hours. Benjamin Zucker's passion and dedication to his work was always an inspiration. Elaine Markson took me in as an intern at fifteen years old and gave me a unique place to grow up. Many years have passed since I left her office, but I can still see the yellow manuscript boxes lining the walls.

I could not have written this book without the help of others in caring for my children. It was an odd thing to do, writing about women taking care of other women's children while there were women taking care of mine. In particular, I will always be grateful to my sister, Christina Washington. And to all the teachers at Kiddy Citi in Brooklyn, especially when I was on bed rest with Georgia. Myca Defty held Georgia for hours on end and got me to the finish line.

I can't begin to thank Claudia, Kim, Vivian, and all of the nannies and parents who told me their stories. My biggest hope for this book is that it does their lives justice and that their personalities truly come alive on the page. Kim is one of the most thoughtful people I've ever met. Vivian is the most spirited. And Claudia is, perhaps, the strongest. She was the source of inspiration for this book. She is its center and its core. I am most grateful that she opened up her life to me. I am lucky to have them all in my life.

Michael Rothfeld has been through every step of this book with me. He pushed me, encouraged me, and gave me the key to getting past the first chapter. I never want to be on this journey without him.

And finally, this book is also for my daughters, Annabel and Georgia, who remind me every day that there is something new to explore.